I0893203

The Color of Democracy in Women's Regional Writing

STUDIES IN AMERICAN LITERARY REALISM AND NATURALISM

SERIES EDITOR
Gary Scharnhorst

EDITORIAL BOARD
Louis J. Budd
Donna Campbell
John Crowley
Robert E. Fleming
Alan Gribben
Eric Haralson
Denise D. Knight
Joseph McElrath
George Monteiro
Brenda Murphy
James Nagel
Alice Hall Petry
Donald Pizer
Tom Quirk
Jeanne Campbell Reesman
Ken Roemer

The Color of Democracy in Women's Regional Writing

Jean Carol Griffith

The University of Alabama Press
Tuscaloosa

Copyright © 2009
The University of Alabama Press
Tuscaloosa, Alabama 35487-0380
All rights reserved
Manufactured in the United States of America

Typeface: Adobe Caslon Pro

∞

The paper on which this book is printed meets the minimum requirements of American National Standard for Information Sciences-Permanence of Paper for Printed Library Materials, ANSI Z39.48-1984.

Library of Congress Cataloging-in-Publication Data

Griffith, Jean Carol.
The color of democracy in women's regional writing / Jean Carol Griffith.
p. cm. — (Studies in American literary realism and naturalism)
Includes bibliographical references and index.
ISBN 978-0-8173-1661-7 (cloth : alk. paper) — ISBN 978-0-8173-8239-1 (electronic) 1. American literature—Women authors—History and criticism. 2. American literature—20th century—History and criticism. 3. Women authors, American—Political and social views. 4. Regionalism in literature. 5. Local history in literature. 6. Democracy in literature. 7. New York (N.Y.)—In literature. 8. Southern States—In literature. 9. West (U.S.)—In literature. I. Title.
PS151.G8 2009
810.9′9287—dc22

2008051153

This book is dedicated to the memory
of Jean Carol Hinkle Griffith
My mother and an avid reader

Contents

Acknowledgments ix

Introduction: Writing Region in the New Century 1

PART I. "Is New York Such a Labyrinth?": Street Life and Amalgamation in Wharton's and Glasgow's City 19

1. Men of the Mob and "Fascinatingly American" Women 21

2. "'Et Que Cétait comme dans Le Livre'": Wharton, the Harlem Renaissance, and All That Jazz 50

PART II. "Virginia Is Not Dead but Sleepeth": Segregation and the "Family Black and White" in Glasgow's and Cather's South 71

3. Family Reunion: Slavery as Usable Past 73

4. A House Divided: The Interracial Family and the White Supremacist Community 99

PART III. "Fortunate Country": Old Immigrants and New Women in Cather's and Wharton's West 129

5. How the West Was Whitened 131

6. New Women and the World of Business 156

Conclusion: "Always, Everywhere, Inferior" 177

Notes 183

Bibliography 201

Index 213

Acknowledgments

As David McWhirter knows all too well, I am rarely at a loss for words, but I find it difficult to express adequately my gratitude to him for his ongoing encouragement and eagerness to share his wisdom. With my own growing experience comes the knowledge of how fortunate I am to have him as a model of what it means to be a scholar, a teacher, and a colleague. I am also the happy beneficiary of the advice and support of other cherished mentors in the graduate program at Texas A&M University, most especially Pamela Matthews and Janis Stout, and of the expertise Elizabeth West lent to this project in its earliest stages. The Center for Humanities Research (now the Glasscock Center for the Humanities) and the Women's Studies Program at Texas A&M provided me with fellowships during my years as a graduate student, and I am thankful for both the material benefits and the ego boosting that came with such support. Since completing my graduate studies, I have been lucky to work with several colleagues at Oklahoma State and Wichita State Universities whose encouragement of me as a novice was and is essential, as are the needed inspiration and distractions my students consistently provide. Michael McCamley, Sam Robertson, and my dear Esther Lopez provided both distractions and understanding, astutely knowing when I most needed which. Heidi Ardizzone's willingness to correspond with me about her research on the Rhinelander family proved indispensable to my analysis of Wharton and the Harlem Renaissance. This project benefited from the sage advice of readers for *Studies in the Novel, Western American Literature,* and especially from The University of Alabama Press, consummate professionals, who made the publication process as painless as it can be. A portion of chapter 2 was published in *Studies in the Novel* 38.1 (Spring 2006), 74–94, and an earlier version of chapter 5 was published in *Western American Literature* 41.4 (Winter 2007), 393–417. I am grateful to both journals for their permission to reprint this material.

I'd also like to thank those family members who provided me with encouragement as I completed this project. My humble thanks go to the Griffith clan and its various subsidiaries, a family whose ability to change and (quite literally) grow is an adventure, and to my husband's family, especially Mary Ryder, whose sympathy knows no bounds. And finally, my thanks to Ross, who was there long before this book or the very idea of it entered my head, and who will be there after other books (hopefully) follow it. You are what endures.

The Color of Democracy in Women's Regional Writing

Introduction

Writing Region in the New Century

Edith Wharton once summed up her attitude about modern America thus: "I wanted the idols broken . . . but . . . by people who understood why they were made."[1] Wistfully lamenting the destruction of cultural "idols"—beliefs not necessarily true in an empirical sense, but nonetheless symbolically significant—Wharton especially regrets that they are being destroyed by those who do not understand their origin. She shares this characterization of turn-of-the-century America, though not precisely the same attitudes about it, with the two other writers who most concern me here, Ellen Glasgow and Willa Cather. In her autobiography, *The Woman Within* (1954), and in many of her novels, Glasgow attributes an "evasive idealism" to the Old South, a contradictory phrase suggesting that antebellum southern society had attempted to reach some standard of perfection only by eluding reality, by practicing misdirection. Cather echoes both writers in a review of George Bernard Shaw when she asserts that nineteenth-century culture was built upon a chimeric foundation, one that is being threatened in the present: "Why not leave us our illusions," she asks, "since this is a short journey and cold, and mostly in the dark, and we believe, at least, that they comfort us."[2] For all three women, what is not true in the strictest sense ("idols," "illusions," "evasive idealism") was nonetheless influential in shaping and perpetuating societies that, in their own historical moment, are in danger of erasure. And for all three, as Wharton makes most clear here, this danger is associated with outsiders. Facing the passing of the old century and the birth of the new one with much ambivalence, these women set themselves apart from many of the traditions in which they were raised, particularly those enforcing restrictions on women, but they also distanced themselves from several characteristics of modernity. The feelings of temporal liminality, of being neither wholly of the nineteenth-century past nor of the twentieth-century present, that they expressed in letters, criticism, and autobiographical writings often manifest themselves as spatial liminality in their fiction. Constituting what Glasgow, referring to several of her Virginian novels, calls a "social history" of a region in transition, Wharton's depictions of Old and modern New York, Glasgow's of the Old and New South, and Cather's of the pioneer and settled West share a similar contrast between the past and modernity: while all three former societies are characterized as naïve, orderly, and cloistered, the turn-of-the-century region is depicted as chaotic, corrupt, and crowded.

Peopled with societies at once cultivated and pastoral, the regional past, according to these writers, was a necessarily fleeting age wedged between the establishment of American civilization and the overcivilization associated with American modernity. Glasgow's Old South, Cather's pioneer West, and even Wharton's Old New York are provincial and peripheral, as are all pastoral societies, to the north, the east, and Europe, respectively. But as much as these writers point to the follies of the past and mock the close-mindedness of past regional societies, they also insist that these societies made important contributions to the nineteenth-century development of a uniquely American culture. Their descriptions of the past evoke the pastoral as "a means of rearticulating, rather than abandoning, worldly concerns,"[3] for their works attribute a stability to regional communities that is achieved by keeping people socially as well as geographically in their places. In *A Backward Glance* (1934), for instance, Wharton tells us that her Old New York ancestors were "the heirs of an old tradition of European culture," yet because they possessed a distinctly American "standard of uprightness in affairs," this group "shaped the national point of view."[4] Considered by Wharton to be the descendants of the Dutch and English founders of her native city, Old New Yorkers in her works trace their ancestry back to the European aristocracy, or at least to the well-to-do merchant classes, and are thus imagined to be as different from their fellow countrymen of other classes and ethnicities than they are from their ethnic peers in the Old World. The "strict" standards with which Wharton endows the society into which she was born require a rigid adherence to tradition and the vigilant maintenance of boundaries between Old New Yorkers and outsiders, what *The Age of Innocence*'s Henry van der Luyden calls "republican distinctions."[5] "Like all agreeable societies," Wharton writes of her social circle, "ours was small," a "little 'set' with its private catch-words, observances and amusements, and its indifference to anything outside of its charmed circle; and no really entertaining social group has ever been anything else" (*Backward Glance,* 79).

Like Wharton's Old New York, Glasgow's Old South is saturated in sentimentality—"evasive idealism"—and at the same time committed to vigorously guarding its boundaries. Though critical of her ancestors, Glasgow nonetheless attributes a similar sense of blamelessness to traditional measures of social control. What held elite southern society together before the Civil War was, more than anything else, a "native element, dearer than Brussels lace," which, as Wharton's Old New York did, included an "old inestimable air of exclusiveness."[6] That exclusion divided the region's inhabitants into distinct but oftentimes codependent groups (planters, poor whites, and slaves) whose status was usually fixed by birth, with marriage, kinship ties, and a strong sense of class solidarity helping to define membership in the planter class just as they did in Wharton's Old New York society. Even in the years following the Civil War, Glasgow writes, the Virginian elite perpetuated social boundaries formed by birth rather than by wealth. Dictated by "ritual and rubric" and "utterly wanting in curiosity about the new and the strange," these societies displayed an innocent yet insistent ignorance about other regions—geographical and social—beyond their borders (140).

Cather's pioneer West imposes the pastoral in its classical sense, including the settling of "new" land and the breaking away from, as well as carrying over of, remnants of life elsewhere. In "Nebraska: The End of the First Cycle," Cather writes that this settlement process, initiated by the "dreamers and adventurers" who traveled through the territory and then taken up by "the first courageous settlers" who came to stay, constituted both a test of character and "a moral victory."[7] Indeed, she finds "the splendid story of the pioneers" to be so grand in scale that "no new story worthy to take its place has yet begun" (7). The creators of this "splendid story" were both Americans and, Cather makes abundantly clear, immigrants from Europe. Admitting that these immigrants faced some measure of nativist prejudice from their American neighbors, Cather nonetheless insists that the West of the pioneer era was amenable to foreign newcomers because there was little pressure to assimilate. "When I was a child," she writes elsewhere, "all our neighbors were foreigners," and what distinguished Nebraska in the past were the ways that foreign and "native" elements interacted—and did not interact:

> Nobody paid any attention to them outside of the attention they wanted. We let them alone. Work was assigned them, and they made good houseworkers and splendid craftsmen. They furnished their houses as they had in the countries from which they came. Beauty was there and charm. Nobody investigated them; nobody regarded them as laboratory specimens. Everybody had a sort of protective air toward them, but nobody interfered with them. A 'foreigner' was a person for-

> eign to our manners or custom of living, not possible prey for reform. Nobody ever cheated a foreigner. A man lost everything in the esteem of the community when he was discovered in the crime of a false barter.[8]

Cather's West of the "first cycle," then, reinforced the same sort of social divisions that Wharton's well-to-do New York and Glasgow's exclusive Old South did: the foreign population provided good servants and craftsmen (to whom "work was assigned"), but this population was "left alone," unhindered by snooping Americans and, therefore, free to re-create their lives along old-world patterns. In the case of all three writers, the societies of a region's past are shaped by uniquely American conditions but remain rooted in European class distinctions and culture. And there is an innocence, a benevolence, that accompanies these authors' renderings of the past, here manifest in the ways "natives" showed a protectiveness toward foreigners and ostracized those in their own groups who cheated them. Although it is as difficult to believe that "nobody ever cheated a foreigner" in the Old West any more than it is to believe that Old New York's elite was, as Wharton repeatedly insists, "middle-class," such qualities are essential components of these writers' images of the regional past.

Also essential to their portrayals of the regional past is the element of threat we saw in their attitudes toward modernity; as John Grammer defines it, pastoral "as a historical vision" includes the hope that a region will remain stable as well as "the fear that that realm will at last be destroyed."[9] Even as they benefited from the increasing social, political, and economic opportunities turn-of-the-century America provided women, none of these writers could wholly embrace all of the social transformations that made those opportunities possible. Concerned with the nation's supposed erosion of "taste," all three women linked the regional past to a superior culture, a linkage that, as Raymond Williams has written, is fundamental to the pastoral mode.[10] "When I was young," Wharton writes in *A Backward Glance,* "it used to seem to me that the group in which I grew up was like an empty vessel into which no new wine would ever again be poured. Now I see that one of its uses lay in preserving a few drops of an old vintage too rare to be savoured by a youthful palette" (5). Modern American culture, for Wharton, overturns all that she retrospectively comes to admire about Old New York because it rejects its European roots and increasingly displays a fascination for the lowest elements of society, or "the man with the dinner pail," as she puts it (206). Wharton admits to helping these modern trends along only to see, too late, the ramifications of her disloyalty. "I was a radical when everyone else I knew was conservative," Glasgow similarly confesses in *The Woman Within*, "and now I am a conservative when most other people appear to be radical," a response she attributes to the ascension of "modern iconoclasts . . . without culture" (42, 140). As Glasgow does, Cather defines the "new social restlessness" of the modern age as one that "spring[s] from a desire to do away with the exceptional."[11] These comments echo others at the time that, as Alan Trachtenberg has shown, deploy a discourse of high "culture" as a corrective to what many thought to be the startlingly low influences that were seemingly shaping turn-of-the-century society.[12]

Such a loss of cultural continuity and discrimination was the result, according to all three writers, of living in a democracy, the increasing proliferation of which they saw as responsible for dismantling the boundaries that held past regional societies together and kept outsiders at bay. Wharton, for instance, characterizes the turn-of-the-century New York elite (the group she explores in *The House of Mirth*) as nineteenth-century New York's opposite: while Old New York is isolated from outsiders and maintains "a strict standard of uprightness in affairs," modern New York society lacks "inherited obligations" and a "traditional sense of solidarity," both a code of behavior and a coherent group identity.[13] A great measure of the despair Wharton evinced about turn-of-the-century America stems from her perception that democracy was being taken to dangerous extremes; writing in 1919 about Henry Canby's lecture on "The America of Today," Wharton remarks that although Canby "has some good things—or nearly good—to say," she finds "tiresome" his invocation of a supposedly common "distinction between aristocratic & democratic forms (as if democratic were the necessary synonym of illiteracy)."[14] Wharton understands Canby's distinction between the aristocratic and the democratic as one in which democracy is becoming synonymous with a lack of culture; indeed, she bemoans that democracy, as Canby and others construct it, stands in opposition to culture and valorizes literary renditions of "crass manners," "navvies & char-women," and "cowboys de chic" (93, 91). In *The Woman Within*, Glasgow associates the "rising tide of uniformity" in American literature with a popularization of "Sensation," "so effortless, so unbridled, so direct in motive, and so democratic in method" (276, 267). For Glasgow, modern democracy is comprised of moral opposites ("ugly fact" and "fine ideals," "crooked deeds" and "straight feeling," as the narrator of *Life and Gabriella* puts it) and therefore has unclear ramifications for American society.[15] As Wharton and Glasgow do, Cather links a distinctly modern propagation of democracy with what she sees as a degradation of cultural standards: "The novel, as we know it today, is the child of democracy, and is not a high form of art," an association that, Cather adds elsewhere, means that it shares "all of [democracy's] virtues, but likewise all of its faults."[16] Note that in the case of all three writers, the term "democracy" is associated with the present rather than with the nation's founding and is being used, at least in part, pejoratively. Locating in modernity a fuller realization than in the past of democracy's supposed tendencies to level out class hierarchies and ignore racial and ethnic differences, these writers mixed the faith in American exceptionalism that was common in the Progressive Era with an equally common concern about what being an exception—especially compared to European nations—might mean culturally. What Dale Bauer argues of Wharton thus seems equally true of Cather and Glasgow: the increasing emphasis on creating a more democratic social realm may have had some "virtues," as Cather puts it, but it nonetheless degraded culture by making it a buyable commodity.[17]

Thus the contrast these three authors present between an old and a new regional realm is one that ultimately serves to explore larger debates about the nature of culture in a democracy. Long seen as white America's highest achievement, democracy was becoming increasingly synonymous with the burgeoning racial and ethnic heterogeneity imagined to threaten American whites. While the more limited scope of democracy associated with the past—one that chiefly benefited and was supposedly created by well-to-do white men—was linked to individualism, the fuller democratization of the modern age, as we will see repeatedly, was associated with images of an amorphous yet conformist "mob" or "crowd." In *The Epic of America* (1934), James Truslow Adams, a frequent commentator on American democracy, claimed that "the ideal of democracy and the reality of the crowd are the two sides of the shield of modern government"; others argued that democracy, coupled with the nation's racial and ethnic heterogeneity, was responsible for producing that "crowd."[18] As Matthew Frye Jacobson has shown, "racial" difference in the early twentieth century was thought not only to divide whites from Jews, blacks, and Asians, for instance, but also to distinguish between whites of differing classes and, often corresponding to class status, whites from western and northern Europe ("old" immigrants) from those of southern and eastern European origin ("new" immigrants).[19] Such instability in social boundaries that had—supposedly—been fixed in previous decades contributed to a heightened preoccupation with the very word "democracy" in the modern era. Were the qualities often associated with democracy—cultural discrimination, civic responsibility, a strong work ethic, and, most commonly, the ability to govern oneself—acquired? Or were these inherited prerequisites to democratic fitness, and divvied out differently according to gender, class affiliation, or race? Were the ideals of democracy themselves possible to achieve, and if so, *should* they be achieved? Such questions elicited a range of responses, from the paranoid to the celebratory, to the changing demographics of the nation, leading observers like Horace Kallen, who promoted diversity as the key to a thriving American culture, to note that it was democracy, above all, that was "at stake" in the United States.[20]

Kallen's claim that racial equality was an important indicator of the health of American democracy struck many others as outrageous, for according to his opponents, democracy was possible only in a homogeneous society of the type Wharton, Cather, and Glasgow associate with the nineteenth-century region. In 1924, the same year that Kallen made his statement praising diversity, eugenicist Lothrop Stoddard wrote, "The fact is democratic parliamentary institutions have been a real success only among peoples largely Nordic in blood."[21] The apprehensions generated by an extension of rights and privileges to groups deemed "unfit" for them could even veer toward questioning the wisdom of democracy itself, for it seemingly lent itself to an expanding number of challenges to those (Anglo elite men) "naturally" ordained to rule over all others. Stoddard's *The Rising Tide of Color* (1920) posited that the elevation of the so-called colored races and of the lower white races equaled the stagnation of the best white race (most commonly called Anglo or Nordic). For this reason, he found "American idealism," which he understood to be the expansion of democracy to non-Nordics, thoroughly "short-sighted."[22] The paradox with which eugenicists thought their society was grappling pitted American Nordics' supposedly misguided, if charitable, push for diversity and equality against what was, to the eugenicists' way of thinking, an inescapable "racial reality": non-Nordics, more fit for physical survival than so-called better white races, were incapable of self-government. Their full inclusion in and access to America's democratic institutions (from schools to political clout) could only result, therefore, in the destruction of those institutions and of the race most closely associated with them. In his introduction to Stoddard's work, Madison Grant doubted the benefits of democracy (as did Stoddard himself) because it too often led to what was, in the eugenicists' view, a disastrous mixing of superior and inferior races.[23] Equally disastrous, according to such views, was modern democracy's blurring of class boundaries. For the eugenicists, the working-class status of African Americans or of most Italian immigrants, for instance, made plain their racial inferiority, a view shared by non-eugenicists like Wharton's friend Barrett Wendell. As Thomas Gossett put it, Wendell and the like-minded "came to regard the triumph of democracy as inevitable and as an unrelieved disaster."[24]

Often mixed with such perspectives as Wendell's was a greater faith in Americanization than the eugenicists possessed. For those who touted the benefits of the melting pot, the notion that all races underwent a similar evolutionary trajectory meant that all could share democratic rights and privileges equally *someday* (usually in the far distant future), but because "evolutionary *change* was not as salient . . . as were evolutionary *stages*, . . . cultures were described in a static manner," and each generation's capacity for self-government, or for hard work, for example, was more often seen as essentially fixed.[25] Theodore Roosevelt was perhaps the most famous figure to promote this link between democracy and racial advancement: "self-governance," he argued, "came to a race only through the slow growth of centuries, and then only to those races which possess an immense reserve of strength, common sense, and morality."[26] While certainly not free of prejudice against the European groups that eugenicists considered inferior to Nordics, men like Roosevelt and Frederick Jackson Turner nonetheless rejected the notion that democracy was the result of a specific European group's racial greatness, arguing that America was spawning a unique, supreme white race of its own. According to this view, white Americans were racially superior to *all* Europeans precisely because they were a mix of different European elements (usually western and northern European) and because they had evolved apart from an aristocratic ruling class, in the fullest flowering of "democratic conditions."[27] The paternalism implied by the notion of America as a melting pot, then, often coexisted with a belief that American institutions, unlike those of Europe, were a level playing field. Hence this notion of a white American race superior to the Anglo or other old-world white races usually entailed an element of nonelite protest. From this perspective, upper-class Anglos were not racial exemplars but racially degraded, deficient in the prevailing American spirit and shamelessly dependent on obsolete, old-world distinctions.

Even more critical of the link between whiteness and democracy, cultural pluralists like Kallen argued that widening the scope of democratic privilege would actually contribute to the health of the nation, that diversity was the antidote to what ailed white America.[28] For Kallen, racial diversity was not antithetical to but synonymous with democracy (which was precisely what worried his eugenicist opponents), and, furthermore, democracy was not opposed to but "an essential prerequisite to" a flourishing cultural realm.[29] Democracy may create increasing anxiety about racial heterogeneity, which, Kallen acknowledged, strained the nation insofar as it defined itself as "unified." But "cultural growth is founded upon Cultural Pluralism. Cultural Pluralism is possible only in a democratic society whose institutions encourage individuality in groups, in persons, in temperaments, whose program liberates these individualities and guides them into a fellowship of freedom and coöperation."[30] Agreeing with Kallen, Randolph Bourne wrote that "democracy involves, not the elimination of differences, but the perfection and conservation of differences," and went further in pointing to the hypocrisy of linking democracy with Anglo-American supremacy: "We act as if we wanted Americanization to take place only on our own terms, and not by the consent of the governed."[31] Bourne called for a severing of the association of democracy with Anglo status: "Let us cease to think of ideals like democracy as magical qualities inherent in certain peoples. Let us speak, not of inferior races, but of inferior civilizations. We are all to educate and be educated."[32] Despite their paternalism, these perspectives echoed many aspects of what those from immigrant and minority communities had been saying for years, for whom democracy had long represented both the promise of a new future and its betrayal, at least insofar as it continued to benefit some more than others. "Your country?" W. E. B. Du Bois reminded whites who thought democracy and their own racial status were synonymous, "How came it yours?"[33] As this brief summary of responses to the nation's growing awareness of its hybridity suggests, the struggle to achieve a greater democracy can be, and indeed has been, motivated by antiracist as well as racialist or even racist impulses. While Stoddard and the eugenicists, on the one hand, and Kallen and the cultural pluralists, on the other, represented two extremes in these debates, many white Americans, as we will see, took positions somewhere in between, adopting oftentimes disparate, sometimes downright contradictory responses to how diversity should shape democracy.

Region was a key site of the anxieties generated by this turn-of-the-century debate. The erosion of class boundaries of which Wendell spoke was the product, he argued, of the settling of the West by the worst of what he called "Northern [New England] blood," who were creating a new region "whose political and moral condition now leaves most to be desired."[34] By contrast, Turner saw the West as creating a new and improved white race—indeed, as carving out an America finally free of European influences—that would reinvigorate decedent whites from the Northeast and the South. For eugenicists like Stoddard and Grant, it was the South, at least before emancipation, that stood as a testament to Anglo-Saxon superiority. According to this perspective, the greater urbanization and industrialization of the North proved the threat that a democracy that encourages immigration posed to Anglo or Nordic superiority, as the "higher" races were not as fit for city life as were "lower" races like the Slavs. Strongly opposing the eugenicists' assessment, Bourne maintained that the South provided the greatest evidence against Anglo-Saxon superiority: "Let those who feel the inferiority of the non-Anglo-Saxon immigrant contemplate that region of the States which has remained the most distinctively 'American,' the South. Let him ask himself whether he would really like to see the foreign hordes Americanized into such an Americanization."[35] Kallen was perhaps the least reliant on regional stereotypes in his understanding of the importance of geographical differences to constructions of democracy. The most "hyphenated" Americans, he claimed, were the ones whom new-immigrant detractors like the eugenicists praised: Germans and Scandinavians in the Midwest. Kallen argued that regional differences made racial fusion impossible, as "each section, East, West, North and South, is peopled by white men of different European stocks and traditions. They add diversity to diversity, and when one speaks of their inward Americanization, one wonders also to just what local type this inward change must assimilate itself."[36] Linda Frost argues that in the decades surrounding the Civil War, both Northerners and Southerners used the language of racial difference to disparage their regional enemy.[37] Although it is generally supposed that such sectional antagonism was subsumed by the success of turn-of-the-century measures of unification, by the closing of the frontier, the easing of tensions between the North and South, and by the countrywide proliferation of a consumer culture, for instance, these very conditions served to accentuate geographical discrepancies in contending with a racially varied populace. And greater mobility across the nation in the forms of travel and migration made regional comparison and contrast—if not sectional antagonism—an important element in debates about democracy. As Kallen argued, American regions "add diversity" to an ever diverse nation, a fact that was highlighted for turn-of-the-century Americans by more contact between people of different locales. And Kallen's comments crystallize a growing awareness that, given its regional diversity, the nation had never been particularly homogeneous. Coinciding with the nation's growing heterogeneity, then, the increasing opportunities for regional comparison helped to destabilize the link between democracy and white status.

The ability to make such comparisons also marked a critical transition in literary regionalism, a transition that Wharton, Cather, and Glasgow helped to pioneer. For these writers, fuller democratization of the nation was linked to the destruction of past regional cultures and of the boundaries that made those cultures possible. Their conflicted responses to the past and to the modern regional realms shape the equally ambivalent attitudes these writers held toward the writing of place. On the one hand, their works are closely aligned with particular geographies, ones that each woman felt most comfortable with and capable of portraying. In "My First Novels (There Were Two)," Cather tells us that writing her first novel *Alexander's Bridge,* set in

Boston and London, "was like riding in a park, with someone not altogether congenial," but that writing her first novel of Nebraska, *O Pioneers!* "was like taking a ride through a familiar country on a horse that knew the way, on a fine morning when you felt like riding."[38] Although New York is an important setting for Glasgow's work, she, in a way that is similar to Cather, regrets her decision to set her first novel there rather than in her native Virginia. "I knew my part of the South," she tells us in *The Woman Within,* "and I looked deep enough within and far enough without to learn something of human beings and their substance. We write better, I had discovered by my experimental failures, when we write of places we know, and of a background with which we are familiar" (129–30). Finally, Henry James's advice that Wharton "*Do New York!*" which, in her short fiction, Wharton had already been doing, nonetheless made something of an impact on her choosing of subjects for subsequent longer works. For with the 1905 publication of *The House of Mirth,* Wharton would increasingly defend her choice to write about the region—upper-class New York—to which she "happen[ed] to be nearest" as well as to resist the representation of regional types, "cowboys de chic," for example, that she thought were popular with American readers.[39]

Despite the prominence of local communities in their works, these writers rejected (implicitly or explicitly) an association with their women regionalist predecessors. As Donna Campbell observes, "Wharton seemed determined . . . to distance herself both from the local colorists and from those other women authors who, like herself, were determined to correct their excesses," but as much as Wharton may have separated herself from writers like Glasgow, whom Campbell mentions in this connection, she nonetheless shares with her and with Cather a similar treatment of region.[40] These three writers adapted regional writing to accommodate their sense of historical liminality, believing that the regions emerging from modern democratization could not be adequately expressed within the paradigms established by local color, a literary tradition that was, for them, as pastoral as regional histories themselves were. Just as Wharton claims to refuse "the rose-coloured spectacles" of writers like Mary Wilkins Freeman and Sarah Orne Jewett, preferring, instead, "to draw life as it really was," Glasgow roots her belief that the novel is "a mirror of life" in her disdain for local-color works, which she characterizes as "little vessels of experience" (*Backward Glance,* 293; *Woman Within,* 97–98).[41] The extent to which Cather rejects or adopts aspects of her regionalist predecessors' writings is more complicated, given her friendship with and respect for Jewett. Although her "Miss Jewett" essay bestows considerable praise upon the older writer, Cather's veneration for Jewett seems circumscribed, and her descriptions of the strength of Jewett's work, like the assessments of local color made by Wharton and Glasgow, include adjectives that are both diminutive and stereotypically feminine: "a lady in the old high sense," Jewett and her work both display "charm," "grace," and delicacy.[42] Cather's insistence that Jewett did not live for her art and that Jewett herself understood that her work occupied a small place on the American literary scene suggest that what Cather most liked about Jewett was that the older woman understood her limitations: "Her stories were but reflections, quite incidental," of the country life that she loved (87). Contrary to Glasgow and Wharton, who both found Jewett's work insufficiently lifelike, Cather writes that *The Country of the Pointed Firs* contains "not stories at all, but life itself" (78). Yet since Cather stressed verisimilitude as a virtue for fiction less than Wharton and Glasgow did, she may well be suggesting here that Jewett's work, in being sufficiently lifelike, isn't sufficiently literary.[43]

So while Wharton, Cather, and Glasgow all denied creative affiliation with the woman-dominated tradition of local color, they did not refuse the narrative possibilities available in regional writing. Instead, the treatment of region in these writers' works corresponds to a new emphasis on how democracy redraws social boundaries and reinterprets (often to their chagrin) what constitutes art and culture. As Sherrie Inness and Diana Royer note, "throughout U. S. history, regional writing has been a way for women to write about their unique experiences," as regionalism "involves our investment in community, whether that community is a small town or large city."[44] Sometimes in protest, sometimes in celebration, the regional works of these women replace harmony with discord and stasis with fluidity, for in confronting the pressures of changing regional life they thought earlier women writers had overlooked, Wharton, Glasgow, and Cather entered increasingly anxious debates concerning emancipation and segregation, immigration, and the social as well as geographic mobility made possible by a growing consumer culture. My point is not that earlier regionalists had ignored the social transformations occurring in their own societies, but that these three women writers thought they did, and that this belief led them to reformulate the genre in order to examine regions as spaces of conflict.

Imagined to be the result of a growing number of Jews streaming into New York, of emancipated African Americans upsetting the South's political house of cards, or of new immigrants struggling for a place on the midwestern plains, these conflicts dramatically alter the relationships between natives and strangers, the shifting identities of which, as Stephanie Foote cogently argues, constitute the "defining textual economy of regionalism."[45] Also complicating those relationships is the development of a consumer culture that increasingly obscured the class boundaries that helped to define the Old South, Old New York, or the pioneer West. Local-color literature, as Wharton, Cather, and Glasgow understood it, elucidates quaint and humble "folk" who are happily stuck in idyllic rural areas and ignorant about those beyond their borders. Sandra Zagarell identifies the "accentuated harmony" of local color as functioning to celebrate ethnic purity and to establish fixed class hierarchy as "the authentic American way of life." In contrast, the works on which I concentrate locate such stability in the past and often lack what Zagarell calls the "presumption of knowability" about regional folk—commonly described by Wharton, Glasgow, and Cather as a locally inflected "mob"—that local-color literature possesses.[46] In many works by nineteenth-century regionalists most characters stay in place, both geographically and socially, but characters in turn-of-the-century regionalism constantly move and change. Glasgow's Virginians flee the South to enjoy the anonymity of New York. Wharton's nouveau riche westerners besiege the fortress of the old eastern elite. And Cather's immigrants and migrant southerners move west to the promises and the pitfalls of a society still in the making. All bring with them the perceptions and attitudes of their homes, which must be negotiated with their adopted cultures in ways that "add diversity to diversity," to borrow Kallen's phrase again. In this sense, as Nancy Glazener has illustrated, regional novels do not necessarily advance democracy in themselves (as William Dean Howells had argued), but some, like those by these three authors, certainly take the modern democratization of regional culture as their subject.[47] These writers' constructions of local change register, above all, an anxiety about the very flexibility of the discourses of democracy, the chameleon-like quality that makes it adaptable for a variety of contradictory and competing claims.

While they explore the tensions between competing definitions of democracy and how these tensions were felt regionally, their works also illustrate that the privileges of self-government did not extend to all whites, or even to all Anglos, equally. These three authors were writing at a time when white women played a crucial symbolic function in defining the nation, particularly when it was thought to be in jeopardy from racial others. But to the extent that they continued to be barred from the political, social, and economic rights of citizenship, white women were not permitted the full privileges of citizenship, and hence of whiteness. Instead, as Mason Stokes argues, they were "silent markers in a system of exchange" that naturalized the link between whiteness and democracy.[48] Yet this system had to compete, during the decades in which Wharton, Cather, and Glasgow wrote, with a growing push to incorporate white women more fully in democratic privilege. As Louise Newman points out, white women at the turn of the century assumed an increasing number of public, professional positions, wherein they "staked out new realms of possibility and political power" and articulated "new arguments about race and gender to assert themselves as the political, social, and racial equals of white men."[49] In keeping with this trend, Cather, Wharton, and Glasgow use regional writing to explore social transformation in a form of fiction associated with and acceptable for women. Indeed, because regionalism was already construed as feminine, these writers could position themselves as innovators of the genre, at the forefront of a new means of writing about community and place that to them seemed more suited to the pressures of modern life. If earlier writers like Jewett had—or seemed to have—stayed in their place by writing in a mode deemed proper for the "lady" writer, the three writers whom I discuss transform that same mode to step out of their places and grapple with many of the most pressing social questions of their day.

Because they imagine white women's participation in democracy to be mediated by the relationships between race and region, these writers complicate ongoing scholarly debates about the liberal or conservative agenda of women's regional writing. One side of this debate, the foremost proponents of which are Marjorie Pryse and Judith Fetterley, posits that as white women's regional writing critiques gender hegemony, it also and equally critiques hierarchies of race, class, and ethnicity. In contrast, scholars like Amy Kaplan and Richard Brodhead argue that writers such as Jewett actually use regionalism to participate in these nationalist, classist, and racist agendas.[50] On both sides of this critical rift, the nation is configured as a kind of no-place or as an undifferentiated "urban" space disassociated from a particular city.[51] That no-place, more importantly, is seemingly the origin of racialist and imperialist as well as patriarchal thought. Yet the regional fiction Wharton, Cather, and Glasgow helped to develop reframes this relationship, challenging us to view the nation as a series of regions, each with a distinct way of defining a white woman's place in relation to changing conceptions of democracy and difference. Although we tend to associate each of these writers with one locale—Wharton with New York, Glasgow with Virginia, and Cather with Nebraska—their works actually portray a number of oftentimes competing settings that allow them to explore a dizzying array of turn-of-the-century constructions of democracy. For Glasgow, the fluid nature of identity in New York serves as a counterpoint to the fixed notion of one's place that she associates with Virginia. While Virginia looks similar to Cather, she constructs the West as the place that is most framed by a modern democracy that eschews class boundaries and embraces racial diversity, at least among Europeans. And for Wharton, outsiders with "new money," either foreigners or westerners, buy their way into New York society and proceed to collapse the very distinctions—between culture and commerce, between the private and the public—that held that society together. As Nancy Bentley contends, Wharton's works are "less about local social patterns" per se than they are about "the disruption and global dispersion of those patterns," a disruption that marks Glasgow's and Cather's works as well and one that, I argue, constitutes not a departure from regionalism, but rather a reinvention of it.[52] In this sense, these writers are "regionalist" for two reasons: both because they are associated with writing of the place where they were born and because their fiction repeatedly compares that home base to other places.

This comparative treatment of setting constitutes an important means by which these women changed regional writing. The binary of the local and the national assumed to be inherent to local color simply cannot be applied to such works because they lack a homogenizing or oppressive center (the nation) and are at once firmly rooted in place and endlessly roaming. These works thus challenge us to reconceptualize Fetterley and Pryse's opposition between (white) woman-centered, antiracist region and racist, patriarchal, and urbanized nation, for they present both white women and regions as occupying liminal spaces. In doing so, they illustrate how both regions and white women are at once marginalized and in possession of the potential to marginalize others. Laura Donaldson's argument that white women in modern Western culture occupy a "contradictory social positioning" wherein they are "colonized patriarchal objects and colonizing race-privileged subjects," a phenomenon she calls the "Miranda Complex," thus can be applied to regional spaces as well, insofar as a region both shapes and is shaped by other places and can colonize those within its borders.[53] *The Color of Democracy* examines Cather's, Wharton's, and Glasgow's interest in regional contributions to American origins and scrutinizes these writers' explorations of the fate of those origins once democracy expands beyond the boundaries they associate with the nineteenth century. The "strict standards" Lily Bart acquires throughout the course of Wharton's *House of Mirth,* for example, save her from the marital suit of a New York Jew and preserve the purity of her racial status. Yet they also preclude the possibility of her survival, for it is not Lily and her kind but racial and regional outsiders (newly wealthy Jews and westerners) that will shape the "the national point of view" in the future. While Glasgow's Virginian women, like Lily, hail from a traditional regional elite, they more successfully navigate the labyrinth of a region's racial terrain in ways that allow them increased access to democratic privilege: by "mastering" black labor in the New South (as Dorinda Oakley does in *Bar-*

ren Ground) or by reinventing themselves as New Women in New York. For Cather, the same signs of prosperity (dress, mannerisms, speech) that prove the self-governing capabilities of Alexandra Bergson of *O Pioneers!* and Lena Lingard of *My Ántonia* constitute a disruptive force when they are assumed by the southern black woman, Nancy, in *Sapphira and the Slave Girl.* Region shapes race in these works, which in turn shapes the limitations upon, as well as the options available to, the women characters at a given novel's center. Even as their works illustrate the relationships between the marginalized (women, region) and the marginalizing (men, nation), then, they also tell us much about the relationships between white women and other marginalized groups.

Because they rejected the world of the local-color text, and perhaps because their own works explore the relationships between regions, these writers' contributions to regionalism have generally been overlooked. This is especially the case with Wharton, whose association with regionalism is often confined to *Ethan Frome* and *Summer,* both set in rural Massachusetts. Yet we have failed to see the regionalist qualities of Wharton's New York novels in part because we fail to recognize how urban life can be shaped by local customs as much as rural life is.[54] Foote's claim that what unites all regionalist texts is an exploration of who is "native" and who is a "stranger" allows us to see the works of these writers as directly engaging with regionalism's chief concerns, no matter where these texts are set. Foote's definition should also serve to remind us that literary regionalism—and the work of these writers is no exception—lacks a fixed political agenda as much as white women, as a group, do. Easy assumptions about marginalized hinterlands and oppressive urban centers all too often continue to shape scholars' assessments of literary regionalism and of its reflection of the distribution of power in American society, for if in many cases such assumptions are accurate, they are not always so. Consider, for example, the now-famous—or infamous—red-state, blue-state map of the 2004 presidential election. Much of the tension that map seemed to generate was grounded in its ironic overturning of stereotypical ideas about the rural and the urban, the North and the South, the coasts and "flyover country," and the dynamics between them all. Indeed, where on this map are we to locate the geographical and social center of authority, the "nation," and where the margin or oppressed hinterland? And as early twentieth-century regionalism illustrates, regional categories change over time as much as those of race or ethnicity do. Some attention to spaces in between—between the writing of place in the nineteenth century and the twentieth, between regions, between region and nation, and between white women and racial or ethnic minorities—helps to reveal the ways democracy has been shaped by all members of American society, however much or little social authority each possessed at a given time.

By reading the works of Wharton, Cather, and Glasgow alongside local histories and other writers of New York, Virginia, and the West, I place these women in the context of literary as well as historical debates about the racial dynamics of democracy. Chapter 1 examines Glasgow's and Wharton's New York, a city portrayed as one that develops a new kind of street life that brings women of the traditional elite together with ethnic men who could increasingly afford the trappings of the respectable. Using the naturalist "fall" to return to values associated with the regional past, Wharton's *House of Mirth* and Glasgow's *The Descendant* show how these interactions both compromise an older conception of democracy rooted in Anglo supremacy and bolster the value of white women to symbolize that democracy. By the 1920s, as I discuss in chapter 2, the city's street life was leading genteel women uptown, into jazz cabarets. The ensuing dance craze (bemoaned by the New York press as well as by Wharton's *Twilight Sleep*) seemed to epitomize twentieth-century democracy's erosion of cultural standards, fostering a symbolic amalgamation of black and white. Disagreements about the ramifications of jazz's mixed associations, which go to the heart of much Harlem Renaissance literature as well as to Wharton's work, reveal the ambiguities inherent to life in a city at once racially segregated and closely associated with cultural diversity.

Nowhere in the nation did a racially segregated democracy flourish more than in the South, though, a fact that informs Glasgow's Virginian novels as well as Cather's *Sapphira and the Slave Girl.* In part 2, I show how James Baldwin's notion of a "blood relationship" between whites and blacks provides a particularly useful framework for scrutinizing the ways segregation, designed to deny African Americans access to democracy, also threatened whites by denying them access to African Americans, without whom it was seemingly impossible to construct a regionally distinct notion of white citizenship. White southerners mitigated this crisis by continuing relationships with blacks in the private realm, relationships they imagined to be much like apologists' views of slavery as fostering a "family black and white." Residual images of an interracial family, as I argue in chapter 3, proved especially valuable in designing laws that restricted blacks in the workplace and in augmenting the position of white women. Striking a balance between public segregation and private integration was no easy matter, though, and at times these family connections jeopardized the sense of racial superiority they were meant to safeguard, an issue I take up in chapter 4.

In the West, the region explored in part 3, various types of "new" women emerge to fill the vacuum of a supposedly blank geographical space and an increasingly inchoate national culture. While the South was commonly assumed to be the place most informed by the link between whiteness and democracy, the West, the ostensibly newest region, played a similar role in the nation. Yet it did so by reinventing whiteness and by developing novel forms of white manhood and womanhood. Cather's prairie, for instance, intervenes in disputes about democracy by synthesizing two distinct, and, as we have seen, typically opposed sides of the debate: cultural pluralism, which severed democracy from Anglo status, and eugenics, which attempted to make democracy synonymous with Anglo status. In combining aspects of both eugenics and cultural pluralism, *O Pioneers!* and *My Ántonia* fix the racial traits of old and new immigrants and celebrate how that fixity results in diverse expressions of gender. Along with its immigrants, the West was also noted for fostering a new culture of divorce, which supposedly made the family a commodity. In the Midwest of Cather's later works, such as *A Lost Lady,* as well as in Wharton's depictions of the region (a subject absent from work on her, but central to novels such as *The Custom of the Country*), white women discard genteel men, who symbolize the regional past, and embrace a business ethos propagated by "new" men who lack regional and communal ties. In doing so, these women represent a region and a nation divorced from "republican distinctions": an America, as Cather and Wharton imagine it, divorced from the best elements of Americanness.

My conclusion further considers the association of regionalism with marginalization by revisiting some of the comparisons I make earlier between Glasgow's, Cather's, and Wharton's works and those by ethnic or racial minorities. What such comparisons indicate is that to claim a regional identification—always a troubling business for groups oppressed on the basis of race and ethnicity—is to claim a national one, too. In other words, in writing of the region, Wharton, Glasgow, and Cather both explore their own marginalization and claim their authority to speak on the marginalization of others. These writers' works, in short, scrutinize what their authors considered to be a sometimes promising, sometimes dubious democratization of culture, exploring how the advantages and disadvantages of this twentieth-century process affect white American women and the literary genre that remains most closely associated with them.

PART I

"Is New York Such a Labyrinth?": Street Life and Amalgamation in Wharton's and Glasgow's City

It is democracy turned upside down that I object to, . . . There seems a lack of decency about it—as if we were to awake some morning to find the statue of Liberty on its head, with its legs in the air. I believe in the old conservative goddess of our fathers—Freedom shackled by the chains of respectability.

—Dr. Salvers in *Phases of an Inferior Planet* (1898),
by Ellen Glasgow

Mrs. Preston says this war is to give everybody a chance to lift up his head like a person. It is to bring together the people on top who got everything and the people on the bottom who got nothing. She's been telling me about a new word—democracy. It got me on fire. Democracy means that everybody in America is going to be with everybody alike.

—Hannah Hayyeh in "The Lost 'Beautifulness'" (1920),
by Anzia Yezierska

1

Men of the Mob and "Fascinatingly American" Women

I. THE CROWD

On May 5, 1912, ten thousand women marched for suffrage down Fifth Avenue, starting at Washington Square. It was the largest suffrage demonstration in the city to date, as well as the most diverse: society queen Alva Belmont, a prominent figure in the gossip columns, marched in the lead of thousands of female factory workers. The *New York Times,* which had treated woman suffrage with passing disdain in many previous articles, finally took notice—after all, ten thousand women, with an Alva Belmont to boot, were hard to ignore. In the weeks that followed, the *Times* printed a number of features debating woman suffrage, and on May 12 ran a piece claiming that the cause "is indeed a great river into which a vast number of small streams flow."[1] This article details the array of women—politician's wives, upper-class matriarchs such as Belmont, women of the working class, and New Women professionals—who marched that day and, illustrating the regional range of the cause, notes the attendance of a "delegation from Virginia" headed by "two women known all over the country": Mary Johnston and "Miss Ellen Glasgow, author of 'The Descendant,' 'The Voice of the People,' and other well-known novels."

Whether or not Glasgow marched down Fifth Avenue with thousands of others in support of woman suffrage that day in May, it is certain that she had ample opportunity throughout her career to observe and to be a part of New York's bustling street life. Although she continues to be more or less exclusively defined as a Virginian, Glasgow paid extended visits to New York annually before the war, and her experiences there, she tells us in *A Certain Measure* (1943), were incorporated into much of her fiction.[2] And in both her fiction and nonfiction, she displays a fascination with the dynamic public life of the city, particularly with the crowds. In the 1916 novel *Life and Gabriella,* for instance, the city's crowds symbolize the title character's ambivalence to what Hannah Hayyeh in Yezierska's "The Lost 'Beautifulness'" calls a democracy in which Americans will "be with everybody alike."[3] A Virginian lady who has fled the regional stagnation that she fears to be her birthright, Gabriella Fowler nonetheless holds herself "aloof from the masses," especially the "lethargic foreign faces" that obscure "the finer American type" like herself.[4] Throughout the course of the novel, though, and largely in response to her growing love for a self-made Irish American, Daniel O'Hara, Gabriella learns that her despondent Anglocentrism is a remnant of her southern background and that, contrary to her first responses to O'Hara and to the crowds, "there is no hope . . . for America except in the clear vision of the future" (490). The narrator's approval of Gabriella's eventual acceptance of O'Hara makes plain that a clear vision of the future requires that she, a "finer American type," must come to understand herself through her relation to, and not her difference from, other Americans. Glasgow's use of the city's crowds serves, then, as a method of foreshadowing Gabriella's eventual acceptance, in the form of O'Hara, of social mobility.

Not surprisingly, one writer not present at the 1912 march for suffrage was Edith Wharton, who not only did not support women's causes with any special interest but also had little enthusiasm for New York's street life. Emelyn Washburn, a girlhood friend of Wharton's, was perhaps the first to note this: "I wish," she wrote, "Edith had had some street life, and known all sorts and conditions of men as I did—and learned to love New York."[5] Wharton never did, of course, learn to love New York, but despite this, and even despite her decades-long expatriation and her view of herself as a "wretched exotic," she never stopped thinking, reading, and writing about the city of her birth.[6] If Washburn's comments are correct, Wharton's ambivalence to New York was related to her limited knowledge of its diversity. In another sense, that attitude can be attributed to what she thought she knew about its diversity; to extend upon Washburn, Wharton failed to appreciate New York because she failed to appreciate the multiplicity of its people. Although Glasgow's works approach New York life with consistent, if ambivalent, fascination, Wharton's considerable canon of novels constructs a history of the city's elite in which the "tight little citadel" of *Old New York* (1924) or *The Age of Innocence* (1920) becomes the society of whirling "atoms" in *The House of Mirth* (1905) and beyond.[7] In such novels the nineteenth-century elite of New York understand themselves in relation to "family," in which class and racial identities are formed through kinship ties and the marrying of like and like. The elite of the turn of the century, on the other hand, understand themselves in relation to "society," a purchasable (and increasingly affordable) status that redraws the upper class along the pattern of the masses. Amy Kaplan has demonstrated that in Wharton's works, "the gaping mob both defines and threatens the upper class, which depends on the mob's admiration and its exclusion."[8] Yet the conglomeration of "old" and "new" money that constitutes Wharton's turn-of-the-century elite itself often resembles a mob, albeit a well-dressed one. In *Age,* for instance, the spectacle of May Welland in her bridal splendor must be carefully shielded from anonymous would-be onlookers, her very aloofness signifying the tense but codependent relationship between elite status and the public life of New York that Kaplan describes. For much of the novel, though, May also must be shielded from the likes of Mrs. Struthers, and it is precisely when she ceases to be kept apart from the arriviste that, we are to understand, the transformation of elite New York from a "family" to a "society" is complete. Wharton's disdain for Old New York's dependence upon and fear of the mob, as well as its eventual absorption into it, account for her attitudes both toward the society into which she was born and toward the street life Washburn thought she lacked.

Glasgow's and Wharton's concerns with the puzzling multitudes speak to the ways "the crowd" seemed to epitomize the supposed dangers of extending democracy too far. According to Gustave Le Bon, the period's self-proclaimed authority on the crowd, "one of the principal characteristics of the present age" was the ascendancy of the masses, which resulted in a "substitution of the unconscious action of crowds for the conscious activity of individuals."[9] This modern replacement of conscious individuality with unconscious groupthink, Le Bon feared, portended no less than the destruction of civilization. Le Bon's *The Crowd* (1896), like many other Chicken-Little warnings about civilization's demise, endowed the "unconscious action of crowds" with attributes imagined to belong to "inferior forms" of individuals, to "women, savages, and children, for instance" (16). The characteristics of a particular crowd, according to Le Bon, depend upon its class and racial makeup (Latin crowds are more prone to allegiance to a dictator and more feminine than Anglo-Saxon crowds, for instance), and the most inferior kind of crowd, not surprisingly, is a heterogeneous one (157). Although Le Bon did not fault specific aspects of democracy (universal suffrage, public education) with bringing about the rise of the masses, he did see those institutions as linked with modern degeneration at the crowd's hands, partly because democracy had spread to races unfit for it: "When we see certain countries, such as the United States, reach a high degree of prosperity under democratic institutions, while others, such as the Spanish-American Republics, are found existing in a pitiable state of anarchy under absolutely similar institutions, we should admit that these institutions are as foreign to the greatness of the one as to the decadence of the others" (79). In addition, Le Bon argued that democracy was dangerous to the "conscious activity" of the evolved because it tended to disrupt class barriers, giving members of the working class "a violent dislike to the state of life in which they were born, and an intense desire to escape from it" (3). Like the ideas that galvanized the barbaric crowds of the past (religious faith, tribal chauvinism), democracy's power and its biggest danger to civilized society, according to Le Bon, lay in its openness to interpretation. Not only did different classes and races adhere to differing understandings of the term (to Anglo-Saxons, for example, it secures the rights of the individual, but for the "Latin races" it secures the power of the state), but so, too, did different geographical locales, Le Bon asserted (196). To Le Bon, the problem with democracy, in short, was that it is a system of social thought and political organization that tends toward the needs and wants of the many—to the crowd—and not to the few who have made Western civilization great. Like Cather's, Wharton's, and Glasgow's observations about modern America, Le Bon's study of the "popular mind" aligned racial heterogeneity and social mobility with a form of cultural degeneration thought to be particular to democracy.

The New York works of Wharton and Glasgow do not portend quite so dire a forecast for modernity as Le Bon's did, but they do employ New York's street life in order to explore the consequences of democracy's tendency to promote diversity and fluid social status, and in the case of both authors, the city is a "labyrinth," to use Ellen Olenska's phrase, because it mixes together members of distinct racial and class backgrounds (75). Images of the city's crowds in their works thus constitute responses to a broad range of pressures facing the city, including the huge influx of immigrants to New York in the latter half of the nineteenth and the twentieth centuries. By 1855 two out of three adult New Yorkers were foreign-born, and by 1910 there were 1.252 million Jews in the city, mostly crowded on the Lower East Side, as well as a quarter of a million Italians residing near them in Mulberry Bend.[10] And because even by the mid-nineteenth century, the thirty-four blocks along Fifth Avenue between Washington Square and Forty-second Street housed only four hundred families—twelve families a block—while one East Side tenement block housed seven hundred families, responses to New York's multitudes were often responses to its changing racial character.[11] Yet another source of fascination with the crowd was, to be sure, the development of a consumer order—from Lower East Side peddling to Ladies' Mile shopping and Broadway theatergoing—that created a "novel kind of city," as historian William Taylor writes, "designed as a showcase, at once a stimulus and a gratification to the mass of consumers whose identity was being redefined by a new concept: the public."[12] Like Taylor, Edwin Burrows and Mike Wallace argue that among the most "closely watched phenomena" of urban life in the press was "the crowd," a term they claim suggested both a threatening mob and a "vibrant street life," both foreign hordes and endless opportunities for consumer indulgence.[13] Such a double meaning troubled those like Walter Lippmann who linked class status to one's degree of cultural sophistication. Lippmann, who shared with Wharton an acquaintance with Bernard Berenson, asserted that the problems with American democracy were cultural; Americans, he claimed, now lived like immigrants: "transient" and "rootless," with the vulgar tastes of the nouveau riche.[14]

With its bases of corporate and cultural power occupying the spine of the island, New York's geography manifests abstractions about centers, margins, and the porosity between them. As Elizabeth Ewen argues, "two conflicting forces were set in motion" in the turn-of-the-century city: "an urban consumer economy created distinct classes, geographically set apart, while an urban mass culture carved out public spaces that made possible a limited degree of cultural integration."[15] The city center itself was further demarcated by gender: downtown, associated with business, was a thoroughly masculine domain, while Midtown—with Central Park, shopping districts, hotels, and even ladies' bank windows—became increasingly female or mixed-gender commercial spaces. Even those places most associated with the upper and middle classes could not be segregated easily from the "masses," of course, for if immigrants and members of the working class did not live in Midtown, they went there to work for, be entertained by, and observe those who did. And as the early twentieth century progressed, Midtown would increasingly ape the entertainment forms of those living on the city's poor margins (the Lower East Side, Harlem). New York's consumer culture excelled at transforming the "othered" or the "foreign" (jazz, Yiddish stage music) into fodder for Broadway and hence for the typically "American." As Taylor writes, such a combination of consumerism and non-Anglo cultures made New York at once the "epitome of America" and "utterly alien to it."[16]

Such a combination also made New York the American city that is most commonly associated with the social mobility promised by the American Dream ("if I can make it there, I'll make it anywhere," as the song says). This mobility was made possible in part by the city's influence on the national economy. Provoking both admiration and ire (think of Jason Compson's tirade against Wall Street in *The Sound and the Fury*), New York's economic clout over the rest of the nation became a frequently noted aspect of the turn-of-the-century city. Some contended that this characteristic was its only notable one, for unlike cities dominated by church or state structures grounding and synthesizing the landscape around them, the New York skyline seemed to express the city's investment in business, with each structure conceived in isolation.[17] Even as far back as the 1850s (one of the decades when Wharton's Old New York was at its height), a *Harper's* commentator asked, "Why should [New York] be loved as a city? It is never the same city for a dozen years together," an observation likewise made by the narrator of James Baldwin's *Another Country* more than a hundred years later: "So superbly" is New York "in the present that it seemed to have nothing to do with the passage of time."[18] At the dawn of the twentieth century, both the nation's present wealth (from the "new" West and the "defeated" South) and its future economic potential (corporate consolidation, imperialism, consumerism) flowed into New York and took up residence on Wall Street.

This was not the case, of course, in the more insular Old New York of Wharton's works, and it is precisely the transition from Old to modern New York that her oeuvre documents. Despite the personal distance she put between herself and her New York kin, Wharton shared with other elite New Yorkers a belief that the city's commercial roots, once unfettered by "inherited obligations," fostered a polyglot society. William Dewitt, for example, described Old New York as a "race" that was being "outnumbered and outrun in its own land."[19] Dewitt's comments refer to the influx of "new money" among the city's elite and the attendant reconstitution of upper-class status by wealth rather than by birth. While it is clear that many Old New Yorkers like Dewitt bemoaned the arrival—or invasion, as Wharton's novels put it—of this "new money," it is also probable, as Burrows and Wallace argue, that the success of arrivistes in penetrating the exclusivity of the elite led to increasing restrictions on wealthy Jews, who had been relatively welcome among the upper classes in the nineteenth century. One famous example of this growing prejudice against Jews is the case of Theodore Seligman, who was blackballed from the Union League Club, an organization his own father helped to found.[20] Characterizing Old New York as a consanguineous family and stressing class and racial kinship equally, Wharton's novels reflect this growing anti-Semitism at the same time that they question the creation of an elite society forged out of a combination of what Burrows and Wallace call "blood and money." So while the fate of Lily Bart, subject both to the nouveau riche and to a Jew, is entirely up for grabs throughout *The House of Mirth,* May Welland's, subject to neither, seems settled from the start of *Age,* and their differing relationships to the mob in turn reflect differently upon the status of their race. While Lily represents an endangered species,

May symbolizes the steadying security of Old New York; "What a new life it was going to be," Newland Archer thinks of his coming marriage, "with this whiteness, radiance, goodness at one's side!" (21). As an "embodied image of the Family," May, with her youth, naïveté, and her dread of anything new or foreign, serves as one of Wharton's most developed symbols for both the chief flaws and the chief virtues she saw in her society (335). Nancy Bentley illustrates how both Old New York and the author herself gain authority by the language of primitive tribal organization with which the novel describes May and Old New York: that society's ability to lend itself to ethnographic description gives it authenticity, and gives Wharton expertise as a novelist.[21] But Wharton's ethnographic investigation, not to mention her ambivalent description of May, proves that any comparison between Old New York and "primitive" cultures can be stretched only so far. Despite May's obsession with ritual and her defensiveness toward outsiders, her absolute loyalty to the values of her society and her innocence give her a kind of sophistication. Wharton's ethnography, that is, highlights the metaphors as metaphors, and highlights the ways American imperialism increasingly made other cultures available for such comparisons. As a figure for the city's pastoral elite, May stands between the aristocratic corruption and degeneracy of the Old World and the consumerist dissolution of the new masses, between Ellen Olenska's Polish count and newcomer Mrs. Struthers, the shoe polish poster girl.

The ambivalence with which Wharton treats May and, by extension, Old New York are similar to the ambivalence with which Glasgow treats her women characters who are particularly representative of the South before the turn of the century, women like the appropriately named Virginia Pendleton Treadwell of *Virginia* (1913). The fullest flower of "the women of her race" (genteel southerners? Anglo-Saxons?), Virginia "embodied the feminine ideal of the ages," an ideal that encompasses qualities that Glasgow's character shares with May: self-sacrifice, unquestioned adherence to tradition, and absolute dependence upon marriage and husband.[22] Like May, Virginia remains mired in the past while everyone around her—her friends, children, and husband—grows and changes with the times. Both May and Virginia embody the pastoral innocence of their regions' pasts, but Wharton attributes perpetual youth to May, while Glasgow attributes premature age to Virginia. This difference in women characters otherwise so similar is significant, for Virginia and the southern womanhood she represents is set in contrast not to a region in transition (as May is) so much as another region entirely: New York. As Wharton does, Glasgow often filters regional change through the traditional local elite's point of view, but using New York rather than Virginia as a setting frees her to explore social change without constant reference to her own group. Her New York novels, including *The Descendant* (1897), *Phases of an Inferior Planet* (1898), *The Wheel of Life* (1906), and *Life and Gabriella,* create a crowded, multicultural city, a city of "freedom, exile, squalor, and disorder," but, above all, a place that empowers individuals to redraw social boundaries.[23] Other novels like *Life and Gabriella* present a variety of Virginians, especially women, who go to New York to start careers and to escape the strict gender and class codes of the South, but *Virginia*'s Southern Lady goes to New York only to tag along with her playwright husband. In both cases when she travels to the city, Virginia experiences much the same mix of fascination for and revulsion of the New York crowds that Gabriella does. But unlike Gabriella, Virginia is incapable of becoming one with the masses, not because she shares Gabriella's distaste for the "lethargy" of the foreign, but because she herself is too outdated for modern New York. Her premature age, brought about by her racial predisposition toward excessive self-sacrifice, surfaces on her second trip to the city, when she is only in her forties. Most of the other characters—her husband, her husband's actress-lover, her best friend, "even the white-haired women" she sees at a New York theater—are as old as or older than she is herself, but they all seem much more youthful than Virginia (356). And Virginia is old because the regional society she represents is old, a society that stands in opposition not just to the New South but also to the crowds of New York.

It is perhaps ironic that the nonnative Glasgow would give us a more varied picture of the city than Wharton, but it is also probable that Glasgow spent more of her adult life in New York than Wharton did. Taken together, the critical conceptions of the two authors establish an interesting conundrum: Edith Wharton is not considered a regionalist because she wrote of New York, a region often made to be synonymous with the nation. Ellen Glasgow, despite the fact that she wrote of New York, is considered a regionalist of Virginia. Yet both authors understood the racial dynamics of American citizenship regionally, and both subjected one region to a fictional lens provided by another, a hallmark, as I have already suggested, of the regionalism they and other turn-of-the-century writers initiated. And for both, New York was closely aligned with a construction of democracy increasingly unmoored from traditional means of exclusion, its street life allowing members of the mob to mix with those above them and thereby propel themselves to the status of the elite. For social-climbing men like Wharton's Simon Rosedale and Glasgow's Daniel O'Hara, Lily and Gabriella represent what, in Abraham Cahan's *The Rise of David Levinsky* (1917), David calls "fascinatingly American" womanhood.[24] David is speaking here of American-born Jewish girls, but Glasgow's and Wharton's women represent the very pinnacle of the genteel (and Gentile) femininity to which these girls aspire. According to both writers, it is the two-pronged aspect of the crowd as a threatening horde and as a means of consumer indulgence that makes these relationships possible, for the development of a consumer culture meant that people who are not in the well-to-do family can afford the trappings of that family and pass as one of its members. In addition, new mores in gender, and in particular women's increasing ability to occupy public spaces, meant that genteel women could mix and mingle with the crowds, experiences Glasgow typically portrayed more positively than Wharton did, as we shall see. What in large part defines the New Women in both Wharton's and Glasgow's New York novels, whether they be Midtown department store shoppers or Lower East Side social gospelers, are those activities that put them into contact with those outside their own social group to a degree much greater than that experienced by their home-bound sisters like Virginia and May. In regionalist terms, then, we might say that New York draws to itself strangers who become, or try to become, native by intermingling with women with the social credentials to which they aspire.

II. REGIONALISM RESISTING MISCEGENATION

At first glance, neither *The House of Mirth* (1905) nor *The Descendant* (1898) seems a particularly likely candidate for the label of "regionalist fiction." Both novels utilize multiple settings: in Wharton's case, Europe and New York; in Glasgow's, New York and Virginia. More importantly, both novels adopt aspects of naturalism, exploring the social and hereditary pressures that confront the individual and lead to their inevitable downfall. As Donna Campbell has shown, Wharton and other writers working in this vein rejected the world of the local-color text, aiming instead to capture "the dislocations and paradoxes of a new age."[25] Campbell cites Mrs. Mainstay of "Mrs. Mainstay's View" and the women in the *Bunner Sisters* as examples of Wharton's naturalist criticism of the values of local color, values that include renunciation, resistance to change, and respect for the past. In *The House of Mirth* it is members of the old order like Mrs. Peniston who best represent Wharton's critique of those values. Belonging "to the class of old New Yorkers who have always lived well, dressed expensively, and done little else," Mrs. Peniston practices a settled idleness distinct from the laziness of the newer sort like Norma Hatch, the "unplaced" newcomer for whom Lily briefly works (32, 213). Unlike the dislocated western woman, Mrs. Peniston is very much fixed in place, her character defined by the confines of the old home in which she lives and by the society she represents. As the van der

Luydens of *The Age of Innocence* do, Mrs. Peniston upholds the old ways by abstaining from the new; while she revels in the minute details of the Van Osburgh wedding, for instance, she does not attend the event. Fetterley and Pryse note that earlier regionalist works "became associated with the figure of the spinster" in the minds of writers, like Wharton, who wished to distance their own work from them, and such distance can certainly be measured in the narrative attitude toward Mrs. Peniston and the niece, Grace Stepney, for whom she disinherits Lily.[26] Both are single women (Mrs. Peniston is widowed and Grace a confirmed "spinster") who live in a claustrophobic domesticity sheltered from masculine society. Honoring the past—or, as Wharton would have it, being entirely dependent upon it—Mrs. Peniston considers the ways of the new elite to be "synonymous with immorality, and the mere idea of immorality was as offensive to Mrs. Peniston as the smell of cooking in the drawing room." What constitutes immorality for Mrs. Peniston is dislocation, people as well as odors being out of place (99). The narrowness and hypocrisy of Mrs. Peniston's views leave little doubt how Wharton felt about several aspects of Old New York as well as of local-color writing.

Similarly, the Virginians of Glasgow's *Descendant* keep faith with the conservative values of the past in ways that border, from the narrator's perspective, on sadism. Their fundamentalist principles prompt them to treat the lowly, orphaned Michael Akershem, born out of wedlock to a working-class mother and an anonymous father of the leisure class, as a "moral plague spot," and to temper their scant charity to him with a condemnation that constitutes "the only excitement they permitted themselves."[27] This is, after all, Plaguesville, Virginia, a setting that inverts the community-centered values of local color as if they were reflections in a fun-house mirror. The town's minister, the only member of Plaguesville to recognize Michael's intellectual gifts, is nonetheless glad when the outcast leaves the community. What precipitates Michael's final break with Plaguesville is the townspeople's perception that he has become a danger to genteel young women, particularly to the minister's own daughter, to whom Michael develops an attraction. The local values of Plaguesville, like those of Old New York as represented by Mrs. Peniston, are perpetuated by keeping individuals firmly fixed in the socio-geographical places in which they were born.

Thus like Jay Gatsby and so many other rags-to-riches American dreamers, Michael moves to New York in order to rise in social status. Full of the vigor and magnetism with which Glasgow, like other naturalist writers, often endows her working-class men, Michael possesses a "genius of endurance" that gives him the strength to elevate himself (19). Instances of Michael's evolutionary health abound: his strong brow, commanding height, and incessant energy all indicate his power, as does his razor-sharp intellect. As Marcelle Thiébaux points out, though, Michael possesses individual "fitness," but he has not inherited the Darwinian "social impulse" needed to curb his ego.[28] Both his "fitness" and his lack of a "social impulse," the narrator tells us, are due to his mixed "blood," the blood of "two diverse natures [that] met and mingled, and they formed a third—a mental hybrid" (23). Such a mixed nature perhaps explains his brownness: Michael is a sort of mental mulatto. As such, he is what Eva Saks calls a "miscegenatious body," made "doubly deviant" by virtue of his physically manifesting a "conflation of difference."[29] Such ambiguity amid the apparently straightforward biological determinism of the novel highlights the complicated nature of Michael's hybridity. His mixed parentage combines distinct class identities that, if kept apart, "might have formed a wholesome simplicity," but instead "warred with one another" and formed "a poisonous complexity" resembling Le Bon's descriptions of the crowd (68). But if Michael's conflict-ridden nature makes his fall inevitable in this arguably most naturalist of Glasgow's novels, his rise is not: it is the tumultuous welter of modern New York that allows him to rise at all. Arriving in New York, he is "born again to start upon life with no ties in the past to bind one—with no past, only a future," but once there, he is forced to live among the anonymous working-class crowds of the city, to whom he feels a sense of disgust inherited by his genteel father (28). Michael thus experiences what to him is a political awakening, and he begins to make a successful career of mobilizing the huddled masses. The novel's plot makes clear, however, that Michael's commitment to social justice is nothing more than the means by which he tries to compete with those above him: he becomes genteel by trying to destroy gentility.

Two key qualities of New York that *The Descendant*'s Virginia setting lack are an upper class that neuresthetically craves the primitive, hybrid nature Michael embodies and an immigrant working class ready to follow any leader who taps into their "natural" resentment of those above them. John Driscoll, an upper-class friend of Michael's, is the novel's primary example of the former group, a man who longs to forego the "nervous energy called civilization" and immerse himself in a more primitive, less genteel (and less white) realm (54). Both responsible for advancing civilization and sick with being overcivilized, Driscoll fancies himself as a sort of amateur ethnographer, reading, to borrow from Nancy Bentley, "the exotic world of savages" as "the site of greatest theoretical clarity, visible to the trained eye in a way the confusion of modern society was not."[30] Wanting to escape to that theoretical clarity, Driscoll dreams of buying a Caribbean island where he will "shoot the first thing in clothes that sets foot upon it" (245). Driscoll's remarks assume the right, by virtue of his whiteness, his masculinity, and his gentility, to claim any space he wishes, but it is precisely the exercising of this right by others that makes it impossible for him to free himself of civilization. Even more ironically, Driscoll seeks the primitive in distant places only to find it closer to home, in Michael, the friendship between the two men exemplifying Campbell's point that in the naturalist text "an excess of civilization" often leads to "a degeneration in some cases identical with that which the emergence of the brute signals."[31] When Michael senselessly murders Kyle, one of his own followers, Driscoll comes to regret his own role in elevating Michael beyond his station, for "knowing Michael's undisciplined nature and his own disciplined one, he told himself that he was a fool to judge him as he judged himself—or any other man" (246). In other words, Michael is a primitive hybrid, and thus an evolutionary throwback, not a "man." The consequences of Driscoll's shirking of his duties to inferiors like Michael are accentuated by the fact that his friend becomes most primitive just when he most aspires to respectability.

Michael's career of invective equally depends upon having followers among the working-class mob, "men who, spending their lives in physical labor, are willing to save themselves mentally by taking their opinions secondhand" (121). Not only does the narrator imply that Michael's activism among the masses is a force of "evil," but as such, it depends upon the sheeplike inability of the working class to discriminate in moral matters. Glasgow draws on the same language of a threatening under caste that Jacob Riis uses in *How the Other Half Lives* (1890), language that likewise echoes Le Bon's warnings about the crowds. Calling himself a "war correspondent" bringing the city's well-to-do knowledge of its menacing enemies, Riis asks his readers what they plan to do about "a proletariat ready and able to avenge the wrongs of their crowds."[32] The kind of vengeance of which Riis speaks is precisely the same as that which Michael tries to exact through his control of the masses. But the narrator's most scathing irony is directed against those masses themselves, particularly Irish men like Kyle and McTibs, who work for Michael's paper, *The Iconoclast*:

> In a moment of missionary zeal Kyle had succeeded in opening McTibs's eyes to the futility of things hoped for, and the enormity of his making an honest living when he might make a dishonest one. . . . McTibs realized that Communism was the one thing needful; the road to Communism lay in throttling Society. He attempted to throttle So-

> ciety, which resulted in his being in *The Iconoclast* editorial rooms and his children in the city poor-house.
>
> As for his wife—well, Kyle had converted her also. He had persuaded her that marriage was deceitful, and morality was vain; and, being persuaded, she had hanged herself. (127)

The working class's vulnerability to Michael's teachings varies according to ethnicity: the Irish are the most predisposed to his nonsensical radicalism, followed by the city's Italians (who arrive in the New World already "skilled in beggary," we are told [197]). To the more conservative Germans, however, Michael's teachings are "rot" (180). These portrayals are in keeping with popular turn-of-the-century racial classifications, which held that old immigrants like the Germans, seemingly fit for democratic citizenship because they shared Anglo-Americans' Teutonic origins and therefore a "natural" ability to self-govern, rejected radicalism, while the Irish—at once resentful of and dependent upon their betters—brought radicalism with them from the Old World.

Like Michael Akershem, *The House of Mirth*'s Simon Rosedale is associated with the masses: dubbed by Judy Trenor as "the same little Jew who had been served up and rejected at the social board a dozen times," Rosedale is meant to stand for Jews as a whole (16). And like other Jews in Wharton's works, Rosedale's physical traits (especially his glossiness) serve as "outer signs of an essential, immutable, inner moral-intellectual character."[33] Just as Michael's hybridity at once exiles him from respectability and gives him the vitality to break its ranks, Rosedale's Jewishness functions both as the source of his social ostracism and as the basis of his triumph over obscurity: the "instincts of his race" help him cope with New York's initial rejection, and the "tradition of his blood" gives him the determination to keep trying despite society's disdain for him (96, 141). Lily and her kind exist in a "great gilt cage in which they all huddled for the mob to gap at," and Rosedale's task is to exchange his place outside the cage for a spot inside, his financial success assuring that, as Trenor notes, "a few years from now he'll be in whether we want him or not" (45, 65). The stereotypes upon which Wharton relies to develop Rosedale's character act as a kind of narrative shorthand, what Toni Morrison calls the "economy" of stereotype, based on the reader's acceptance of Wharton's version of Jewishness.[34] Although readers are asked to ascribe most of Rosedale's negative qualities to his race, none of these qualities differ too greatly from those of the non-Jewish characters, especially socially secure men like Gus Trenor and Percy Gryce. The novel nonetheless incessantly compares Rosedale to these men, and, despite their obvious unpalatability, it is Rosedale who falls short. Lily's social demise, in fact, is marked by the distance between Rosedale and Gryce, whom Lily half-heartedly hopes to snag at the beginning of the novel. Despite the fact that he comes with a large fortune, a puritanical mother, a banal set of Americana, and little else, Lily knows that "if she did not marry Percy Gryce, the day might come when she would have to be civil to such men as Rosedale" (46). The events of the novel are arranged so that readers will make similar comparisons, such as when Lily looks for Gryce at Jack Stepney's wedding and instead finds Rosedale, or when she waits for Selden to arrive for a visit and Rosedale appears instead (73, 139). At times Rosedale seems to function solely to make Selden, in particular, look better than he would without the contrast. When Rosedale appears in her aunt's drawing room with the marriage proposal Lily thought Selden would bring, "the contrast" between them, between Jewish and Anglo masculinity, is, we are told, "grotesque" (140). The plotting of Lily's downfall requires that we see Rosedale as the least desirable of Lily's marital options.

Yet it is Trenor, not Rosedale, who most threatens Lily's social position and her very self, his sexual expectations turning her into a kind of "charity girl," a type frequently bemoaned in the turn-of-the-century New York press. Kathy Peiss notes that single working-class girls at the time, like most New Yorkers, were attracted to the variety of new leisure activities the city offered but often had no means by which to pay for them, so they resorted to a practice the local press called "treating," wherein men paid for a woman's entertainment and were repaid with sexual favors ranging from hand-holding to intercourse.[35] Trenor's language in the scene in which he tries to force himself on Lily suggests that he expects just such a payment for his "investments" on her behalf: "the man who pays for the dinner is generally allowed to have a seat at the table" (114). Long before Lily is forced to consider Rosedale's proposal, then, she is re-classed by Gus as a charity girl. I disagree with Christian Riegel's assertion that Wharton "see[s] things as virtues in Gentiles and vices in Jews," for she does lambaste Trenor, but I do agree that the novel advances a "double standard" because its assumption that readers will understand Rosedale's character mostly in terms of his race is contradicted by the fact that he is simply not that different from anyone else.[36] Seemingly to mitigate whatever danger Trenor, as opposed to Rosedale, might represent for Lily, the novel manages to implicate Rosedale in Trenor's attempted rape: as Trenor is forcing himself upon her, he tells Lily that Rosedale and he have exchanged stories about her, and, learning she has been the object of such gossip, Lily feels a "sense of dizziness," as if "the brutality of the thrust" were a "physical blow" (114). In this way, the novel deflects some of the physical violence with which Gus threatens Lily by implicating Rosedale in metaphoric violence. So is Trenor's would-be rape a result of his unchecked power as an upper-class white man, or is it a result of his "primitive" side, accentuated as it is by his association with Rosedale? The two men's symbiotic relationship suggests that both are true, for Wharton frequently uses Rosedale's Jewishness as a reflection—and a deflection—of Trenor's and other upper-class whites' flaws.

The Descendant and *The House of Mirth* also examine the ways Michael and Rosedale need to solidify their social triumphs by being accepted by the women as well as the men of high society. Although Michael is eager to reinvent himself in New York, once he has achieved some measure of prominence as the city's newest social activist, he finds himself drawn to a southern girl, Rachel Gavin, who represents the society from which he fled. Like Gabriella Fowler, though, Rachel has come to New York to start a career, exchanging her identity as a poor-but-proud daughter of the old Virginian aristocracy for one as a New Woman artist. Rachel risks her reputation by living with Michael (at his insistence) out of marriage, her love for him becoming a kind of descent into madness—an obsessive, self-destructive compulsion to ruin both her art and her respectability. And as their relationship progresses, it becomes more and more apparent that Rachel's destruction is Michael's unconscious motivation, and that this is his revenge against all those in the South who held him in such contempt. The greatest proof of this is that once Michael has pulled Rachel down, in society's eyes, to his level, he ceases to desire her and becomes obsessed with another, more "respectable" woman named Anna Allard. Here Michael exhibits that characteristic of democracy that so troubled Le Bon, in that it engenders a "violent dislike to the state of life" in which Michael is born and "an intense desire to escape from it" (3).

Rosedale, at least, cannot be charged with actually desiring Lily's demise, and he seems to be genuinely ignorant about the social consequences that would befall Lily should she accept his proposal of marriage. He also has the virtue of being honest with Lily about the intentions motivating that proposal: for him, being associated with a well-bred Anglo girl is "like money in his pocket," and his offer of an alliance is, he frankly admits, a business exchange (15). While in *The Passing of the Great Race* New Yorker Madison Grant had argued that procreation between non-Jews and Jews produced Jews (the logic being that offspring of a "mixed" racial heritage take on the race of the parent considered to be of the dominant but "lower" origin), Rosedale seems not to know, or to care, about the potential effects of miscegenation.[37] Yet like the relationship between Michael and Rachel, in which she descends in respectability as he acquires more of it, Rosedale's steps up the social ladder are marked by the female company he keeps as much as, and perhaps more than, the money he makes on Wall Street. After Jack Stepney fails to integrate Rosedale into society at the Van Osburgh "crush," he "showed himself with Rosedale at the fashionable restaurants, in company with the personally vivid if socially obscure ladies who are available for such purposes" (16). According to Lewis Erenberg's study of New York nightlife, there were only a small number of restaurants (Delmonico's, Sherry's) that elite women frequented, and they did so for planned events like the Patriarch's Ball.[38] Otherwise, fashionable restaurants were used by elite men to entertain (with impunity) actresses, singers, and other women considered at the time to belong to a more dubious status. This is why *House of Mirth*'s Carrie Fisher, who makes her living and maintains her position in society by helping newcomers (like the Gormers and the Brys) enter the privileged realm, cannot be Rosedale's initial social contact, for he would compromise the first unmarried elite woman with whom he associates.

It is, of course, one of the central ironies of Lily's situation that the more she is pushed toward a marriage with Rosedale, the more her value to him diminishes, for his climb and her fall, as Hildegard Hoeller points out, are "in perfect contrast."[39] In fact, one of the most significant steps in Rosedale's social triumph comes when he is given the opportunity to snub Lily, not marry her. Running into Lily after her first fall from social grace, Rosedale, "flushed . . . with the importance" of being seen with Judy Trenor at a fashionable hotel, sees how that lady treats Lily and follows suit (178). The big, public hotel stood as a symbol to many of a new openness to accept wealth alone as proof of elite status, as Erenberg notes, and Rosedale's opportunity in such a space to show disapproval for Lily's supposed transgressions brings him closer to assuming the responsibilities of Anglo men as arbiters of women's respectability.[40] As Rosedale succeeds in his invasion and inches closer to erasing his identity as a Jew, Lily moves from the pinnacle of white womanhood to charity girl and workingwoman. This transition is ironically foreshadowed by her tableau vivant of "Mrs. Lloyd." An effort to embody ideal Anglo femininity, Lily's tableau risks becoming a sales ad targeted to a Jew, for at the time the novel was published, as Christopher Gair has shown, Reynolds's painting lay in the private collection of the Rothschild family.[41] In this way, Rosedale's social ascension depends on Lily's demise as much as Michael Akershem's depends upon Rachel's near destruction.

In accordance with both novels' naturalist inflections, the ultimate fates of Rosedale, Lily, Michael, and Rachel all live up to the maxim that "blood tells." A man whose "loud-voiced clamor against custom" masks "a shade of regret . . . that respectability, which he appeared to scorn, had scorned him in reality," Michael's mixed associations make class mobility an allegory of racial assimilation, a point suggested when Driscoll advances the seemingly random view that "the abolition of slavery has more to answer for than is written in history" (104, 211). Interestingly, this assessment of emancipation occurs to Driscoll just when he is beginning to understand how much Michael has "ruined" Rachel. Michael's metaphorical brownness, in other words, becomes recognizable at the very moment when his destruction of her whiteness, symbolized by her sexual purity, is most in jeopardy.[42] While his relationship with Rachel almost, but not quite, drives her mad, his growing obsession with Anna at the end of the novel pushes Michael himself over the edge and prompts him to kill Kyle in what, even to him, is a senseless act of violence. "Blood tells" most, in other words, just when one is trying to dodge its inevitability.

Most readers of *The House of Mirth* recognize that Wharton's unique contribution to naturalism lies in the fact that it is Lily, an upper-class white woman, who suffers a reversion to type. But Rosedale, too, reverts to type. His initial attraction to Lily is grounded in "that mixture of artistic sensibility and business astuteness which characterizes his race," but the two sides of this mixture begin to war with each other just as the elements of Michael's blood do (16). It is characteristic of stereotypes of the Jew that although in business matters he is "civilized" or even overly so, he remains primitive in emotional and sexual matters, or "gross, unscrupulous, rapacious," as Wharton's narrator puts it (195). As Lily watches Rosedale play with Carrie Fisher's daughter, she notes that his behavior toward the feminine sex resembles "the way of the predatory creature with his mate," this glimpse of Rosedale as what the narrator calls a "fireside man" suggesting that despite his honed instincts for making money, in private life Carrie's daughter is more civilized. As Gail Bederman shows, whites often postulated that racial others stopped evolving earlier than they did, so that so-called primitives were as evolved as adults as white children were.[43] This vision of Rosedale brings us back to his implication in Trenor's assault on Lily: Trenor might be the one attempting violence, but Rosedale, as a "predatory creature," certainly seems just as predisposed to it. It is exactly in such scenes—where we glimpse characters in private, away from the business world—that Wharton tests her characters, and Rosedale's race prevents him from achieving anything but a rudimentary domestic life. As Lily's status declines, Rosedale's "artistic sensibility" as well as his predatory nature prompt him to remain attracted to her inherent racial worth. But his "business astuteness" engenders in him a growing distate for her diminished social worth. Indeed, once Lily has become passé in the eyes of high society, Rosedale's attraction to her develops into a "forgotten enemy that had lain in ambush and now sprang out on him unawares" (226).

Rosedale's predatory nature belies the social status he achieves by the end of the novel; his "fall," then, is one for readers' eyes only, a plot device that accentuates the hypocrisy of the society that has forced Lily's more public fall. As a "marriageable girl," Lily is to remain "pure" or untainted by those outside of her own New York society, a task that becomes increasingly difficult with each successful invasion by a stranger to the elite. The life Lily leads at the end of the novel is not just one of hard, dull work and poverty; it is also one in which she will enjoy no differentiation from the masses and no protection from victimization at its hands. Lily's fall from social grace, from her Aunt Peniston's home to a shabby boardinghouse, is literally a move from fashionable Midtown to the working-class, mostly Irish West Side margins, where the racial status she embodies will harm rather than help her. As Jennie Kassanoff points out, Lily "personifies . . . squandered Anglo-Saxon promise," but Wharton's novel insists that something of that promise remains.[44] For just as Rosedale's social instincts compete with his predatory sexuality, Lily's social instincts, which increasingly prompt her to be kind to Rosedale, war with her racial ones, her "intuitive repugnance" often "getting the better of years of social discipline" (16). So as "blood tells" for Rosedale, it does for Lily as well. The most significant use of Rosedale's Jewishness, in fact, is that it throws Lily and Selden "into hyper Anglo-Saxon relief," as Elizabeth Ammons puts it.[45] The chief distinction between Lily and Selden on the one hand and Rosedale on the other is that Lily and Selden lack the courage of their convictions, while Rosedale lacks convictions altogether. By the end of the novel, though, Lily gains the daring she has thus far failed to display when she chooses to do the ethical thing (not to use Bertha's letters) and courts death instead. Again, Rosedale's racial status functions as a key means of contrast here, for Lily does entertain the idea of using the letters, but decides against it when Rosedale suggests she do so: having Rosedale articulate the blackmail plan reflects its "monstrous glare" and forces Lily to see "the whole transaction in a new aspect" (202, 203). Would Lily have developed the sense of ethics she does at the end of *The House of Mirth* without such a contrast? Although, on the one hand, Rosedale is the only person from her old life to visit Lily once she has lost everything, he is also the person against whom she must turn if she is to fulfill the moral imperative of her situation. Bertha's letters, which in reality say more about well-to-do New York society than anything else, nonetheless reach Lily via the other, via either the charwoman Mrs. Haffen or Rosedale. In this way, both characters deflect Lily's and upper-class New York's moral lapses, becoming implicated by the structure of the novel in the sins of the New York elite. This deflection allows Wharton to cast Lily, in death, as an exemplar of a purer race removed from the onslaught of outsiders, and thus race "becomes an essential—if deeply problematic—answer to the cultural vulnerabilities of class and gender."[46]

Paradoxically, it is Rosedale, with his Jewish "artistic sensibility" and "appreciation of value," who provides the greatest proof of the racial superiority that Lily comes to represent. Her growing moral scruples impress him because as he gains "social experience," he acquires "the air of a collector who had learned to distinguish minor differences of design and quality" (234). In other words, both because of his rough sexual impulses and his finely honed "air of a collector," Rosedale secretly resists society's reclassification of Lily. And if he does not question the inherent value of Lily's whiteness, why should readers? Lily's final moral triumph is the realization that she cannot maintain a sense of her own superiority and marry Rosedale, which is why she burns the letters—her last remaining link to him—and, consequently, does the only truly ethical thing she has ever done. The moral and racial superiority she comes to represent both through resisting Rosedale and through her death create a novel that is written "against the grain of the patriarchal masterplot" and one that upholds Anglo-Saxon authority "to the death."[47] In cleansing her of the taint of the mob as well as that of the elite class that is coming to resemble it, Lily's death aligns her with the values Wharton associates with the pastoral regional realm in a way that was impossible in life.

Finally, "blood tells" for Rachel Gavin as well. The end of *The Descendant* establishes a contrast between Rachel's perspective and that of Anna, a charity volunteer, much like *House of Mirth*'s Gerty Farrish, who maintains traditional notions of social boundaries, rejecting Michael's advances both because his teachings encourage her wards to turn away from "training and inherited belief" and because he himself is one of their numbers (175–77). Unlike Anna, Rachel supports the promise of social mobility and is herself a manifestation of such democratization. Whereas Michael's New York self-reinvention is destructive, Rachel's, perhaps because of her superior birth, is creative: she finishes her masterpiece, a painting of Magdalene that is meant to be a symbol of feminine suffering and triumph. In the end, Anna's naturalist warning is unconvincing when paired with the complex and poignantly drawn Rachel, whose point of view comes to dominate the novel. So even as Glasgow's work punishes Michael for his rise, it can't bring itself to doom Rachel for her belief in his right to do so.

In the case of both novels, the characters' naturalist "fall" prompts a return to regionalist values: Lily comes to represent the best of Old New York, and Michael comes to stand as a warning against the full-fledged abdication of the local hierarchies dominating Plaguesville as well as the pitfalls for women like Rachel in wholly abandoning their privilege. As Donna Campbell has noted, however much of a revolt naturalists tried to wage against their local-color predecessors, they nonetheless shared much in common with them: like works that came before them, *The House of Mirth* and *The Descendant* are marked by a "preservation of the self within a matrix of absence and loss."[48] Both Michael's fall and Rosedale's ascent represent great losses, individual and social, but preserved are the women through whom these men try to transcend boundaries: Lily, the dead racial paradigm, and Rachel, the living one. In both novels seemingly "natural" divisions associated with nineteenth-century regional cultures are threatened by, but ultimately triumph over, the widening scope of democracy in the modern era.

III. DEMOCRATIC UNIONS

In their later works Glasgow and Wharton forego a naturalist reassertion of local-color values, exploring instead a full transition of men of dubious origin to the ranks of the respectable. The social transformations of Rosedale and Michael lack a sense of completion because neither character manages to align himself with the woman (Lily or Anna) who symbolizes total integration into the society to which they aspire to belong. Characters like Julius Beaufort of *The Age of Innocence* and Daniel O'Hara of *Life and Gabriella,* however, succeed where Rosedale and Michael fail, and their successes herald a new order patterned not around birth and consanguinity but around fluid, variable identities. Such variability is made possible in both novels by the city's economic preeminence and its new consumer order as well as by the growing number of strangers, domestic and foreign, who are drawn to New York because of these qualities. Critical to the transformation processes that *Age* and *Life* detail is that the troubling New York crowds, and the more troubling men who break their ranks, are strangers to the city who come to make their fortunes there. While the women with whom they associate—*Age*'s Regina Dallas Beaufort and *Life*'s Gabriella—are both southerners, they are somehow not strangers in the sense that Beaufort and O'Hara are. Both men come closer to becoming native only when they ally themselves with women who, by virtue of their class and racial status, aren't really strangers to New York society at all.

In the scholarship on Wharton, much has been made of the marriage of Wall Street and Fifth Avenue, but what has generally been overlooked is the extent to which Wall Street surfaces in her works as a region of strangers, enemy territory that lies very close to the turf of the natives. As it does in Howells's *A Hazard of New Fortunes* (1890), Wall Street functions as a nexus bringing together individuals from distinct groups and—like it or not—placing them on equal footing, not only lifting up the lowly but, because it does so, prostrating the socially prominent. Yet unlike the New York that Howells creates, Wharton's city seems to collapse distinctions between members of the working class and ethnic groups. Howells's Dryfoos, a western man who has come to New York to increase his newly made wealth and buy his daughters Knickerbocker husbands, is set in opposition to the immigrant, Lindau. The two, in fact, engage in an ideological battle (Dryfoos is a laissez-faire social Darwinist and Lindau a committed socialist) that hurts most those, like the Bostonian Basil March, who represent an older, more stable regional gentility. In contrast, ethnic others like Rosedale and Beaufort and "new" men like Elmer Moffatt and Abner Spragg of *The Custom of the Country,* sharing similar acquisitive values, are all equally "fit" for Wall Street life.

Beaufort's relation to Regina has secured him a social position in Old New York, but his marriage would never have occurred had he not succeeded on Wall Street in the first place. As Ralph Marvell in *Custom* observes, "The daughters of their own race sold themselves to the Invaders; the daughters of the Invaders bought their husbands as they bought an opera-box."[49] Furthermore, the social positions of the "Invaders" rely upon the measure of control they can exert over Old New York's money, which is why there is such anxiety around Beaufort's financial dealings throughout *The Age of Innocence.* As a region within a region, Wall Street not only facilitates the social transformation of men like Beaufort but it also forces the established elite to become shamelessly dependent on the other. Nothing makes Wharton's association of Wall Street and outsider status clearer than her male characters who do not succeed there. Few, indeed, are the number of men born into the Old New York family who succeed in navigating the hostile terrain of Wall Street, for "aboriginal" characters like Ralph Marvell—whose attempt to support the financial demands of his wife by adapting himself to the daily grind of Wall Street literally makes him ill—are simply unfit for such a task (47). And as is indicated by Ralph's business dealings with Moffatt, which spell the beginning of the end for Ralph and for his son, part of Old New York men's incapacity to function on Wall Street has to do with their inherited predisposition toward a "standard of uprightness in affairs" that men like Beaufort and Moffatt constitutionally lack.[50]

Although both Wharton and Glasgow construct Wall Street as a region inhabited by strangers, financial success there signals something very different for Glasgow than it does for Wharton. Despite Gabriella's initial disdain for O'Hara, the novel's point of view praises the rags-to-riches example of hard work he embodies and extols the fruition of a democracy that supposedly assures that "You can always get on if the stuff is in you" (412). The challenge that Glasgow sets for Gabriella (similar to the challenge New York posed to Glasgow herself) is to give up her prejudiced notions that connect status with birth and culture with character. That O'Hara, being born a poor Irish American who has made his own way, is therefore devoid of taste, neither Gabriella nor the novel questions. But Gabriella learns that O'Hara's having been born with honor but without the trappings of the honorable makes him, in some ways, superior to her: "Before this man, who had sprung from poverty and dirt, who had struggled up by his own force, . . . she felt suddenly humbled. Without friends, without knowledge, except the bitter knowledge of the streets, he had fought his fight, and had kept untarnished a certain hardy standard of honour" (457). Not "pruned" by custom or tradition, O'Hara recalls both the "triumphs and the failures of American democracy" (480). Glasgow leaves no doubt that whatever democracy holds for the future, Gabriella will be part of it, because she learns to forego the social prejudices—most of them, anyway—that mark her past.

While O'Hara is, of course, key in this transformation of Gabriella, she is also in a sense primed to undergo such a change because of her experiences in New York. After the breakup of her marriage to an Old New Yorker, Gabriella must navigate a city that continually challenges her inherited notions of privilege. As we saw above, she attempts to maintain her mental distance from the "lethargy" of the foreign hordes, but the location of her home on the West Side, which Glasgow locates very near an immigrant enclave stretching from Canal to Seventieth Street, suggests that such distance is difficult to maintain. Living in an apartment house that lacks private baths and kitchens (based on Glasgow's own apartment in the Windermere building), Gabriella's children play with Italian and German immigrants, and she herself chats with the "mothers of the Jewish babies" (322–23). But the poverty and, as she imagines it, the unseemliness of the immigrants around her haunt Gabriella with a "malignant demon of melancholy" even as she engages in the most commonplace exchanges with them (322). Interestingly, when Gabriella moves from this neighborhood to the more middle-class West Twenty-third Street, she becomes more rather than less concerned that her children "form friendships in their own class" (392). It is here that she meets O'Hara, so while the neighborhood poses a greater challenge to her regionally inflected sense of privilege, it also holds out greater rewards for her.

Like Gabriella, Ellen Olenska establishes herself "far down West Twenty-third Street" alongside bohemians and artists in a house that reminds Archer of a "far-off bazaar," thereby disobeying her family's "feeling against living in *des quartiers excentriques*" (72). Not recognizing that in New York, "everything may be labelled—but everybody is not," Ellen fails to understand her family's wish that she remain apart from the mob (75). Ellen ignores many other dictates Old New York sets for the social geography of the city, including being seen on Fifth Avenue at "the crowded hour" with Julius Beaufort (29). Despite her geographical disobedience, she agrees with Archer that certain things—such as the news of one's engagement—should not be spoken of in "a crowd," a discernment that seems in keeping with the regional values Archer himself most respects. As M. Rivière learns, Ellen is a "kind" of American to whom "things that are accepted in certain other societies, or at least put up with as part of a general convenient give-and-take," are "simply unthinkable." In other words, she is an Old New Yorker of the best kind, as Wharton saw it (256). Even as Ellen acknowledges its flaws, she articulates one of Wharton's most eloquent defenses of Old New York when she explains to Archer why he cannot break his promise to marry May:

> New York simply meant peace and freedom to me: it was coming home. And I was so happy at being among my own people that everyone I met seemed kind and good. . . . But . . . I felt there was no one as kind as you; no one to give me reasons that I understood for doing what at first seemed so hard and—unnecessary. . . . But . . . you understood; you had felt the world outside tugging at one with all its golden hands—and yet you hated the things it asked of one; you hated happiness bought by disloyalty and cruelty and indifference. That was what I'd never known before—and it's better than anything I've known. (172)

The fundamental irony of *The Age of Innocence*—and the primary means by which Wharton launches her critique of Old New York in the novel—is that Ellen, in part through her ability to inhabit a variety of spaces, comes to honor the regional values of Old New York even if its members manage to exile her from it.

One of the things that is "unthinkable" for Ellen is a relationship with Julius Beaufort; despite Archer's anxieties, Wharton makes a point of showing that Ellen has no interest in such a liaison. But the gossip about them helps to establish a pairing of Ellen with Regina Beaufort. By absconding herself from New York to keep away from Archer, the man with whom she is tempted to engage in a tryst, Ellen proves her loyalty to the Old New York family. It is precisely that family loyalty that Regina Beaufort, ensconced on Fifth Avenue, lacks. Beaufort, who "passed for an Englishman," is even more menacing to the purity of Old New York—and its women—than a character, like Rosedale, who can be dismissed as a "little Jew" (3). Old New York relies upon marriage to reproduce itself, which is why the marriage of May and Archer, a union of two already established clans (geographically, we might say a marriage of Fifth Avenue to itself), is celebrated but the marriage of Beaufort and Regina (Fifth Avenue and Wall Street) is not. Marriage functions in the novel both to keep outsiders at bay and, paradoxically, to let them in, so that everything hinges, in a mixed marriage, on whether one marries up or down. This helps to explain why Catherine Spicer Mingott, the "Matriarch of the line," is drawn to outsiders like Ellen and Beaufort—for she was once an outsider, a "vulgar Spicer," herself—and why she furiously opposes the ending of both of their marriages (10, 153). As an outsider turned matriarch, Mrs. Mingott stands in opposition to the other rulers of the clan, the van der Luydens, because while the Manson-Mingott marriage is one of opposites, the marriage of the van der Luydens is based upon similarity to the point of being quasi-incestuous (they even look alike). But Mrs. Mingott consistently upholds the marriage tie, either between opposites or those suggestive of siblings, commanding that Regina Beaufort share her husband's social shame and financial ruin and answering Regina's plea of consanguity—"But my name, Auntie—my name's Regina Dallas," with a retort that reminds Regina that she has forfeited the family tie: "It was Beaufort when he covered you with jewels, and it's got to stay Beaufort now that he's covered you with shame" (275). Mrs. Mingott upholds the one New York institution that ensures her own place in the tribe, for if Regina Beaufort can revert to being Regina Dallas, she herself could revert from Mrs. Manson Mingott to Catherine Spicer.

Because Regina has married an inferior, she, unlike Mrs. Mingott, has made her social role extremely precarious: "When one was related to the Mansons and the Rushworths one had a 'droit de cité' . . . in New York society; but did not one forfeit it in marrying Julius Beaufort?" (17). Regina does, indeed, forfeit her status, for in a patriarchal society a wife assumes her husband's identity, even his race, and relinquishes her own. This is why Grandfather Newland's advice—"Whatever you do, don't let that fellow Beaufort be introduced to the girls"—seems so prophetic (33). Even the ridiculous Lawrence Lefferts understands that "if society chose to open its doors to vulgar women the harm was not great, though the gain was doubtful; but once it got in the way of tolerating men of obscure origin and tainted wealth the end was total disintegration" (341). As much as Wharton disdains Lefferts, he is more hyperbolic than incorrect here. Old New York men like *Custom*'s Ralph Marvell may doom themselves and the purity of their family by marrying outsiders, but their status as Old New Yorkers remains unquestioned. In fact, Ralph comes closer to embodying the pastoral values of Old New York—the nation's "Aborigines," as he calls them—after he has married newcomer Undine Spragg (47). Regina's status, on the other hand, becomes just as mysterious as Beaufort's origins: she is no longer a member of "one of America's most honoured families" but one of the "pet common people"—or, as the narrator speculates, perhaps something even worse—that Old New York occasionally tolerates (16). Unlike Lily Bart, who in becoming Mrs. Simon Rosedale would have become the wife of a "little Jew," Regina joins a more menacing category that cannot be classified.

As a flat character in a novel full of complex ones, Regina is not just enigmatic, she is devoid of any discernable selfhood, her personality repeatedly effaced by her husband's and replaced by him with the markers of conspicuous consumption. "The knowing people," the narrator tells us, attribute all of her domestic accomplishments to her husband; it is Julius Beaufort who "trained the servants, taught the chef new dishes, told the gardeners what hot-house flowers to grow . . . and dictated the little notes his wife wrote to her friends" (17–18). All of the things that make May and her kind socially prominent women of Old New York make Regina, instead, a walking advertisement of her husband's supposed vulgarity and of her own relegation to marginal status, for "Regina always does what [Beaufort] tells her" (33). Regina's impeccably dressed appearance at the opera before the start of her annual ball symbolizes "her possession of a staff of servants competent to organise every detail of the entertainment in her absence," and her reappearance there a year later, wearing a new, expensive necklace, reassures Old New York that their fortunes will not be lost by Beaufort's misdeeds on Wall Street (16). Often functioning as little more than a model for the display of fashionable clothing and fine jewels, Regina embodies the aloof elite and the looming mob simultaneously. By making Regina wear her clothes as soon as they arrive from Paris instead of following the nineteenth-century custom of packing them away, Beaufort not only starts a new and, to Old New York, disturbing fashion trend, but he also exposes Regina to the mob and to Old New York's censure. "All Regina's distinctions," Janey Archer puts it, are needed to overcome her association with Beaufort, the implication being that Beaufort, in actuality, makes Regina indistinguishable from more common women (260). That he does so primarily through fashion is perhaps the surest sign her husband leaves upon her of his own race, for Jewish men dominated the jewelry and the fashion industries in New York, the latter a process that Abraham Cahan details in *The Rise of David Levinsky*. In making "the average American girl a 'tailor-made girl,'" the business advances of Russian Jews like Levinsky "had the effect of cheapening the better class of garments prodigiously," the effect, in other words, of making women like Regina less distinguishable from those "fascinatingly American" Jewish women with whom David associates.[51] When Beaufort loses his money (and other people's), Old New York at first pities Regina, but her pleas to Mrs. Mingott for support—the only direct action she takes in the novel—associate Regina even more closely with his foreignness. It is at this point that her status as a symbol of Julius's financial power and his racial designation are most obvious. What motivates her request is never made clear: is she really, as she says, thinking herself a natural, immutable member of the family, or did her husband orchestrate this too? The question is never answered, and once Regina takes this action she again fades into obscurity. But because she "had not the excuse . . . of pleading that she was a 'foreigner,'" she becomes her husband's scapegoat, proof that "there was nothing to do but to accept this awful evidence of the indissolubility of marriage" (281). For Regina, that indissolubility is to the death. For Beaufort, who maintains his position if not his physical presence in New York and manages to score places for his children there, it is not. That is the consequence, Wharton suggests, of the democratization of New York, and the consequence of marrying a man who passes for an Englishman.

In contrast to Wharton's Regina, Glasgow's Gabriella is required to accept the promise of a mixed marriage if she is to survive. While Gabriella's initial rejection of O'Hara is motivated by the Irishness of his name (which at this point is all she knows about him), his character—unlike the other Irish characters in the novel—is relatively free of stereotypes. Just Irish enough to test Gabriella's prejudices, but not so Irish that he cannot emerge in her view, or the novel's, as an American, O'Hara is repeatedly associated with the turn-of-the-century extension of democratic privilege. He admits that he is interested in the process of making money, not in having it—a problem, as Gabriella sees it (just as Glasgow herself and, for that matter, Wharton and Cather did), that is common to "the uncultivated rich" (468). O'Hara's tastes are drawn from popular culture (he speaks in slang and hums ragtime) and he expresses himself in action, not language (Gabriella speculates that he probably thinks "Hamlet" is a town out west, and she often remarks upon his "great difficulty with words") (407). Gabriella's initial response to him—

even when she will admit his good qualities—is that "blood tells" (391). His "blood" is Irish, but, as Gabriella learns, his background is western, having been sent to the West as an orphaned boy. Orphaned Irish children were sometimes sent by the city's genteel charities to work on western farms, a practice denounced, not surprisingly, by the Catholic Church. The influence of his relocation is the first thing Gabriella finds redeeming about him: "It's wonderful, isn't it, what the West can do with a man? Now, if he'd stayed in New York he would have been merely impossible, but because he has lived out of doors he has achieved a certain distinction" (472). This depiction of the West, where masculinity thrives and, apparently, everyone lives outdoors, is a safe background for O'Hara's "bigness," permitting him to succeed without competing with elite men of the North and South. Burrows and Wallace point out that this was exactly the purpose of western relocation programs: "clumped in New York, [orphan boys] were a festering menace; dispersed over the continent, their individualism and opportunism could be put to good account."[52]

Gabriella's disdain of O'Hara's Irishness, then, is mitigated by his status as a relative stranger to New York and by his association with the West, a region many hoped would function as a safety valve for tense relations between working-class immigrant groups and genteel native groups in the East. This accounts, in part, for the novel's very different attitude toward other Irish characters, particularly Madame Dinard, the owner of the Fifth Avenue dress shop where Gabriella works. For Gabriella ultimately embraces the new America represented by her and O'Hara's West Twenty-third Street neighborhood, but she does the opposite at work on Fifth Avenue, maintaining older divisions between the Anglo and Irish, aristocratic and common. As Glasgow describes her, Madame Dinard, born O'Grady, is an Irishwoman passing for a Parisian whose success in fashion is countered by her stereotypical bad luck with husbands. Her cynical attitude toward others and her stinginess in business matters, not to mention her vanity and her absurd physical description (she is "voluble, painted, powdered, bewigged"), make her read more like a caricature than a character based on an actual person, as Glasgow claims she was (254).[53] Despite the fact that Dinard seems to be successful—we see many ladies of fashion, or at least of money, visit her store—Madame's talents are deficient: the shop is vulgarly decorated, the poor-quality merchandise is overpriced, and the employees are snobbish and crass. In fact, Madame Dinard's success with the shop seems contrary to her nature, as artificial as her French accent. As she grows older, the narrator tells us, Madame slips back into "her naturally careless methods of work"; "her tendency to . . . be inexact and unsystematic" becoming increasingly apparent to the more capable Gabriella, who eventually takes over the dress shop (321). Gabriella's opportunity to do so comes because "Madame, who had been born an O'Grady," lacks her "grace, her good-breeding, her indefinable charm," qualities that aid Gabriella in dealing with Madame and other Irish upstarts like the "plutocrat" Mrs. Pletheridge (278–79, 303):

> Perhaps, too, though she assured herself that she was without snobbishness, there was a secret satisfaction in the knowledge that one of her ancestors had been a general under Washington while the early Pletheridges were planting potatoes in a peasant's patch in Ireland. Her dignity was more assured than Madame's; for she was perfectly aware of a fact to which Madame was blind, and this was, that, in spite of her position in the social columns of the newspapers and her multitudinous possessions, Mrs. Pletheridge was not, and could never be, a lady. (303–04)

That Gabriella is assured that she is not a snob, of course, is the way the narrator assures readers that she is. But the narrative distance achieved in the first sentence collapses in the second: Madame doesn't know that Mrs. Pletheridge isn't a lady because Madame herself isn't. Linked by their Irishness and their working-class roots, these two women lack knowledge of their "true" positions that Gabriella, a saleswoman, possesses by right of birth or "good-breeding." So just as Gabriella has a difficult time giving up the self-supposed benefits of her illustrious family history, so too does the narrator. And they apparently should not do so, for even the immigrants with whom she rides a cramped subway car appreciate Gabriella's "aristocratic racial outline" and understand that she exemplifies "the American spirit at its best" (326, 349).

Glasgow writes that the time she spent in New York composing *Life and Gabriella* was one of growth for herself and for the nation, but despite whatever progress she and her character make in embracing modern democracy, Gabriella's professional success remains in tension with her personal triumph over past prejudices.[54] Gail Bederman notes that nominal whites like the Irish who were "primitive" according to the prevailing notions of "civilization" were thought to be so in part because their societies had no gender differentiation: part of being civilized was being strongly gendered.[55] So perhaps Glasgow portrays O'Hara and Dinard so differently in order to combat anti-Irish sentiment, but if that is the case, she does the opposite with her Anglo characters, for Gabriella is every bit as (and often more) hardworking, levelheaded, and self-controlled as the men of her own group. While critics like Marcelle Thiébaux have read Gabriella's choice to marry as an awkward reversal of the novel's ostensible objective to narrate the life of a professional woman and thus a betrayal of feminist principles, we must place her decision in the context of traditional constructions of race and class as well as those of gender.[56] In agreeing to marry O'Hara, Gabriella augments her own sense of social worth. Her choice not only justifies him (character really is more important than culture) but it also justifies *her,* for she is embracing a more open, inclusive society. Yet the dissimilar ways Glasgow genders Anglos and Irish make equally clear that even a democracy needs some of what Gabriella represents: class, culture, good breeding, and the wherewithal to know when to draw upon these and when to reject them.

This is, perhaps, the lesson for all of the women characters I've discussed here. And like these characters, Wharton and Glasgow seem to waver between abandoning and accepting both the old values of the past and the democracy that turn-of-the-century New York seemed invested in promoting. For just as the landscape, economy, and street culture of the city encourage the passing of woman suffrage or other advances in women's rights, they also encourage the transformation of other kinds of New Yorkers, a circumstance that posed a double bind for both authors as they imagined the turn-of-the-century city.

2

"'Et Que Cétait comme dans Le Livre'"

—Wharton, the Harlem Renaissance, and All That Jazz

I: "PLEBEIAN INTRUSION[S]" AND JAZZ-AGE NEW YORK

In 1927, the same year that she published *Twilight Sleep,* a searing indictment of New York society in the Jazz Age, Edith Wharton wrote to Galliard Lapsley about another novel of the 1920s city published the year before, Carl Van Vechten's *Nigger Heaven* (1926). Linking, as she often did, literary tastes to social developments (despite not having returned to the United States since early in the decade), Wharton told Lapsley that she found Van Vechten's work "nauseating" "rubbish" that made her "despair of the Republic."[1] While her response to *Nigger Heaven* is hardly surprising, what is a bit unexpected is that she was familiar with the novel at all, her conscientiousness about keeping up with American literary trends notwithstanding. But she apparently did not keep up enough to prepare herself for what she took to be Van Vechten's accuracy in describing the cultural mecca du jour just north of Manhattan proper. "I thought the whole thing [Van Vechten's novel] was made up," Wharton confesses to Lapsley, "but the other day Mr. & Mme. Bourdet ... came to lunch, & they told me they had been to New York for the 'premiére' of the play there & had been taken by the 'Jeunes' into nigger society in Harlem 'et que cétait comme dans le livre.' And now I must stop & be sick—." Wharton's incredulousness stems not just from Van Vechten's novel itself—which she takes to be a bad enough sign of the state of her native city—but even more so from the existence of a "real" Harlem whose "nigger society" (probably a contradiction in terms for her) was popular among a range of whites, from Van Vechten to the Bourdets. As James de Jongh and other scholars have argued, the Harlem Renaissance "was taken to be a harbinger of change in who blacks were," which, as Wharton's letter indicates, also portended a change in relations between blacks and whites.[2] Made sick by Harlem culture and the fascination it held for some members of her own race, Wharton nonetheless felt compelled to respond to that fascination in *Twilight Sleep,* her take on what Langston Hughes calls "that fantastic period when Harlem was in vogue."[3] Although the novel is clearly a satire of the Van Vechtens of New York society, *Twilight Sleep* ironically shares some of the same concerns about the Harlem vogue exhibited in *Nigger Heaven* and, for that matter, in fiction by African American writers, especially Hughes's "Rejuvenation through Joy" (1933), Nella Larsen's *Passing* (1929), and Claude McKay's *Home to Harlem* (1928). Both Wharton's novel and *Passing,* for instance, feature love triangles pitting Progressive Era, New Woman types against vampish flappers. Both novels as well as *Nigger Heaven* end in violence, and, most importantly, all four of these works examine cabarets, the popularity of jazz, and the interracial mingling that Harlem nightlife was thought to foster.

Such comparable elements can further augment our understanding of how local culture influences literary production, as the question of how to interpret and portray Harlem in its relationship to white New York illustrates both the continued centrality of place in fiction and how chaotic and contested modern regional spaces were imagined to be. Van Vechten's notion of Harlem as "Nigger Heaven" was based upon a metaphor of New York as a theater, whose gallery seats—the highest and worst seats—divided African Americas from whites in the orchestra below.[4] What Hughes calls Van Vechten's "unfortunate" title, then, expresses how New York combined disparate cultural traditions in its artistic life and, at the same time, practiced an unwritten segregation of the population that enjoyed that art.[5] "The Mecca of the New Negro," as several characters sarcastically call Harlem in Van Vechten's novel, might be exotic fodder for the white novelist to praise (as Van Vechten did) or, as in Wharton's case, to scorn. But the "gallery of this New York theater" also put African Americans on display, as *Nigger Heaven*'s Byron argues in what is clearly the authorial point of view:

> That's what Harlem is. We sit in our places in the gallery of this New York theater and watch the white world sitting down below in the good seats in the orchestra. Occasionally they turn their faces up towards us, their hard, cruel faces, to laugh or to sneer, but they never beckon. It never seems to occur to them that Nigger Heaven is crowded, that there isn't another seat, that something has to be done. It doesn't seem

> to occur to them either . . . that we sit above them, that we can drop things down on them and crush them, that we can swoop down from this Nigger Heaven and take their seats. (149)

In his autobiography, *The Big Sea* (1940), Langston Hughes explains Van Vechten's use of this spatial metaphor thus: "to Mr. Van Vechten, Harlem was . . . the only place where Negroes could see or stage their own show, and not a very satisfactory place at that."[6] Hughes appreciates Van Vechten's efforts to integrate "this new city of Harlem (which is a part of New York)," to honor, as Hughes sees it, the principles of democracy by uniting two distinct sections of the city.[7] Recalling the annual birthday party that Van Vechten gave for himself, James Weldon Johnson, and Alfred A. Knopf, "a Gentile, a Negro, and a Jew," Hughes writes that Van Vechten always served three birthday cakes—one red, one white, and one blue. For Hughes, this annual event epitomized Van Vechten's contribution to the "New York theater": "Carl Van Vechten is like that party. He never talks grandiloquently about democracy or Americanism. Nor makes a fetish of those qualities. But he lives them with sincerity and humor."[8] Whatever can be said for or against Van Vechten's intentions or Hughes's defense of them, this construction of a "New York theater" provides an interesting lens through which to view Wharton's response to the Harlem Renaissance. For *Twilight Sleep* is motivated by the fear that African Americans may not be so safely segregated in Harlem, that, according to Van Vechten's Byron, New York itself, "which already had been Indian, Dutch, English, and finally the melting-pot for every nation," might "become a Negro island" (190). Added to the ambiguities arising from the presence of a black "city within a city," as James Weldon Johnson calls it, is the fear that the divisions between the two are rapidly eroding.[9]

Twilight Sleep, Wharton's most direct confrontation with such an erosion, has consistently suffered from a lack of critical scrutiny in part because some critics find the satire rather too strident, but also, I suspect, because when it is paired with earlier novels like *The House of Mirth*, *The Age of Innocence*, or the equally biting *Custom of the Country*, it appears somewhat anomalous—Madame Wharton, novelist of elite drawing rooms from New York to Paris, does the Jazz Age. Looked at from one angle, of course, Wharton's interest here in flappers, cabarets, and Cubist art is out of keeping with the works she had been writing before that point, but from another angle the concerns of *Twilight Sleep* are very much in keeping with those of the rest of Wharton's oeuvre (interestingly, *Nigger Heaven*'s Byron refuses to write about upper-crust Harlem because it would be "too much like [writing of] Edith Wharton's set" [107]).[10] The threat of a Harlem invasion in the twenties is not due simply to postwar modernist malaise for Wharton; rather, it is merely a point further down the slippery slope from earlier invasions of the pastoral New York of the nineteenth century by Simon Rosedale and other newly wealthy arrivistes such as Undine Spragg. In this way, *Twilight Sleep* plays a key role in Wharton's regionalist project as one of the final chapters in her history of the New York elite, from the "tight little citadel" of *The Age of Innocence* (44) and *The House of Mirth*'s society of "atoms whirling away from each other" (248) to a point at which society has become so mixed with various ethnicities, classes of origin, and regional affiliations that what holds the New York elite together is no longer "family" (as in *Age*) or even money (as in the "society" of *House*). In the Jazz Age of *Twilight Sleep*, we see that many of the invaders whose escapades her earlier works explore have attained full ascendancy over elite New York society. In the absence of "inherited obligations, or any traditional sense of solidarity between the classes," these invaders and those they have vanquished form an elite class that is nothing more than an incoherent mish-mash of people with incompatible backgrounds who have little connection to, and even less sympathy with, each other.[11]

Further, *Twilight Sleep* shares with Wharton's other works an interest in examining the ramifications of Americans' growing acceptance of divorce, particularly upon the "family" that had once defined and guarded membership in society. Along with *Custom* and her later novel *The Children, Twilight Sleep* is perhaps Wharton's most pessimistic commentary on the future of the American family: Pauline Manford, the social-pariah-turned-powerhouse at the center of the novel, has had two husbands, the first a derelict Old New Yorker, Arthur Wyant, and the second a newly wealthy westerner, Dexter Manford, like herself. Though she hardly has Undine Spragg's marital track record, Pauline nonetheless has produced a family in which no one's roles are clear: Nona, Pauline's daughter, spends more time with Wyant than she does with Manford, her own father, while Jim, Pauline's son with Wyant, relies more on his stepfather, Dexter. Furthermore, it is hinted by Lita, Jim's rapacious wife, that Jim is not Wyant's son at all but Dexter's. Having married Dexter after he served as her divorce attorney in her suit against Wyant, Pauline still maintains a relationship with "poor Arthur," as she calls him, because his "Old New York blood" gratifies her social pretensions.[12] Pauline believes that this arrangement proves that she herself and her culture have reached the pinnacle of civilization, but the novel's plot suggests otherwise. This Jazz-Age "blended family" implodes when Dexter has an affair with Jim's wife and Wyant, in an attempt to defend his son's honor, shoots Dexter but wounds Nona instead.

Like Simon Rosedale, Pauline and Dexter Manford may have attained a place in society, but that makes them no more fit than Rosedale is for the roles they assume there. Pauline's "pioneer blood," tinged with a "plebeian dye" by ancestors who were miners in Pennsylvania before making their fortune in a western town named, unsubtly enough, Exploit, is supposedly a source of pride to her, aligning her with the social transformations thought to be a product of modern democratization (53, 15). But she still manages to confuse the Gainsborough painting in her dining room for a portrait of more illustrious relations than those she actually possesses (16). Both her feigned attachment to her working-class roots and her obvious lack of "paintable" ancestors—a key marker of the Old New Yorker, according to historians Edwin G. Burrows and Mike Wallace— seem inappropriate to her current social status.[13] Indeed, there is something paradoxical about "new money" in Wharton's works: the American Dream allows characters like Pauline to have the material trappings of the upper class without those immaterial elements—refinement, discernment, taste—that are supposed to justify them. The same is true for Pauline's husband, Dexter Manford. Achieving a prominence for which he is socially, emotionally, and intellectually unfit, Manford is probably correct that he should have chosen a life more suitable to his western, working-class origins, one in which success would be measured by "farming on a big scale, with all the modern appliances his forbearers had lacked, outdoing everybody in the county, marketing his goods at the big centres, and cutting a swathe in state politics" (71). As a prominent New York attorney married to a society matriarch, however, Manford is in a position that belies his true nature, which becomes obvious through his atavistic attraction to his stepson's wife, Lita. Likewise, Pauline's paradoxical social position leads to other contradictions in her character, particularly her confused principles. Coupling "loveliness and poetry" with "advanced industrialism," Pauline believes in the perfectibility of society and, in particular, in her own abilities to perfect it, but those are the only things she believes in with any consistency (18). Embracing alike technology and its opposite, the "return to Nature" movement advocated by the Mahatma, her spiritual guru, Pauline at one point in the novel begins to give a speech she has written in support of birth control at a luncheon given to promote motherhood (96). As much as she likes to assume control of those around her, she is not only an unsuitable role model but also a bad mother, too concerned with her own importance to pay attention to her family, not unlike the figure of the modern mother Theodore Roosevelt and others faulted for hastening "race suicide."[14]

In moving from Exploit, "a city absorbed in making money," to New York, "a society bent on enjoying it," Pauline has changed both her class and her regional affiliations, attempting, as Janet Goodwyn argues, to live "without a specific geography."[15] As a result, she has lost her authenticity: "Had [she] been a pioneer's wife, and seen her family stricken down by disease in the wilderness, she would have nursed them fearlessly; but all her life she had been used to buying off suffering with money, or denying its existence with words, and her moral muscle had become . . . atrophied" (261). According to Pauline, though, women like herself embody the triumph of democracy, or what the narrator classifies as a narrow-minded modern culture in which the only freedom is the freedom to conform: "Don't you think it's glorious," Pauline asks Nona, "to belong to the only country where everybody is absolutely free, and yet we're all made to do exactly what is best for us?" (190–91). Pauline's ostensible patriotism extends to wanting to share such "freedom" with others, with the victims of an earthquake in Bolivia, for instance, whose tragedy, as Nona jokes, could be avoided in the future if Pauline and her friends "sent out a commission immediately to teach Bolivians to do something they didn't want to do—not to *believe* in earthquakes, for instance" (12). As a member of "the only country where everybody is absolutely free" only to follow the latest fads, Pauline believes it is her duty to enforce her values on foreigners, but she, in her turn, needs the Mahatma's "Return to Purity" to cope with the stress of (or, more precisely, the "resulting wrinkles" from) being responsible for the Bolivians. Lacking a true sense of identity and belongingness as well as the taste they were thought to engender, Pauline looks to what the novel portrays as nonsensical and "low" cultural influences like those promoted by the Mahatma—to the gallery seats of the "New York theater"—to fill the void, fostering a disingenuous cultural realm that leads to what Wharton considered to be the worst excesses of the twenties. Taken together, Wharton's novels of New York suggest that the erosion of traditional class and ethnic boundaries encouraged by New York's street life promotes the blurring of white and black in the Jazz Age.

II: TWILIGHT SLEEP AND "THE NEW CITY OF HARLEM (WHICH IS A PART OF NEW YORK)"

According to Dale Bauer, novels such as *Twilight Sleep* make plain the point that Americans and others "had less to fear from foreign intruders" than they did from their own "projections of dominance over others," a point that, Bauer argues further, coexists with the novel's association of Harlem Renaissance culture with whites' "uncontrolled sexuality."[16] For Bauer, the fact that Harlem's "nigger society" is used as a metaphor for whites' excesses helps to mitigate *Twilight Sleeps*'s characterizations of African Americans. But Wharton's use of Harlem as a metaphor—no matter whom else it is meant to criticize—comes "at great expense to black life," as John Cooley claims of other white writers who used Harlem material.[17] Jennie Kassanoff rightly asserts that "if class and gender have conventionally structured Wharton criticism, race is the missing but historically crucial component complicating progressive interpretations of Wharton's project," a point that seems critical to *Twilight Sleep*, for in accessing them as a metaphor for whites, Wharton projects her own dominance over blacks even as she portrays other whites as doing so.[18] Further, her censure of Americans like Pauline Manford centers less upon their dominance over others than upon their own lack of discrimination, a quality that is rooted in their class and regional affiliations.

It is poetic justice, therefore, that in her husband's liaison with her daughter-in-law, Pauline is hurt by her own promotion of what the narrator considers to be illegitimate cultural fads ("Psycho-analysis," "mental uplift," and a meeting with a "Man with Persian miniatures") among the younger generation. Paula Fass's work on Jazz-Age society has shown that the popularity of flapper figures like Lita Wyant was part of a larger cultural emphasis on youth. Openly scornful of social pieties, this youth culture, according to Fass, emphasized personal freedom and self-gratification, and was often likened to the so-called primitive cultures of immigrants, the working class, and especially people of color.[19] While the flapper was clearly a national and even international figure, it was New York's entertainment industry and its vibrant street life that promoted the woman whom many credit with being one of the earliest and most famous flappers, Irene Castle. A professional dancer and cabaret owner, Castle was so popular that she helped set fashion and beauty trends for women all over the nation, who attempted to emulate her sporty, thin body type, her cropped hair (what was later called the bob was first known as the Castle clip), and a style of dress that simultaneously evoked boyish innocence and overt sexuality. Although she and her husband, Vernon Castle, invented the fox trot, they spoke out in their 1914 book, *Modern Dancing,* against other so-called animal dances (the popularity of which probably helped propel them to stardom) associated with African Americans. Showing young women how to "cross racial and cultural barriers and adopt some of the elements of both high and low life," the image projected by Irene Castle relied on the blending of cultures, for on the one hand, she was a flapper who popularized cabaret life, but on the other, she was the daughter of a good family from New Rochelle and the wife of a well-to-do Englishman.[20]

Women like Castle made such ambiguity sexy, and made the sincere New

Woman of the Progressive Era look dowdy by comparison, at least to men like *Twilight Sleep*'s Dexter Manford. While Pauline's "killing New York life" is full of efforts to reduce the size of her hips or to ward off wrinkles, Lita's beauty is repeatedly said to be not only effortless but unconscious as well (10). A "primitive angel" with "a gift for posing," Lita is described as fluid and supple, while Pauline, even on the dance floor, moves in a way reminiscent of "something between going to church and drilling a scout brigade" (75, 176, 74). As we have seen, Pauline's ethical code is self-contradictory; Lita, on the other hand, lacks a sense of ethics entirely. The younger woman cares as little for philanthropy as she does for social conventions, and is guided by no sense of responsibility except to her own whims. Her blasé, childish, and unashamed selfishness (she frequently remarks without compunction how bored she is with her husband), in contrast to Pauline's self-serving dedication to duty and charity, is precisely what the men in the novel find so appealing: unlike Pauline, Lita doesn't care enough about anyone else to want to run their lives. A remarkably similar opposition is at work between Irene Redfield and Clare Kendry in Nella Larsen's *Passing* (and, for that matter, between Mary Love and Lasca Sartoris in *Nigger Heaven*). Wharton's Pauline and Larsen's Irene attempt to control others both through their embracing of various "causes" and through the matriarchal roles they assume over their husbands, whose lives they wish "to be allowed to direct for their own best good."[21] Described by the narrators of both novels as sexually repressed, these women no longer have physical relationships with their husbands, whom they look to instead as props for what Irene repeatedly calls "safety," "that security of place and substance" that assures their social positions (190). The works' similarities extend to the other women, Wharton's Lita and Larsen's Clare, in the love triangles as well. As it does with Lita, the whiff of scandal hangs over Clare throughout the novel; with "no allegiance beyond [their] own immediate desires," neither Lita nor Clare is, as Clare says of herself, "safe" in the ways Pauline and Irene are (210). Both Lita and Clare trump their romantic rivals (or imagined ones, in the case of Clare and Irene) by dancing: it is at a dance that we first learn of Manford's growing obsession with Lita, and at a dance that Irene first imagines that her husband is attracted to Clare. The sense of danger and the break in the strict yet meaningless routines that their wives have established for them are what draw Dexter to Lita and, at least as Irene imagines it, her husband, Brian, to Clare. Whether or not Brian is attracted to Clare, it is clear that he, like Dexter, feels that life with social prominence, a successful career, and a perfect, polished wife does not satisfy. These similarities between Larsen's and Wharton's works are important because they suggest that the opposition between the New Woman of the turn of the century and the Jazz-Age flapper generated anxieties about acceptable roles for women that crossed racial lines.

Yet it is also significant to our understanding of Wharton's New York to consider how she and Larsen examine these anxieties from opposite ends of the racially segregated "New York theater." In promoting music and dance styles inspired by ragtime and jazz, flappers like Irene Castle helped to popularize a cabaret culture that increasingly blurred distinctions between New York and Harlem and between respectable and common women, the native-born and immigrants, whites and blacks in ways that were troubling to a number of Americans, Wharton among them, who thought that too many barriers had already been broken down in American life. While turn-of-the-century white New Women (like *House of Mirth*'s Gerty Farrish) interacted daily with men outside their race and class, their younger sisters of the Jazz Age extended this interaction into the evening hours. Lewis Erenberg has shown that before the development of New York's cabarets, most genteel social events were private and highly regulated: guest lists, seating arrangements, and music and dance styles were meant to govern behavior, to define hierarchy, and to keep outsiders at bay. Cabarets, which drew the elite as well as the masses to their doors, redefined leisure: dining tables, dance floors, and performers like Castle (who often sat at dining tables for part of the evening) were all in close proximity.[22] Earlier dances that were popular among the elite included large groups and accentuated rigid body positions; cabaret dances like the Charleston, the turkey trot, and the black bottom stressed freer movement and improvisation, "self-expression and the development of 'personality,'" isolating couples and bringing them into closer contact with one another, often at the pelvis.[23] Young female initiates could learn the steps by day at the Castles' dance school, and by night could show off their abilities at cabarets like their Castles in the Air.

The dance craze that swept New York in the teens and twenties generated a considerable amount of criticism, especially from New Yorkers of Wharton's generation, because not all of the entertainers who popularized cabaret dances possessed the social credentials the Castles did. Jewish and Italian performers—gigolos, as they came to be called[24]—were hired by dance palaces as instructors and as partners for unaccompanied young women. Opponents outraged by such pairings lamented that "the spell of the dance" would undermine the racial and sexual purity of white womanhood altogether, charging gigolos with the symbolic rape of white civilization.[25] The press portrayed non-Anglo gigolos according to established stereotypes (they were both sexual predators and effeminate, unable to function in the male sphere of moneymaking), but what seemed new was young Anglo women's apparent willingness to associate with them. Cabarets, critics charged, were allowing "lower" influences to infiltrate the better classes rather than, as reform was meant to do, elevating these others by example. One editorial argued that the new dances were "a reversion to the grossest practices of savage man," based, supposedly, "on the primitive motive of orgies enjoyed by the aboriginal inhabitants of every uncivilized land."[26] In a defense of cabarets that perhaps only served to confirm alarmists' fears, Ellin Mackey, a "society girl" interviewed by the *New York Times,* claimed that cabarets allowed her to select her own dance partners and thereby avoid what she called the "pale-faced youths" and "colorless" men frequenting private dances.[27] Justifying her generation to those who "miss the dowagers on gold chairs and other features of the old-time balls," Miss Mackey asked her elders, "What does it matter if the flapper and her fattish boy friend are wriggling beside us as we dance? We like our partner and the flapper likes hers, and we don't bother each other."[28] It mattered apparently more than young women like Miss Mackey could understand, and many critics of the dance craze focused their reform efforts on genteel girls like her: in 1912, for example, six hundred citizens gathered at the venerable Sherry's restaurant to see the new dances demonstrated and to learn how to discourage them at elite events.[29] Other reformers monitored working-class dance halls. But whether elite whites or the nominally white, largely immigrant working-class masses were to blame for New York's dance craze was debated in the press without consensus. The fault for the proliferation of the new dances rested, all of their critics agreed, with a young woman, but whether she was genteel or working-class, Anglo or "ethnic" was unclear.

Further troubling critics of the dance craze was the fact that, by the twenties, young white women like Miss Mackey were dancing with African American gigolos in cabarets located in the heart of the most thriving African American culture in the nation.[30] Especially after the 1921–22 run of the Broadway musical *Shuffle Along,* Harlem's culture, and jazz in particular, attracted the attention of and was appropriated by an unprecedented number of white New Yorkers. As one character sarcastically remarks in *Nigger Heaven,* "I don't know that we even have Harlem, . . . so many white people come up here now to the cabarets" (45). But jazz provoked the same criticism that the dance forms associated with it did. As Kathy Ogren summarizes: "Detractors criticized both [jazz's] musical characteristics and its origins in lower-class black life. Jazz-lovers hailed it as everything from exciting entertainment to an antidote for repressive industrial society. In either case, Americans found jazz symbolic of fundamental changes they identified in postwar life."[31] And as the criticism (including Wharton's *Twilight Sleep*) of it makes clear, jazz connected African American culture to a larger American pluralism: in his 1925 essay "Jazz at Home," published in Alain Locke's manifesto of the Harlem Renaissance, *The New Negro,* Joel Rogers celebrates the multicultural aspects of a music he claims to be rooted in "the Indian war dance, the Highland fling, the Irish jig, the cossack dance, [and] the Spanish fandango."[32]

A uniquely American music (some argue the only uniquely American music), jazz was often associated with various social groups—African Americans, white female flappers—that were usually kept separate. Far more troublingly, all that jazz—the African American music that set the flapper's white body to dancing in what Susan Gubar has termed a "racechange"—signified a racial association that the color of her skin belied.[33] In McKay's *Home to Harlem,* jazz connects people, however briefly, not only across the dividing line of the "New York theater" but also more broadly, as the narrator tells us of the latest tune: "Broadway was wild about it and Harlem was crazy. All America jazzed to it, and it was already world-famous. Already being jazzed perhaps in Paris and Cairo, Shanghai, Honolulu, and Java."[34] In McKay's novel, jazz and cabaret dancing embody a primitivism associated with the black diaspora at the same time that they encourage open displays of sexuality and facilitate interracial mixing. And in both *Home to Harlem* and *Nigger Heaven,* cabarets are imagined to eliminate racial difference. As Van Vechten writes of one cabaret crowd, "seated at tables around the three sides of the hall unoccupied by the band, were parties of white people, parties of coloured people, mixed parties, but the amber light which flooded the gold and black hall gave everybody present much the same complexion" (242). The fetishistic description of skin color variations in the black community itself, especially in McKay's novel, is likewise meant to serve as a reminder that in Harlem, "you never can tell for sure about a person's race": "Ancient black life rooted in its base with all its fascinating new layers of brown, low-brown, high-brown, nut-brown, lemon, maroon, olive, mauve, gold. Yellow balancing between black and white. Black reaching out beyond yellow. Almost-white on the brink of a change" (320, 57). A "strange un-American world where colored meets and mingles freely and naturally with white," the Jazz-Age nightlife scene was viewed by many, like McKay, both as the epitome of blackness (and all of what its supposed primitive essence could offer repressive white culture) and as already multiracial (106). Like Van Vechten's, McKay's description of cabarets could reinforce the notion that jazz is chaotic, nonsensical, and therefore ethically disorderly, for as much as it helps people to cross racial boundaries, it also has the opposite tendency of exposing racial differences. "The key" to the black race, jazz is also symbolic of what divides African Americans from whites: "No wonder [whites] hated them," McKay's character Ray thinks, "when out of their melancholy environment the blacks could create mad, contagious music" (266, 267). While Ray believes that jazz grows out of blacks' exclusion from an older democracy associated with the "white citizen of a nation that can say bold, challenging things," optimists like Joel Rogers touted jazz as a "joyous revolt from convention" that, in uniting disparate sources and drawing listeners from a variety of backgrounds, could "truly democratize" (154).[35]

In Wharton's novel, too, jazz reflects a tendency on the part of American culture to standardize its multiracial population at the same time that it is linked to a shadowy cast of nonwhite characters. Just as she employs the New York street life in *The House of Mirth* to explore the loss of an elite made up of "family" and the birth of a society that commingles "blood and money," so too does she use what Toni Morrison aptly calls "the consequences of jazz" in *Twilight Sleep* to represent the failure of the new elite to forge a communal identity that is distinct from the masses.[36] In particular, Wharton utilizes a musical form called "unspeakable" by its critics to epitomize the ways elite young white women like Lita Wyant were pursuing disturbingly new social and personal agendas, turning away from so-called civilization and glorifying the supposed "savagery of [jazz's] creators."[37] As the mother of the Wyant heir, Lita plays a critical role in the family. But it is one she consistently abdicates in favor of the freedoms of cabarets such as the Housetop, a nightclub many of the characters attend in the middle of the novel to see, in Nona's words, some "nigger dancing" (144).[38] Wharton's initial description of the Housetop—a parody of clubs such as the Castle-owned New York Roof—highlights the theatrical aspects of the cabaret experience:

> The Housetop was packed. The low balcony crammed with fashionable people overhung them like a wreath of ripe fruits, peachy and white and golden, made of painted faces, bare arms, jewels, brocades and fantastic furs. It was the music-hall of the moment. . . . On the stage—a New Orleans cotton market—black dancers tossed and capered. They were like ripe fruits too, black figs flung about in hot sunshine, falling to earth with crimson bursts of laughter splitting open on white teeth, and bounding up again into golden clouds of cotton-dust. (147)

Both the rich whites and the black performers in this "New York theater" are "like ripe fruits," but the whites are so because of their dress, their painted faces, and their accessories, while the blacks are so because of their very bodies: teeth, lips, the laughter that ripples out of them. Apparently natural to the performers themselves, this staging of slavery's past, to borrow Kevin Mumford's phrase, is "black music for white people, black bodies for the white gaze."[39] Yet Wharton's novel displays a considerable amount of apprehension about jazz's supposed ability to bring the races into contact with each other at all. Although Nona Manford initially finds the Housetop scene "all warm and jolly and inconsequent," once she finds Lita there without her husband and in the company of a racially mixed group that includes a Jewish filmmaker and an African American jazz musician, "all the ugly and disquieting realities" of the threat her sister-in-law poses to her family resituate Nona in relation to such racial mixing (147).[40]

"Old fashioned in spite of the jazz," Nona, Wharton's narrative center, understands that young white women like herself have been hurt by their mothers' "beaming determination" to ignore past tradition as "some obsolete European superstition unworthy of enlightened Americans" (46, 45). Lacking Nona's tragic awareness of this cultural void, Lita, as Wharton put it in her notebook for the novel, "is—jazz."[41] Being a flapper and a mother, a contradiction no less severe than Pauline's social status or Harlem's "nigger society," Lita portends the total dissolution of the family that Wharton thought jazz and other twenties cultural trends engendered. More an embodiment of jazz than a fully dimensional character, Lita takes only two things seriously: her own desires and her abilities as a dancer, practicing with Italian waiters (gigolos) when partners of her class aren't available (which has the added value, she thinks, of being shocking) (242). While Lita has little to say throughout the novel (except how bored she is with her husband), "all her expression was in her body, in that long *legato* movement like a weaving of grasses under a breeze, a looping of little waves on the shore" (75).

It is her interest in dance that most often draws Lita away from her family and to a motley group that includes Tommy Ardwin, Wharton's parody of a gay modernist (à la Van Vechten). An interior designer, Ardwin decorates Lita's home in ways obviously meant to suggest her shortcomings as a wife and mother:

> The drawing-room . . . was very expressive of the modern marriage state. It looked, for all its studied effects, . . . more like the waiting-room of a glorified railway station than the setting of an established way of life. Nothing in it seemed at home or at ease—from the early kakemono of a bearded sage . . . to the three mourning irises isolated in a white Sung vase in the desert of an otherwise empty table. The only life in the room was contributed by the agitations of the exotic goldfish in

> a huge spherical aquarium; and they too were but transients, since Lita insisted on having the aquarium illuminated night and day with electric bulbs, and the sleepless fish were always dying off and having to be replaced. (31)

While the home of the stuffy Aggie Huston is a testament to Old New York's commitment to maintaining its own purity, a fortress barring "plebeian intrusion," as the narrator calls it, Lita's home is just the opposite: a blank, impersonal, public space filled with Orientalist objects that have no relation to the space they fill or to the people who occupy it (200). Ardwin's own home likewise celebrates "slumming" and artificiality: he blocks up a real window that looks out onto the "stupid old 'night piece' of Brooklyn Bridge and the East River" only to paint a "sham" window on another wall that simulates "a geometrical representation of brick walls, fire escapes and back-yards" (78). Frederick Wegener argues that Wharton's association of modernism with "a loss of scruples" is "a social rather than an ethical or aesthetic concern," but as the novel's portrayal of domestic design makes amply clear, these concerns are inseparable, for "failure to understand interiors in relation to those who inhabit them augurs other kinds of failure" related to the well-being of the family.[42] Ardwin's window overlooks the Brooklyn Bridge and the East River, so it is possible that he lives somewhere in Lower Manhattan and that his window faces east, and, if this is the case, his fake window imaginatively resituates the view to look west, toward the Lower East Side tenement district with its brick walls, fire escapes, and backyards. In any event, Ardwin functions in *Twilight Sleep* as Jack Stepney does in *The House of Mirth*: both introduce young women of the elite to racial outsiders. Jack is the first to introduce Lily to Rosedale, while Ardwin, in the even more permissible Jazz Age, introduces Lita not only to the Jewish filmmaker Klawhammer (who wants to cast her as Herodias in his next film) but also to the "octoroon" jazz pianist, Jossie Keiler. While Stepney limits his effort to integrate Rosedale ("oh, confound it, you know, we don't *marry* Rosedale in our family" [125]), Ardwin is the head of the group "trying to persuade Lita to go into the movies," creating a "restlessness" in her that ultimately drives her not to the screen but into her father-in-law's arms (*House of Mirth,* 125; *Twilight Sleep,* 76). Whether in films, music, or décor, the "eclecticism" Ardwin and his group represent amounts to a "symbolic miscegenation" brought on by "an invasion of the elite social strata by more vulgar castes from below."[43]

Like Rosedale and Mrs. Haffen in *The House of Mirth,* members of those vulgar castes in *Twilight Sleep* function atmospherically, signaling danger more through their racial and class affiliations than through their actions themselves. For instance, Jossie Keiler's mixed-race status symbolizes a threat far out of proportion to anything she actually does, which is very little, despite the fact that her acquaintance with Lita is a considerable source of worry for Nona. Wharton attributes to the musician an excessive, grotesque appearance ("pudgy feet," "sausage arms," and "bolster legs" [78]) that hints at "the consequences of jazz" on the family, but practically the only dialogue attributed to Keiler is when she joins in a joke made by Ardwin, who flippantly answers Nona's question as to whether he has seen the always-missing Lita: "Is Lita here? Jossie Keiler, you're not Mrs. James Wyant disguised as a dryad, are you?" (78). Hardly worth the menace surrounding her, Keiler's reply—"knew I'd get found out"—nonetheless substitutes her for Lita, intimating that Lita's origins may be just as mixed as Keiler's. Lita's dancing is often accompanied by Keiler's playing, and her talent is what prompts Klawhammer to want to cast her as Herodias, the biblical figure who shares Lita's penchant for sexual betrayal, her inadequacies as a mother, and her manipulation of men through dancing. Because all of Lita's "ethnic affinities," to use Bentley's phrase, lay in the nonwhite realm, her family's efforts to keep her with Jim by keeping her away from Jews and people of color are doomed from the start.[44] This fact is made clear to the reader by the narrator's description of Lita's upbringing. Raised by a negligent aunt, Lita was often left at the Mahatma's Dawnside retreat, which stands "aloof on its height above the Hudson" probably just west of Harlem proper (211). While orphans raised by aunts are not uncommon figures in Wharton's works—Ellen Olenska's aunt is as irresponsible and silly as Lita's is—it is unusual that no mention is made of Lita's parents, and even more rare that her aunt's surrogate would be a man Arthur Wyant calls a "nigger chap" (44). Speaking with Nona about his wife's desire to divorce him, Jim asks the central question of *Twilight Sleep*: if Lita leaves him, "what does she go to?" (183). Her mysterious antecedents, together with her "ethnic affinities," introduce racial ambiguity into the already confused family structure Pauline has established.

This scenario—an elite family threatened by a wife of uncertain racial affiliation—parallels a so-called miscegenation case involving Wharton's distant cousin Leonard Kip Rhinelander. In 1925, two years before Wharton completed *Twilight Sleep,* Kip filed an annulment suit to end his brief marriage to Alice Jones, who, he claimed in the suit, married him under false pretenses because she did not tell him that she was black. Although the two had dated for several years, they married only after Kip reached the legal age to inherit his family's considerable fortune, a circumstance leading to the widely held belief that his father, and not Kip himself, orchestrated the suit. At the beginning of the trial, some consensus had to be reached about just what race Alice was: her mother was English and her father was West Indian, which meant to him that he was not "black" but "colored," a distinction lost on Americans. Thereafter, the case hinged on whether Kip knew Alice's racial identity (established to be "black" by U.S. standards) before they married. Attempting to build what historians Earl Lewis and Heidi Ardizzone call a "multi-layered criteria" for determining Alice's race, Lee Parsons Davis, Alice's attorney, read into the record a letter she had written to Kip in which she described going to a "strutting party."[45] Davis asked Kip during his testimony to define a "strutting party" for the jury, and he did: it was a dance. Davis then argued that if Alice used what he called a "typical Negro expression," her lover should have been able to determine her race. This argument is significant to Wharton's novel because it implied that Alice's racial identity was obvious since she attended a "strutting party" in the first place. Likewise important to my discussion of *Twilight Sleep* is that the case posed a considerable dilemma to the jury: accuse a member of Wharton's Old New York family of miscegenation or admit that race is not self-evident. Alice successfully defended herself from her husband's accusation in part by "baring her breasts, back, and legs before the court," proving, by way of her appearance, that Kip must have known she was black, since the couple had been sexually active prior to marriage.[46] Miscegenation cases, or "Rhinelanders," as they came to be called, became more and more common in an America that was less and less sure of its systems of racial classification, exposing the paradoxes inherent to designations of racial difference.[47] For the scientific and legal rhetoric of race was meant to ground difference on some surer biological footing than appearance (on "blood" or genetics, for instance), but one's "race" was impossible to determine without reference to appearance. Such a paradox led to an increase in antimiscegenation laws designed to stabilize "the flux in blood and the problem of its representation" that followed from marriages such as Kip's to Alice.[48]

The Rhinelander trial was among the most publicized, both nationally and internationally, of these miscegenation cases. White women packed the courtroom for the duration of the trial but, with the exception of a few female reporters, were ejected when sexually explicit testimony was given.[49] The courtroom revelation that Alice's mother had birthed a child out of wedlock made for a titillating display of sexual taboos, while the testimonies of musicians Irving Berlin and Al Jolson (Alice, being a jazz enthusiast, had mentioned Jolson in their letters) proved good fodder for the press, which covered the trial obsessively. Zora Neale Hurston's pleasure at seeing Alice vindicated by the jury was quoted in the *New York Daily News,* while from the pages of the *Crisis,* W. E. B. Du Bois scoffed at the way the trial, the most humiliating blow to white America's "[m]agnificent Nordic morality" in recent history, was based upon a hypocrisy: "[I]f Rhinelander had used [Alice] as concubine or prostitute white America would have raised no word of protest."[50] In *Passing* Irene worries that "the Rhinelander case" has set a precedent that may endanger her marriage to Brian: for if Clare's husband finds out that she is passing, he, like Kip, might seek to dissolve the marriage, leaving Clare, as Irene imagines, free to pursue Brian (228).[51]

I doubt that Wharton knew Kip Rhinelander personally, but we can imagine her chagrin at having the name of her mother, her godfather, and many other members of her family become synonymous with miscegenation cases, "Rhinelanders." As she avidly read both American and European newspapers, it is likely that the considerable press coverage of the trial reached her during the period that she was writing *Twilight Sleep*. We also know that despite her exile and her complaints about her New York relations, Wharton was in touch with some of the Rhinelanders at least through the war, during which time she represented the family at the funeral of the fallen soldier Newbold Rhinelander, son of Thomas and Kit Rhinelander.[52] And we should recall in this connection her reaction in 1927 to Harlem's "nigger society," for, according to the African American newspaper the *Amsterdam News*, "Harlem was for Alice. . . . because she stood as a symbol to Negro womanhood."[53] Indeed, the similarities between the case and Wharton's novel, and between Alice Jones and Lita Wyant in particular, are remarkable. Lita, like Alice, is a flapper who loves to dance. As Alice did, Lita frequents cabarets and theaters that feature heterogeneous cultural displays like those associated with Berlin and Jolson. The white press initially portrayed Alice Jones as a vamp, a filmic extension of the flapper stereotype particularly associated with sexual aggression.[54] Not only is Lita sexually aggressive in her pursuit of Dexter Manford, but she also wants to transform herself from a flapper to a film star, a vamp. The threat of incest, so often twined with miscegenation,[55] is likewise suggested by Lita and Dexter's affair: if Lita's guess is correct, Dexter is the father of her husband and the grandfather of her son. The threat that the Rhinelanders accused Alice Jones of posing to their family purity is reenacted in Lita and Jim's marriage, even as Wharton (unlike the *Rhinelander v. Jones* jury) leaves the race of the wife unknowable. Lita's mysterious origins become all the more hazardous because, unlike Alice Jones, she is a mother: as Laura Doyle persuasively argues, the body of the mother is the matrix where race and gender merge. White mothers can be celebrated, then, as glorious shields against Anglo-Saxon suicide or be demonized as the portals through which otherness can infiltrate the white race.[56] For Nona and for the novel, the danger of Lita's attraction to dancing and cabarets is that the racial mixing associated with them can slip from entertainment and slumming to threatening family and racial coherence.

For in leaving her white family, Lita would be, in a sense, leaving whiteness, either to join an Italian man (Michelangelo, a distant Wyant relation) in a film produced by a Jew about Jews or, worse, to rejoin the "nigger chap" who taught her to dance in the first place, the Mahatma (44). The Mahatma is the source of several dramatic revelations in the novel concerning the extent of Lita's scandalous behavior. Not only do we learn that it was at Dawnside that Lita learned to dance, but we also learn that alongside other scantily clad rich girls, Lita appears in a photograph taken at the retreat and printed in the tabloids that sparks a campaign to debunk the guru. While he is the root of much of the white family's anxiety, readers never encounter the Mahatma directly: we hear of him, his thick lips and oily skin, only in fragments (272). His racial identity is equally vague and metonymic: frequently called a "Hindu sage" with "Oriental" dress, he is also crudely classified as a "nigger." His background is apparently irrelevant because he functions as a symbol of the Harlem Renaissance, the "attribution of 'primitivism'" serving here as a means of "imposing character invisibility."[57] The Mahatma's unclear racial identity and his fragmented physicality work to dehumanize him rather than make him more rounded. In this way, he is like the ominous yet one-dimensional "Cubist statue" adorning Lita's black boudoir, an association that Manford makes (109).

If the Mahatma is a symbol of the primitivism whites associated with African Americans, he is also a catalyst for their own atavistic impulses. At the beginning of the novel, Pauline, grateful that his "holy ecstasy" exercises "had reduced her hips after everything else had failed," is eager to defend the Mahatma from the gossip being spread about him among other upper-class whites whose daughters are depicted in the tabloid photograph (23). She also admires his "mystical teachings about Self-Annihilation, Anterior Existence and Astral Affinities . . . all so incomprehensible and so pure." The Mahatma's teachings answer Pauline's need for a prepackaged, meaningless worldview, and like jazz, Ardwin's decorating, and other examples of the democratization of culture we have seen, this worldview is artificial and self-contradictory: the terms attributed to the Mahatma above are indeed incomprehensible, although the rest of the novel calls into question Pauline's assessment that they are pure. The tabloid photograph should make it clear to Pauline that her earnest pursuit of an ideal is akin to Lita's search for a life in which she can "dance and laugh and be hopelessly low-lived and irresponsible," and it does make her revise, if only for a moment, her impressions of the Mahatma (255):

> She had never seen anything of the kind herself at Dawnside—heaven forbid!—but whenever she had gone there . . . she had suspected that the bare whitewashed room, with its throned Buddha, which received her and other like-minded ladies of her age . . . had not let them very far into the mystery. Beyond, perhaps, were other rites, other settings: why not? Wasn't everybody talking about "the return to Nature," and ridiculing the American prudery in which the minds and bodies of her generation had been swaddled? The Mahatma was one of the leaders of the new movement: the Return to Purity, he called it. He was always . . . praising the ease of the loose Oriental dress compared with the restricting western garb: but Pauline had supposed the draperies he advocated to be longer and less transparent; above all, she had not expected familiar faces above those insufficient scarves. (95–96)

Jazz pollutes the artistic culture of 1920s New York, while the importation of a supposedly nonwhite spirituality linked to jazz pollutes the elite class's philosophical groundings.[58] Although the teachings of the other "healers" that Pauline consults are equally fraudulent, their ethnicity (both Gobine and Loft are eastern European) does not lend itself to the same kind of ominous aura surrounding the Mahatma's racial status, nor that of Jossie Keiler.

Like the "octoroon" pianist, the "Hindu sage" who is also a "nigger chap" plays a crucial role in the novel, even if we never see him directly. As a symbol of the ideological underpinnings of the Harlem Renaissance, the Mahatma should be read against other such symbols of the "Negro vogue" penned by African Americans, whose views were oriented by a different position in the "New York theater." Langston Hughes's short story "Rejuvination through Joy" is, as David Chinitz argues, a satire of the ways whites appropriated and denigrated African American culture, and it is, more specifically, a fascinating commentary on the concerns of Wharton's novel.[59] In Hughes's story, Eugene Lesche assumes a role very much like that of the Mahatma, promoting "primitive man" as the answer to whites' postwar malaise through lectures titled "Negroes and Joy" and, more critically for our reading of *Twilight Sleep,* preaching that jazz is the "music which is the Joy of Life."[60] Patched together by a "Yale man" from a diversity of sources from Freud to Ethel Waters, Lesche's incomprehensible teachings like "rejuvenation through joy" make him the "New Leader" who replaces other promoters of spiritual fads (such as one who preaches "change through change") (83, 92, 89). Like the Mahatma's "return to purity," Lesche's unique spin on non-Christian beliefs raises jazz to the level of a religion, bringing New York and Harlem into close contact, as the narrator's description of his popularity indicates: "Some said the world was turning passionate and spiritual; some said it was merely a sign of the decadence of the times. But everybody talked about it. The papers began to write about it. And the magazines that winter, from the *Junior League Bulletin* to the *Nation,* even the *New Masses,* remarked—usually snootily—but nevertheless remarked—about this Cult of Joy. (Harlem Hedonism, the *Forum* called it.)" (82) Helping to popularize "primitive jazz out of Africa (you know, Harlem)" and the dances associated with it (his retreat, like Dawnside, gives its guests ample opportunities to dance), Lesche and his racially mixed coconspirators, like Wharton's Mahatma, appeal to a variety of bored, rich whites, including the older generation who know nothing of "Harlem Negroes" "except through the rather remote chatter of the younger set" (84, 74). "All the smart neurasthenics from Park Avenue" flock to Lesche's Colony not only to dance, but also to imitate Harlemites in what they believe are other authentically black ways, such as falling into jealous rages over Lesche (one even hurls an African mask at him) (88, 93). Like the Mahatma's, Lesche's associations with African American culture make him both attractive to wealthy white women and the object of unwanted scrutiny. Just as the Mahatma is discredited by a scandal involving white women, Lesche and his con are exposed when a white female patron, imitating a black woman hired to play jazz, tries to kill him because she realizes "how right," "how primitive" it is to "shoot the one you love" (97). And, not coincidentally, both Wharton's and Hughes's texts attribute unclear racial identities to these spiritual leaders. After the shooting shuts down Lesche's Colony, the tabloids accuse him of passing, and Hughes leaves it impossible to determine if they are correct or if this is merely another sign of whites' hypocrisy. The narrator repeatedly makes reference to Lesche's dark hair, his southern dialect, and his identification with African American culture ("they need what we got," he remarks of the "curative values of Negro jazz"), as if to hint that his "ethnic affinities," like Lita's, complicate his whiteness (76). In Hughes's work, Lesche's unclear origin is meant to highlight whites' exploitation of African Americans; his "true" racial status is irrelevant because his identity is determined not by some objective criteria but by what whites think he is.[61]

In Wharton's novel, by contrast, the Mahatma's racial indeterminacy symbolizes how whites' moral lapses destroy the purity of their own culture; there is little emphasis, as there is in Hughes's story, upon how those moral lapses work to control the lives of others. Having rejected their own traditions (in Pauline's case) or lacking traditions altogether (in Lita's), *Twilight Sleep*'s white women characters gravitate to the culture of Harlem, which turns out to be a region at once too full of disparate elements and devoid of meaning. At the end of the novel the family members scatter, fleeing the scandal of Nona's shooting by traveling to colonial outposts like Egypt, where their pursuits of racial otherness will be free from the scrutiny of New York society.[62] Along with traveling, the family evades moral responsibility by using social prejudice to cover up their own deficiencies, blaming Nona's shooting on a homeless man they lead the police to believe broke into their house. But this potential critique of how wealthy whites exploit the underclass does not mitigate the fact that, to borrow Amritjit Singh's argument, racial others "serve as eternal footmen holding the identity coats for whites" in Wharton's novel.[63] In channeling Pauline's latent sexual desire with his "holy ecstasy" exercises, the Mahatma redirects her attention away from husband and family, just as he does by teaching the more insatiable Lita to dance. Just before Lita and Manford consummate their affair, Lita admits that she wants to leave Jim to "dance and laugh and be hopelessly low-lived and irresponsible," which, she also admits, may bring her right back to Dawnside. Thus the Mahatma becomes Dexter's surrogate and another possible answer to Jim's question, if Lita leaves him, "what does she go to?" Pauline's association with the Mahatma's teachings, together with Lita's association with dancing, add up to a failed marriage for Jim and a strained one for Pauline and Manford, exile for Wyant, a gunshot wound for Nona, and a precarious future for the Wyant heir. So even after the white family implodes because of its own moral inadequacies, jazz remains the sign of the times, and the Mahatma the disembodied ghost of the New Negro haunting white New York. "More than a Negro community," James Weldon Johnson argues in his contribution to Locke's *New Negro,* "Harlem is . . . a large scale experiment in the race problem" in part because of the attraction and revulsion it held for white New Yorkers, and *Twilight Sleep* is Wharton's most extensive commentary on that experiment.[64] In linking the Mahatma first to Pauline and then to Lita, Wharton's satire of Jazz-Age New York suggests that the erosion of class and regional boundaries as well as those between Gentiles and Jews leads to the erosion of boundaries between whites and blacks, a slippery slope wherein one woman's guru becomes another woman's gigolo.

PART II

"Virginia Is Not Dead but Sleepeth": Segregation and the "Family Black and White" in Glasgow's and Cather's South

As far as the color problem is concerned, there is but one great difference between the Southern white and the Northerner: the Southerner remembers, historically and in his own psyche, a kind of Eden in which he loved black people and they loved him. Historically, the flaming sword laid across this Eden is the Civil War. Personally, it is the Southerner's sexual coming of age, when, without any warning, unbreakable taboos are set up between himself and his past. Everything, thereafter, is permitted him except the love he remembers and has never ceased to need. The resulting, indescribable torment affects every Southern mind and is the basis of the Southern hysteria.

—James Baldwin, "Fifth Avenue, Uptown: A Letter from Harlem"

There was much natural kindness on the part of white Virginians toward the Negroes, and this feeling was widely reciprocated. [Northern] agitators helped to undermine this state of things.

—Virginius Dabney, *Virginia: The New Dominion*

3

Family Reunion

Slavery as Usable Past

I. "OUT OF THE DIM MISTS OF INFANCY"

James Baldwin's 1955 essay "Stranger in the Village," which describes his experience in a remote Swiss town whose inhabitants have never seen a black man, ends with the observation that despite such insularity, "this world is white no longer, and it will never be white again."[1] Referring to the emergence of independent nations in Africa, Baldwin writes here and elsewhere of the unique contributions Americans can play in this new world order. That contribution rests upon the fact that black and white Americans, he repeatedly insists, share a familiarity with one another that Europeans, even those who have seen a black man, do not have of colonized Africans. "The most profound reality of the American experience," Baldwin characterizes this familiarity in another essay as a "*blood* relationship" that we cannot begin to understand or change "until we accept how very much it contains of the force and anguish and terror of love" (32). The native New Yorker contends that this "blood relationship" between blacks and whites has its origin in the South, or what he calls his "Old Country." We might add to Baldwin's observations that this "blood relationship" has its origin, more particularly, in the state in which both Cather and Glasgow were born, for Virginia was the first English colony to receive enslaved Africans (197).[2] Baldwin argues that white northerners' positions with respect to the debate over slavery as well as their role in the Civil War helped foster the illusion—and it was an illusion in the sense of being false—that Africans have been ancillary to the making of America and to the making of white American identity. As his remark about a "flaming sword" indicates, Baldwin thought the South's principal positions on slavery and segregation, by contrast, placed white identity in the context of race relations in a very direct way, one of which white southerners themselves were acutely aware.

As in the case of Virginius Dabney's remarks about a "natural kindness" between blacks and whites, white southerners in the twentieth century commonly constructed Baldwin's "blood relationship" as a sort of familial one, refurbishing for the Jim Crow era a logic once used to justify slavery. According to this logic, slavery encapsulated one kind of affiliation, in addition to those between husband and wife and parents and children, that linked all members of the plantation (except, conspicuously, the overseer) as a family, albeit one divided by race. "My family, black and white," as the saying went, suggested a series of associations structured by hierarchy and glazed with a patina of benevolence.[3] In another sense, slavery had not only defined freedom for the nation, but it had also defined a particularly southern notion of antebellum democracy. Glasgow's epic novel of the Civil War, *The Battle-Ground* (1902), examines this construction of southern citizenship alongside the plantation "family" in the character of Major Lightfoot, a fiery old plantation owner with an itch for secession. Claiming that he does not support seccession because of slavery itself, Major Lightfoot instead wants to fight for the *right* to own slaves, which to him means perpetuating the democracy he believes his state invented: "We made the Union," he tells his more moderate friend Peyton Ambler, "and we'll unmake it when we please. We didn't make slavery; but, if Virginia wants slaves, by God, sir, she shall have slaves!"[4] Giving voice to the irony Glasgow thought inherent to the age of evasive idealism's notion of democracy, Major Lightfoot asks, "Without slavery, where is our aristocracy, sir?" (63). Despite the clear indictment she makes of white plantation owners' dependence upon their chattel to define their class prerogative over other whites, Glasgow still sees some truth in the observation made by young Dan Montjoy, the Major's grandson, that "you ought to love the thing that belongs to you" (67). The only white owners who do not love their black slaves in this novel are, in fact, the "poor white trash"; the "quality," to use Glasgow's slaves' term, seemingly always love the things that belong to them. That love implies an innocence reflected in the slaves themselves, who seem blissfully ignorant of the implications of both their bondage and their freedom. These are familial ties, beginning in childhood, that materially bind black to white at the same time that they emotionally bind white to black.

Outlasting the peculiar institution for which they were designed, images of such interracial family ties—notable in the names whites used to refer to African Americans to whom they felt attached ("Mammy," "Aunt,"

"Uncle")—coexisted with the development and entrenchment of segregation. Samuel Dennis Jr. writes that planter paternalism, an ideology that "described reciprocal obligations between white planters and enslaved black laborers as members of the same household" and "was expressed in the oft-repeated phrase 'my family, black and white,'" was "revived during the early twentieth century" by "regional writers and artists [who] reinvented a plantation past where enslaved African American men and women lived contented lives under the benevolent care of the white plantation master."[5] Such a revival dovetailed with the fact that despite many Virginians' claims to the contrary, Reconstruction ultimately failed to increase African Americans' access to democratic citizenship. By 1883 whatever threat the black vote held for white authorities was effectively nullified by the passing of the Anderson-McCormack election law, which assured, according to the *Richmond Dispatch*, "the rule of the white man in Virginia."[6] As lawmakers did in other southern states, Virginia's Redeemers passed poll taxes, understanding clauses, and the like to limit black political rights, so by 1902, the year the state ratified its new constitution, white rule was assured and the black male vote was almost nonexistent. At the same time that it was restricting black suffrage, Virginia began segregating its public schools and, in 1900, its railway cars.[7] Segregation was the South's way of incorporating modernity—and what I have been calling modern democratization—without losing its status as the region that most exemplified stability of place, creating what Grace Hale terms "geographical anchors" across the southern landscape that fixed race in the face of an increasingly mobile nation.[8] Enforcing these anchors both legally and extralegally, white southerners made it clear to African Americans that the privileges of democracy promised by emancipation were denied to them, and they made clear to the nation at large that the white South would continue to cling to its sense of itself as a unique region. That regional particularity, in Virginia as elsewhere, included claims to racial "purity" that, like segregation, manifested themselves legally, in bans on miscegenation, for instance, as well as in measures requiring any person born after 1912 to file paperwork stating their racial heritage.[9] As much as such measures suggested a wish to redefine the region's notion of family as racially homogeneous, integration with African Americans in the domestic realm, especially during childhood, continued to be a critical rite of passage for many white southerners, one that would be threatened by the wholesale segregation of the races. Vestiges of the plantation's image of the family black and white thus mitigated this threat by carving spaces where, in the private realm, white southerners could grow into their racial and class privileges via their connections to African Americans. A regional response to a perceived national crisis concerning the widening scope of democracy, this tension between the need for public separation and the desire for private interconnection is an essential ingredient in early twentieth-century southern literature.

As women born in the South, neither Ellen Glasgow nor Willa Cather was immune to this racialized process of self-building. Although Cather, of course, identified herself more as a Nebraskan than as a Virginian, her first nine years in Virginia and her family's southern roots there had a significant impact on her. Joyce McDonald has written that Cather's southernness—manifesting itself in her penchant for utilizing the pastoral as a way to critique history, in her class sensibilities, and in her belief in a natural aristocracy—inform her fiction even if most of that fiction is set elsewhere.[10] Further, Cather's deployment of southern identity was a way for her to embody differing expressions of identity and still return to her "real" self as a westerner. For instance, her claim of being a "dang'ous nigger" (made when she was a child to a gentleman friend of the family) was a youthful protest against the strictures of acceptable behavior for a lady as set down by her mother.[11] On the one hand, claiming to be a "dang'ous nigger" could be read as a severe infraction, a shocking betrayal of the core beliefs of southern culture that thrived on racialized and gendered oppositions. On the other hand, such a claim could not be *more* in keeping with those beliefs. Role playing as such a figure, Cather assumed access to the black male self, using that self as a sort of language to say something about her own identity, "destabilizing gender by performing race," as Lisa Marcus succinctly puts it.[12] Cather was also enacting such a process when she appeared, in a photograph taken in her teens, in her uncle's Confederate Army cap.[13] In both cases, she is adopting a male persona in order to complicate the construction of gender that she embodies, but the transition between identifying with the black man to embodying a white southern one is critical, signifying that Cather has come of age by first aligning herself with, then mastering, African Americans.

Ellen Glasgow's coming of age was equally informed by the presence of African Americans, although to different ends. Whereas Cather used blackness to express her evolving racialized identity as a nontraditional woman, Glasgow used blackness to express her development of an ethical self. Early on in *The Woman Within,* Glasgow recounts two childhood memories, the first of which is watching a dog being hunted, a sight that taught her a "heartbreaking pity for the abused and inarticulate, for all the helpless victims of life, everywhere" (10). This memory is twinned, in her mind, with another of watching an elderly black man named Uncle Henry being taken by force to the almshouse. Having immediately burst into tears at the sight of the dog, Glasgow in the latter memory joins a group of other children who mock the man's cries only to be visited, an instant later, with the same misery at another's pain she experienced upon witnessing the dog's beating. In addition to her initial reaction, this second memory also differs from the first in that Glasgow has come to presume her own powerlessness: "nothing that I can do will stop them from taking the old man away. Nothing that I can do will keep the old man from crying out in his grieving voice that he does not want to be taken. Nothing that I can do will make the world different" (11). Her identification with the powerless, sparked by the first memory, is rekindled in the second, from which she also discovers how thoughtlessly she can imitate those who inflict pain and how little she can do to prevent such suffering. Glasgow has learned to identify not so much with the black man but as one who sympathizes with him but cannot change his situation.

However little she feels she can help the disenfranchised like Uncle Henry, this ethical self deeply informs Glasgow's identity as a writer, awakening in her the feeling of existing in a state of "strange exile to which all writers who are born and not made are condemned" (37). Her initiation into the exile of the born writer continues to be nurtured by another African American, her mammy, Lizzie Jones, with whom the girlhood Glasgow created her first stories: "Out of the dim mists of infancy a hero named Little Willie had wandered into the strange country of my mind, or, it may be, at the start, into Mammy's" (23–24). Glasgow describes her relationship to this black woman as one in which there is hardly a separation between them, so thorough and so pure is Lizzie's love for her. As Baldwin points out, this could hardly be the case, because a black woman caring for white children like Glasgow "knows how bitterly her black family is endangered by her white one."[14] Yet whites' belief in this love is critical, as Hale observes, in justifying the individual's and the region's past, making both usable in the present for women like Glasgow.[15] Her connection to Lizzie is not only significant to Glasgow's developing storytelling skills, it is also important to that sense of ethics first triggered by the dog and Uncle Henry, a fact that Glasgow makes especially clear when she recalls losing Lizzie:

> It was the beginning of that sense of loss, of exile in solitude, which I was to bear with me to the end. Choking back my tears, I watched the carriage roll down the street, while it tore my world apart, and left a great jagged scar on the horizon. It was as if I could look ahead and see that the happiest time of my life was now over. The long rambles were

> over. The circle of my friends, in every shade of white, black, or yellow, had melted away. The stories in the evenings were over. Little Willie had vanished. (30)

This traumatic initiation into racial segregation leaves a "scar" tearing white from black that recalls Baldwin's "flaming sword," but it is also the start of Glasgow's career as a writer; the next chapter of the autobiography, in fact, is titled "I Become a Writer." The sense of exile that Glasgow begins to experience when she sees the hunted dog and Uncle Henry and that remains with her upon Lizzie's departure is a concrete symbol of her native talent and a means of justifying her eventual success. Despite the painful circumstances, the loss of innocence implied by the loss of her mammy and her colorful cast of friends is vital in making Glasgow both a southerner and a southern writer.

While Cather, as we have seen, felt that she hit her stride as a writer only with the publication of *O Pioneers!*—her second novel but the first one set in Nebraska; in another sense the roots of her writing sprang from the South. As Joseph Urgo has pointed out, in her last published novel, *Sapphira and the Slave Girl* (1940), Cather went back to her Virginian origins, inserting herself in the epilogue of the text as a character recalling memories that constitute both "the genesis of the novel and . . . of the author herself."[16] The Cather figure's memories of her own childhood, furthermore, are shaped by memories of an earlier time that she herself is too young to have witnessed, an era revealed to her by the servant Till's recollections and by the dialect song—"*down by de cane-brake, close by de mill, / Dar lived a yaller gal, her name was Nancy Till*"—that is sung to her at night.[17] Eagerly awaiting the return of the former slave Nancy, the Cather figure, by extension, is anticipating the reestablishment of some link to her own family's interracial past. Nancy's reunion with her mother and her former owners takes place in the Cather figure's bedroom so that she can view the scene, which teaches her many of the habits that, she writes elsewhere, she employs in her depictions of the West. She learns, for example, to look and listen, to remain silent instead of interrupting the story unfolding before her and for her benefit.[18] Included in the epilogue's depiction of Nancy's return are several details—of domestic rituals, of a comfortable, homey kitchen, of the ways women honor the past by sharing tales about it—that distinguish so many of Cather's later descriptions of Europeans. And while a Cather-like writer makes a brief appearance in the introduction to *My Ántonia,* this novel—one that, as Cather tells Dorothy Canfield Fisher, began with memories of African American voices—ends in autobiography.[19] The final words of *Sapphira* are, in fact,

"Willa Cather." Even though she acknowledges them less than Glasgow, then, memories of the family black and white became important sources for Cather's works. While there are significant differences in the ways they wrote of Virginia, both writers came of age in a South where white children like themselves are nurtured in an interracial family only to be weaned by segregation.

II. MISTRESSES OF THEIR SITUATION

Perhaps another indication of the importance to Cather of her southern heritage, in addition to her childhood memories and her beliefs about class and history, is that *Sapphira and the Slave Girl,* like many works by Glasgow, searches for a usable regional past. As we have seen, one of the hallmarks of regionalism's turn-of-the-century transition is its comparative slant, but neither when Glasgow compares Virginia to New York nor when Wharton compares New York to the West do they see fit to imagine both regions' pasts. For Glasgow, New York typifies democracy's present, and its present only, just as the West does for Wharton. By contrast, the pasts of both Virginia and the West occupy some measure of prominence in Cather's works, suggesting that Cather identified, at least in part, with both regions, and that she was interested in exploring the effects of modern democratization on both western and southern cultures. Furthermore, Cather fits nicely with other southern women writers like Glasgow in that she centers her depictions of the South's past more on the plantation mistress than the master, a backward glance that is not surprising for the woman writer. Their focus on this figure of the past was influenced by beliefs about white women in circulation in their own time. Because African Americans were imagined to continue to play the supposedly familial roles they had been forced to occupy in slavery, Glasgow and Cather look to the past and to the family black and white in the past as ways to scrutinize the relationships between southern blacks and white women in the present. Recent work on the Jim Crow South by scholars such as historian W. Fitzhugh Brundage and cultural geographer Steven Hoelscher suggests that this was part of a larger trend. Brundage illustrates that in a dizzying array of "Daughters" societies (mocked in Glasgow's fiction), organizations sponsoring public monuments and memorial rituals, genealogical associations, and groups campaigning for the professionalization of a "pro-southern" version of history, white women of the genteel classes assumed formidable roles in shaping the region's collective memory, increasing their own importance in the New South by becoming guardians of the past. These "woman architects of whites' historical memory,"

Brundage writes, "by both explaining and mystifying the historical roots of white supremacist and elite power in the South, performed a conspicuous civic function at a time of heightened concern about the perpetuation of social and political hierarchies." And in his essay on the historic tourism industry, Hoelscher writes that elite white women in Natchez, Mississippi, "like their equivalents in Charleston, Nashville, and San Antonio, played a fundamental role in shaping the memory that would instruct and bolster southern politics and economy during the middle decades of the twentieth century."[20] While neither Glasgow nor Cather mystify the Old South—at least not totally—they do take it upon themselves to explain or elucidate the past, and they do so through the eyes of what they considered to be a more insecure and unstable present. For both writers, the challenge was to confront Virginia's past more honestly or directly than they believed earlier women regionalists had confronted their own local histories, yet still salvage something that could be put to use in the more chaotic present.

That is not an easy task when the past includes slavery. In writing *Sapphira and the Slave Girl,* Cather claimed that she was interested in depicting the Old South in order to explore slavery itself, or what she called "the Terrible."[21] This statement can strike readers as suspect, though, because the peculiar institution seems considerably less than terrible in the novel; as Naomi Morgenstern has pointed out, the brutal nature of slavery must be "read back into" Cather's text, for no one is severely scarred by it.[22] To be sure, Cather explores the deep tensions that were present in antebellum life, but the seemingly irresolvable conflicts that arise somehow manage to remedy themselves almost in spite of characters' actions. It is in this way that Cather reaches back into the past—purportedly a "Terrible" one—in order to find resources for the present. Urgo is right to assert that in Cather's work, history "can be utilized, . . . but . . . never . . . objectively known," but this begs the question as to what utilization Cather makes of slavery.[23] While many of her novels emphasize nonfamilial, social relationships (*My Ántonia* and *A Lost Lady*) or personal development (*O Pioneers!* and *The Song of the Lark*), *Sapphira* emphasizes family, a fact to which many of the books' names—"Sapphira and her Household," "Sapphira's Daughter," "Nancy and Till"—attest. In investigating the loyalties and anxieties generated by the family black and white, Cather searches for a usable past; she searches, in fact, for her past.

For the girl who makes her appearance only at the very end of the novel comes from a line of Dodderidges who uphold the plantation family, even keeping slaves who are too old to work "well provided for" (24). As many faults as Sapphira possesses, she is considered by all of the other characters, even by those who oppose slavery for ideological or theological reasons, as loyal to her black family members in the same way her father before her was. This is why her sudden change in attitude toward Nancy confuses white and black characters alike, for "it wasn't a Dodderidge trait to turn on anybody they had once taken a fancy to" (59). Although much of this family tradition escapes Henry Colbert, whose own background is not rooted in slavery, he comes to justify Sapphira's role as a slave owner by the biblical proverb, "*Remember them in bond as bound with them,*" and by the logic that "if Lizzie," Sapphira's redoubtable cook, "was in bonds to Sapphira, was she not almost equally in bonds to Lizzie?" (110). Despite his antislavery leanings, something of Sapphira's ways have rubbed off on Henry, for he believes that Nancy cares for his quarters at the mill out of "dutiful affection" and even out of "love" (193). Indeed, not only Henry but all the Colberts have a "family feeling" toward their slaves, a feeling reciprocated by the slaves themselves (9). So unbreakable are the ties between black and white that they extend even into death, at which point blacks are laid next to whites in the family graveyard, separated only by a gravel walk. The description of the "Double S," with its "coffee brown" stream and wildflowers of "singular whiteness," evokes the interracial plantation family in the way its members are divided yet mirrored images of each other—two halves of a whole (115, 166). The structure of Cather's novel suggests this association by placing a description of the "Double S" in between Henry's musings about the morality of slavery and the beginning of book 4, "Sapphira's Daughter," in which Rachel Blake's abolitionist point of view is most fully developed.

In similarly assessing the usefulness of the past, Glasgow portrays in her works a family structure with the same sort of intergenerational bonds between members. In many instances, personal attendants and their masters are so close that they share the same mannerisms, the black slave a kind of dark imitation or "silhouette," as one character in *The Battle-Ground* puts it, of the white master (23). For *The Battle-Ground*'s Dan Montjoy, the slave Abel functions as a guide to his coming-of-age as a Virginian gentleman, an authority on acceptable behavior for a growing boy of the gentry. Blacks and whites reared in slavery, like Major Lightfoot and his driver, Congo, are connected to each other through their association with the white-owned homeplace, which makes separation (of black from white and of either from the plantation) inconceivable, as the Major incredulously tells Congo in a diatribe against abolitionists: "They say I've no right to you, Congo,—bless my soul, and you were born on my own land!" (87).

In much of the rhetoric of the family black and white—and neither Cather nor Glasgow are exceptions—the ties that bind masters and slaves are imagined to be primary and primal, going back both to the origin of the individual and of the region, and the Civil War seems to do little to disrupt them. Glasgow makes this point most plainly in *The Deliverance* (1904), for the slave owners of the novel, the Blakes, have lost everything except their proud name and the loyalty they owe former slaves like Uncle Isam, who turns in a time of crisis to the young "master," Christopher, whom he has barely laid eyes on.[24] Dependence upon and loyalty to the former master or his children remains characteristic of slaves a full thirty-odd years after their emancipation; "it's God A'mighty or Marse Christopher" to all three hundred former Blake slaves as well as to their descendants (445). And that characteristic is shared by Christopher himself, who goes to Isam's cabin to doctor the freedman and his family through smallpox. Doing so allows Christopher to reconnect with his heritage, the "old love of a 'risk for the sake of a risk'" that Glasgow, through the perspective of Christopher's wise Uncle Tucker, labels as lacking "the moral elements of true courage" (447). Robbing Isam's plight of its "underlying sombre horror," Christopher's loyalty is in reality nothing more than an inherited weakness that lacks the true loyalty felt by Isam and by other black members of the family. That devotion is best displayed by the mammy character in Glasgow's short story "Whispering Leaves" (1923), who returns from the dead to continue to care for her young and helpless master. In caring for the boy from beyond the grave, Mammy Rhody is fulfilling a promise to the child's mother, who died before her.[25] The bonds between generations of owners and slaves implied by Mammy Rhody's promise are so strong that they defy even divisions between the living and the dead.

If the black woman's dedication to the white child in Glasgow's short story takes on ghostly dimensions, the white Mrs. Ambler's devotion to her black "children" in *The Battle-Ground* takes on sentimentalized ones: "of all the souls on the great plantation," Glasgow tells us, "the mistress alone had never rested from her labours" (25). Part of the romantic glow with which Glasgow endows this white "mother," though, comes from Mrs. Ambler's sincere struggle to live within a system that she does not wholly support (a moral struggle that African Americans like Mammy Rhody do not undergo). In particular, Mrs. Ambler suffers a crisis of faith because Christianity seems to uphold slavery and because it gives her the responsibility of caring for the bodies and souls of her husband's chattel (48). If Glasgow uses Mrs. Ambler both to sentimentalize and to critique the Old South, her analysis is somewhat dulled by the ways the heroine of the novel, Betty Ambler, inherits her mother's maternal attitude toward their black "kin": "There was never a sick slave or a homeless dog that she would not fly out to welcome, bareheaded and a little breathless, with the kindness brimming over from her eyes" (82). In this way, Glasgow has Betty destabilize gender by performing race, to use Lisa Marcus's phrase again, but unlike the way Cather does it when she assumes the role of a "dang'ous" black man, Betty defies the strictures of femininity (her head is uncovered and she is not in repose) by performing whiteness.

Cather's Sapphira is also described as a kind of mother to her slaves, although a significantly less maternal one than Mrs. Ambler or Betty. Like her attitude toward Rachel, her own daughter, Sapphira's care of her slaves is compromised by her obsession with exerting power over them. At first, Cather's novel emphasizes the manipulative and controlling aspects of Sapphira as a mother to both black and white: she is overly harsh toward and rejecting of both Nancy and Rachel. As the novel progresses and Rachel plots to put Nancy (and by implication, herself) beyond Sapphira's grasp, Cather increasingly portrays Sapphira as a caring, if strong-minded, figure. Even Rachel learns to appreciate her mother's "singular indulgence with Tansy Dave," a slave who tried to run away from Sapphira only to regret it later, her "real affection for Till and old Jezebel, her patience with Sampson's lazy wife" (220). Acknowledging how "Sapphira's darkies were better cared for, better fed and better clothed, than the poor whites in the mountains," Henry and Rachel temper their abolitionist principles with an appreciation of how loyal Sapphira is to her interracial family (228–29). Sapphira is also redeemed as a mother to her white daughter in the section of the novel titled "The Dark Autumn," when she reconciles with Rachel after her granddaughter Betty's death. Even the uncomplaining way in which Sapphira dies could be read as a reconsideration of her role as mistress, for what seems in the beginning of the novel to be false pride becomes, by the end of the text, "intrepid courage" (267). Henry comes to realize that Sapphira is a good mistress specifically because she maintains the hierarchies implied by the family black and white, that "sometimes keeping people in their place is being good to them" (268). Ironically, it is the disruption of the family black and white (not to mention the black family itself) that makes this reconsideration of Sapphira possible, as only with Nancy's disappearance are the rifts between Henry and Sapphira and between Sapphira and Rachel mended. Perhaps that is because Cather can find value in the past only by excising the more "Terrible" aspects of it that Nancy's near-rape implies.

For as much as Cather draws from her southern heritage a belief in a natural aristocracy, as MacDonald claims, she also understands that Sapphira's position as a (mostly) good mistress of slaves—as a Dodderidge as opposed to a Colbert—bolsters her own place in Back Creek's pecking order.

Indeed, as Toni Morrison argues, Sapphira appropriates her slaves' lives in her own search for self-definition, and therefore her own identity as "mistress of her situation and of herself" requires slaves (268).[26] So invested is Sapphira in justifying slavery and herself as an owner of slaves that she likes or dislikes others solely on the basis of whether she feels they are pro- or antislavery. Having married beneath her station and moved from prosperous Loudoun County in eastern Virginia to Back Creek, Sapphira and her "troop of niggers," we are told, were "not warmly received" by a community in which slavery is not widely practiced and often looked down upon (8, 22). Thus the class difference between Sapphira and her neighbors is important, too, but it ultimately serves to highlight differences with respect to slavery because, from Sapphira's perspective, nonelite status signals abolitionist beliefs that, in turn, fly in the face of her status as an aristocrat. Sapphira's polite, disdainful manner with Back Creek's postmistress, Mrs. Bywaters, for example, is rooted not so much in the latter's class but in her "very different opinions on one very important subject," and readers know, without needing to be told, what that subject is (37). And when Henry tries to befriend Mr. Fairhead, Sapphira has a similar reaction, which Henry rightly connects to her investment in slavery: Sapphira "did not really regard [Mr. Fairhead] as an inferior, but as an equal—of the wrong kind" (81). Sapphira regains the prestige she lost in marrying Henry by being a slave owner, which is why she does not mind her neighbor's disapproval: it only reinforces her superiority. Without her slaves, she is simply Sapphira Colbert of Back Creek, the miller's wife. Indeed, it is only Sapphira and her "troop of niggers" that makes this a novel of the Old South at all. Take them out of it, and we are left with Baptists, abolitionists, and poor white mountain people, not figures usually associated with the South "befo' de war." This helps to explain why whenever Sapphira's position is threatened—especially by Nancy—she becomes almost paranoid, such as when she invites Henry's nephew in a maneuver to conquer Nancy sexually or when she cries out in the middle of the night just to make sure her servant is on the other side of her door. Sapphira cannot live without slaves, and the novel itself does not subject her to such a fate, for she dies before the start of the war. So to say that Sapphira is defined through and dependent upon slavery is perhaps not enough. Cather's novel itself is invested in its main character representing the class that was most tied to slavery; in this way, Sapphira isn't just committed to slavery, she *is* slavery. But to a lesser extent, this is true of the other white characters as well. Slaves become substitutes for the white self and its position with respect to other whites, which makes African Americans largely symbolic and thus interchangeable: "whenever [Sapphira] and her husband were thinking of

Nancy, they invariably talked about Bluebell," and in doing so, Henry and Sapphira are also invariably talking about themselves and their positions with respect to each other (199). On the one hand, Henry possesses all of the power of the patriarch, but on the other, Sapphira is above him in class status and has the slaves to prove it. Slaves reveal both the power of individual whites and the limits of that power, while they themselves live without control even over their own lives.

The same can be said of the slaves in most of Glasgow's works. Dan Montjoy and his grandfather, Major Lightfoot, as we have seen, rely upon slaves to reflect their own position, a fact that Glasgow emphasizes by having Big Abel repeatedly save Dan's life during the war. Major Lightfoot's comment about slavery creating the Virginian aristocracy is ironically borne out again and again in Glasgow's works. In *The Voice of the People* (1902), for instance, gentility is marked above all by charity to dependent African Americans: typical for a Glasgow character of her time and place, Mrs. Burwell reminisces with her husband of "the day you proposed to me for the sixth time, I had just seen you bandage up the head of a little darkey that had cut himself—and I accepted you on the spot."[27] Unlike the sentimental Mrs. Burwell, who ultimately represents what Glasgow took to be the best qualities of the age of evasive idealism, Mrs. Blake of *The Deliverance* represents its worst, a spooky symbol of all the reasons the South's cause was lost. Fooled by her family, her remaining servants, and her own pride into believing that the Confederacy won the war and that "the three hundred slaves" she used to own continue to till "her familiar fields," in reality Mrs. Blake has been displaced by her former overseer, her slaves "scattered like chaff before the wind" (74). She continues to define herself by her former role as a plantation mistress, maintaining a close relationship with the few "slaves" remaining to her as well as a haughty distance from non-slave-owning whites, as Sapphira does. As she is dying, Mrs. Blake requests that both her black and white family be present to say their final farewells, attempting to pass her position as mistress on to her children and telling her son, Christopher, that he must "Always remember that a man's first duty is to his wife and children, and his second to his slaves. The Lord has placed them in your hands, and you must answer to Him how you fulfill the trust" (476–77). With delightfully wicked irony, Glasgow employs Mrs. Blake's true status—a poor woman living in an overseer's house—to suggest that even in her more aristocratic past, Mrs. Blake (and, by extension, the Southern Lady) held an ultimately demeaning position that required her own subservience and the even greater subservience of her slaves to the master, as this advice to her son indicates. Thus the ring she waves around majestically as she gives orders to inferiors (like the non-slave-owning Jim Weatherby), which once held a diamond hocked by her children, is a symbol of her misplaced pride, for it now holds a bit of purple glass donated by Docia, her former slave. Perhaps the most forcefully ironic use Glasgow makes of Mrs. Blake is at her death, when she "frees" Boaz, a former slave she promised to emancipate fifty years earlier, and justifies the delay on the grounds that he will find his freedom "nothing but a burden and a trouble" (477). Mrs. Blake's fake emancipation of Uncle Boaz makes plain that the mistress needs the slave as least as much as the "slave" needs the mistress.

Yet in many of Glasgow's works and in *Sapphira,* the critique of white southerners' dependence upon slaves is tempered by the texts' investment in upholding the illusion that slaves needed masters. Cather's Tansy Dave, for example, literally goes mad once he is away from Sapphira. Jezebel, stolen from Africa in her youth, nonetheless harbors fond memories of her life as Dodderidge chattel, and slaves like Till and Nancy take pride in their places as members of the plantation's family. Sampson, the most independent of Sapphira's slaves, courts whatever danger might befall him by stepping out of his place to help save Nancy's virtue. But he refuses to risk the responsibility for himself and his family that freedom would place upon him (181). As he tells his master, Sampson would rather leave his black family—his wife and children—than his white one. If slaves like Nancy, Sampson, Lizzie, and Bluebell assume their free lives reluctantly—fearful, to paraphrase Nancy, of belonging nowhere (note the slippage here between slavery and regional community)—Till never really assumes one at all. Even more than Sampson, in fact, Till cherishes her role in the white family, exhibiting little response to her affair with (or rape by?) a white man and to her marriage, arranged by Sapphira, to a man she dislikes. To the end, Till's main complaint about her condition is not her lack of freedom but her having to live in Back Creek with "no count" whites.[28] Till's love for her own daughter is tempered by her loyalty to Sapphira, which is why Rachel knows that the task of helping Nancy to escape will fall to her since, from Till's perspective, "Nancy had come into the world by accident; the other relation, that with the Dodderidges, Till regarded as one of the fixed conditions you were born into. Beginning with Jezebel, her kin had lived under the roof and protection of that family for four generations. It was their natural place in the world" (217). In other words, beginning with Jezebel, relationships with black "kin" become less important than membership in a white "family."

If slaves' dependence serves to justify white ownership, African American independence serves to justify the postwar images of the family black and white—by making it seem a choice—and the budding system of segregation, which is imagined to be an unfortunate necessity for those African Americans who choose to sever the family tie. Exemplifying postbellum familial continuity, Till serves Sapphira's descendants and memorializes her own enslavement, telling stories of the master and mistress and preserving Sapphira's "odd bits of finery" as her own "keepsakes and treasures" (291). For other Colbert slaves, separation from the white family proves to be a mixed blessing. Sampson manages well, but Tap, once a "jolly mill boy . . . whom everybody liked," is not "able to stand his freedom" (289, 290). Lured to the city "where every day was like circus day to a country-bred boy," Tap kills another black man in a saloon owned by a carpetbagger (290). Here Cather echoes white southerners, fearful of the social, political, and economic opportunities for blacks in urban centers, who warned that the "attractions" of city life corrupted naïve former slaves, making them discontented workers.[29] William Cohen notes that in the decades following the Civil War, the rhetoric of freedom as "dangerous" for freedmen was commonly used to influence former slaves against moving too far away from their former masters: as one press account held, a "befo'-de-war-" type African American counseled his cohorts that "when yer git too far away from de old marster and de old home you's away from de only freedman's bank whar de nigger is got left."[30] Tap's unhappy fate is attributed to his own incompetence and to a "Yankee jury"; he becomes a victim both of his own inability to assume responsible citizenship and of northerners' insistence that he play a role of which he is incapable.

Likewise, Glasgow's servants like Delphy, Verbeny, Ish, and Cæsar remain in the same familial relationships with former owners they had in the past. In *The Voice of the People,* for instance, we meet the servant Cæsar just after he has broken a piece of heirloom Wedgwood and has been caught in the act by his employer, Judge Bassett, and the light, comic tone Glasgow attributes to their exchange comes from its ritualistic quality: we understand, both from the narrator's treatment of it and from the Judge's complaints, that Cæsar has been breaking Wedgwood for a long time. Despite Cæsar's carelessness with china, the Judge values his former slave's talents, including his bartending ones, and brags that he is "prouder of Cæsar's fame at the bar" than he is of his own (164). Whereas the Judge habitually boasts of Cæsar, his friend General Battle does nothing but complain of his former slaves: "'They will break me!' he would declare a dozen times a day. 'They will turn me out of house and home . . . It's worse than before the war. . . . Then they lived on me and I got an odd piece of work out of them. Now they live on me and don't do a damned lick!'" (57–58). The General's repeated complaints are not, by any means, to be taken seriously. He may pretend to despise the dependence his former slaves have upon him, but the fact that he continues to feed them and worries over them as if they were his children indicates that he wouldn't have it any other way. Rich in what Hale identifies as an "integrationist dream,"[31] Glasgow's *Voice* features an entire chapter devoted to recording the former slaves' reminiscences of their bondage, of old freedmen's random interjections about the past (like Ish's repeated non sequitur, "Ole Miss wuz in her grave, she wuz"), and their negative evaluations of the present ("Doze wuz times, en dese ain't times!") (100, 101–2). African Americans thus mark the passage of time but exist out of history, forever the keepers of whites' past rather than their own. General Battle dies midway through the novel, and the Judge is ill at novel's end, but Cæsar remains unaffected by age. Ish, perpetually ancient, never dies; in fact, in a particularly disturbing joke, the General claims that Ish wouldn't die "if he were strung up with a halter round his neck" (58–59). African Americans' roles as markers of the past justify their inferior places in the present; when Eugenia Battle, for example, returns from boarding school, the servant Verbeny "enthusiastically" proclaims her resemblance to her mother: "Can't I see her now same ez 'twuz yestiddy, . . . sayin', 'You b'longs ter me, Verbeny, en I'se gwine ter take cyar you'" (173–74). Here Verbeny not only provides a sense of white cultural continuity—Eugie looks just like her mother—but also a continuity to her own servitude, for Eugie's looking like her mother apparently authorizes her "care" of the black woman. Such stability between the past and present lives of African Americans suggests that emancipation had no practical results except upon whites. Thus even as they expose the immature pretensions of white slave owners, neither Cather's novel nor Glasgow's works fully confront the possibility that the enslaved did not need their masters, or, especially, their mistresses, for to confront that possibility would be to fully segregate black from white in their own time.

Yet in both authors' works, a largely benign interracial family coexists with the more menacing possibility of interracial sex, which is imagined to make the memories of the southern past distinctly unusable, particularly for white women. Unlike the dominant narratives of interracial sex in the twentieth century, in which white women play so conspicuous a part as the "victim" of a black male attacker, accounts of interracial sex between white masters and female slaves tended to push white women out of the picture entirely, except in a supporting role as woman scorned. Cather's novel, in contrast, places the white mistress, not the master, in control of the slaves' sexuality, for it is Sapphira who decides if and whom the slaves should marry. But while Sapphira has effectively dominated both Till's body and her mind, Till's daughter poses a dilemma for her. Her plan to have Martin rape Nancy gives

Martin, and by implication, Henry, more control over Nancy than Sapphira herself would possess (and indeed, one wonders if Sapphira is jealous of Nancy for her supposed influence over Henry, or of Henry for his influence over Nancy). For the novel itself, the sexual underbelly of the plantation family also threatens to expose the baser side of slavery and of Sapphira. Cather's text meets this threat, first, by having several white characters, especially Rachel, recognize the importance of Nancy's virtue—despite the historical improbability of such a recognition on whites' part—and, second, by portraying the attempted rape scene, or the cherry-tree scene, as it is often called, in terms, once again, less than terrible. Sexuality, as Naomi Morgenstern notes, is "staged as the desire of three white 'knowing' characters for one black 'innocent' one," a fact made possible by the way Cather so thoroughly desexes many of the black male characters, like Tansy Dave and Jeff, the "capon man," so as to make black women's sexuality a matter of concern only to whites.[32] Like Henry's inherited tendency toward lechery, which he suppresses by believing that Nancy is innocence incarnate, "free from care, like the flowers and the birds," the violence of Nancy's near-rape by Martin in the cherry-tree scene is softened by the girl's own response to it. That response is a mixture of fear for her virtue and her "foolish, dreamy, nigger side," highlighted by her sitting in a tree, monkeylike (67, 178). Contradictorily, Nancy is innocent both because she wants to remain sexually "pure" and because her race justifies whatever sexual freedom she wishes to exercise, just as the dialect song about her is both an innocuous nursery rhyme sung to the Cather figure and the means by which Martin lulls Nancy before grabbing her.

The sexual implications of the family black and white jeopardize Glasgow's vision of the southern past as well. In *Virginia* Gabriel Pendleton keeps faith with the past by raising his daughter to be the human equivalent of a hothouse flower, as we saw in chapter 1, but he also does so by remaining loyal to his old mammy, Aunt Mehitable. A minister whose happiest memories are of fighting the Lost Cause, Gabriel himself is lost in a chapter pointedly titled "The Problem of the South." Called to the aid of Aunt Mehitable's grandchild, who is being attacked by a group of poor whites, Gabriel is killed in the fray, dying because he is caught between the Old South, in which an "unbreakable" tie bound black and white, and the new, in which even his beloved mammy appears to him "alien and enigmatical" (282). Yet another aspect of the problem of the South, as Glasgow constructs it, is the miscegenation that continues in the new era, and the black and white family this produces is far less innocent than is the one implied by Gabriel's loyalty to Mehitable. Even as Gabriel is ineffectually attempting to rescue Mehitable's hapless grandchild, his fellow war veteran Cyrus Treadwell is being called upon by a black woman, his former lover Mandy (who is even more "alien and enigmatical" than Aunt Mehitable is), to prevent the lynching of their son. But because Cyrus is more a product of the segregated New South, he takes a tack opposite to Gabriel's, refusing to intervene in his son's plight by citing the sovereignty of "the law" (and whether he means lynch law or more official versions of racism, Glasgow leaves strategically ambiguous) (276). The differing choices Gabriel and Cyrus make in response to the "problem of the South" at once gesture toward shared memories of their time in the Confederate Army and toward those qualities that distinguish the two men. On the one hand, both need African Americans—Gabriel his mammy and Cyrus his mulatto mistress—in order to highlight their own status as white men. Glasgow emphasizes this dependence by having them, despite their mutual hostility, wax nostalgic about the glories of the war. On the other hand, Gabriel and Cyrus's opposing reactions to what Glasgow terms the problem of the South hint at the tensions between segregation, meant to separate blacks and whites, and the connections, past and present, that continue to bring the races together.

Ultimately, both writers' works dismiss the peril posed to a usable past by attributing the sexual exploitation of black women to disreputable white men (Martin Colbert, Cyrus Treadwell), instead of seeing that exploitation as the region's business as usual. Having disposed of the "Terrible" aspects of slavery by first smoothing over the violence Martin tries to enact upon Nancy and then by turning Nancy from a family member and a native to a stranger (a process about which I will have more to say in chapter 4), Cather is able to draw from both the pro- and antislavery sides of her family's past. And while the ghoulish results of Cyrus's interracial sex risks revealing only the sinister side of the family black and white, Glasgow, like Cather, provides alternative views of the past in order to make it worth remembering, for Cyrus's treachery to Mandy cannot undo Gabriel's heroic, if ineffectual, loyalty to Mehitable. Striking such a balance, though, is not an easy matter for either writer. For example, many of Cather's characters—even Rachel—suggest that blacks raised in slavery believe in slavery, a belief upheld by the actions of slaves themselves. Their loyalties, as we have seen, are more with the white members of their family than with the black ones. But if that is the case, why do the other Colbert slaves dislike Nancy for being the mistress's favorite, as Bluebell claims they do (185)? Cather's text provides what could be a more democratic example of a multiracial family in the form of the Quakers, whom Henry respects and who are responsible for helping Nancy to freedom. The minister who first meets Nancy across the river comforts the frightened young woman by pointing out that she is simply moving from one kind of family to another: "Dey ain't strangers, where you're goin,' honey. Dey calls theyselves Friends, an' dey is friends to all God's people. You'll be treated like dey raised you up from a chile, an' you'll be passed along on yo' way from one kind fambly to de next" (238–39). Even as Cather opens the possibility of a more democratic interracial family, though, her novel does not validate that model over slavery's family, just as it does not validate Rachel's position over Sapphira's. Like *Sapphira,* Glasgow's works often leave tensions unresolved in their effort to recover the past. In *The Battle-Ground* the songs of slave women being sold register "a childish joy in a coming change" as well as "a mother's yearning over broken ties," a mixture of motives so impossible that one cancels the other out (4). Henry's characterization of Nancy's flight applies equally well to the transition that all of Cather's and Glasgow's slaves undergo as they move from what the authors imagine to be a mutual dependence to an isolating individualism and "from the dark lethargy of the cared-for and irresponsible" to a state in which "nobody is altogether free" (228).

Further, for both writers, slavery becomes an abstract rather than a specific wrong, one that can be condemned without condemning even its most staunch supporters, and thus the past becomes usable to the present by virtue of the fact that despite the injustice of slavery, no one is held responsible for it. But however usable the past is, both Cather and Glasgow understand that it's still past, that the Old South has been irrevocably lost and that the southern mistress has become a historical relic. In the case of both *The Battle-Ground* and *Sapphira,* the mistress is ill, blind, or, most often, dead by the end of the war. Yet the Old South's family black and white takes on an innocence that, as it is in Tap's case, stands in contrast not to the means by which "the Terrible" was eradicated, but to stress points in black-white relations stemming from a new culture of democracy. In one sense, then, Baldwin's description of the Civil War as a "flashing sword" tearing old from new and black from white is perhaps too strong, because it seems that something of the old remains, if only as fodder for the present. The mistress's death, as well as her memory, supplies indispensable lessons for the birth of a New Woman for a New South.

III. MASTERING THE NEW SOUTH

In *The Sound and the Fury* William Faulkner emphasizes the continued salience in the New South of the family black and white by describing the early-morning haggles between Mrs. Compson and Dilsey over a hot-water bottle. In a ritualistic manner, Mrs. Compson stands at the top of the stairs calling her servant, "without inflection or emphasis or haste, as though she were not listening for a reply at all. 'Dilsey.'"[33] On the pretense that she wants Dilsey to fill the bottle, Mrs. Compson calls to her in the fear that she might not be there—"I've been lying awake for an hour at least, without hearing a sound from the kitchen"—and with the pitiable hope that the call will usher the black woman into existence (267). In reality, though, and it is a reality of which Dilsey, with eyes that "penetrate the walls and ceiling," seems aware, Mrs. Compson's call ushers her own self into existence, for without Dilsey and her labors on behalf of the white family, Mrs. Compson would cease to be the woman she is (270). It is "not the bottle which Mrs. Compson wanted," but a confirmation of her own racial prerogative, her own idleness and comfort, in Dilsey's work. Yet Dilsey—and here is where, perhaps, Faulkner portrays his own racially privileged point of view—also needs Mrs. Compson to be idle, for the white woman's repeated threats to take on the African American woman's work, to start the fire in the morning, for instance, seem to annoy Dilsey almost as much as her mistress's incessant calling does. These women are tied to each other by the very things that divide them, by Dilsey's labors and Mrs. Compson's indolence, and by a construction of white southern class privilege unable to imagine itself without an available black domestic labor force. They are tied, in short, to each other as Compsons, black and white.

Unlike Faulkner's novel, works by southern women, from Kate Chopin's *At Fault* and Glasgow's *Barren Ground* to Margaret Mitchell's *Gone with the Wind,* often eschew this unflattering characterization of the useless and idle white woman, instead focusing on white female characters who, through their own hard work and their rejection of traditional roles, become "masters" of the post-plantation farm. Although it is probable that many white women did take on more and more responsibility for the family farm at the same time that many others were increasingly pursuing career opportunities in other fields, the number of female farm "masters" in Glasgow's writing alone does seem out of proportion with reality.[34] Perhaps this figure was attractive to women writers like Glasgow because it combined the public and the private, segregation and the residuals of the family black and white, for if they were beginning to enjoy many of the same freedoms their northern and western sisters did, white women in the South did so in ways that were constrained by anxieties about an emancipated black labor force. In the early twentieth century, white southern women remained both the "physical embodiment" and the "rhetorical repository" of white privilege itself, as Jane Dailey notes, and they increasingly became the standard alibi for racial violence against African Americans and for the restriction of their political and economic rights.[35] In keeping African Americans in their place—that is, working on the old plantation—white women stay in their place, the domestic realm, but they gain increasing power there as "masters" of the New South farm.

Barren Ground (1925) is arguably the best specimen of such southern women's fiction, because unlike Chopin's and Mitchell's works as well as other novels by Glasgow, it totally abandons the love plot, allowing the heroine, Dorinda Oakley, to emerge as the only master of the postwar plantation, appropriately called Old Farm. After a brief engagement to Jason Greylock and a short but formative period of residence in New York, Dorinda returns to Virginia vowing to reclaim her family's land, which, like the other farms in Pedlar's Mill, has lapsed into a wasteland due to a lack of what the narrator calls "free labour."[36] Speaking of another Glasgow work, Francesca Sawaya makes a point that is also central to *Barren Ground*: survival in the New South requires "hereditary adaptability to the changing mode of production . . . from slavery to industrial capitalism," a transformation, of course, that does not take race out of the equation.[37] For as she contemplates how to begin her agricultural mission, Dorinda thinks that finding willing black laborers is her greatest obstacle: "if I could get the labour it wouldn't be so hard" (246). In fact, while the challenge in the novel, for Dorinda and all of those around her, is presumably to reclaim the region's barren ground, in reality it is not the reclaiming of land that is so difficult, but the managing of black hands to do so. The rhetoric of a labor shortage, notable even in states, like Virginia, that had a surplus of labor at the turn of the century, was part of the rationale white lawmakers used to pass measures restricting the rights of African Americans as both workers and citizens. Although the General Assembly of Virginia did not pass as many laws that restricted black labor as other southern states did, it did pass several versions of vagrancy laws (1866 and 1904) and emigrant-agent laws (1870, 1903, and 1911) that helped to secure planters' prerogatives over the rights of African American workers.[38] Vagrancy laws effectively made unemployment a crime, and emigrant-agent laws required whites acting as labor agents (often from the lower South or West, where workers were more scarce) to obtain a license. Together with the convict-lease system, which in effect enslaved prisoners, the vagrancy and emigrant-agent laws passed between the 1870s and the 1910s "represented a major and continuing white effort to reassert hegemony over blacks in all areas of life," even though, on paper, they made no explicit reference to race.[39] Black workers of the postwar decades had to negotiate an agricultural labor system, as Cohen argues, that was dominated by whites' convictions that they "ought to work as long and as hard as they did in slavery," and they often did so by refusing to work for former masters.[40] As best as they were able, freedmen resisted working conditions that resembled slavery, opting for short-term employment rather than long-term contracts because white landowners paid day or short-term laborers more than contract laborers.[41] There were added advantages to remaining without a contract, since southern courts consistently enforced planters' rights over those of workers. Another reason for the much-discussed labor shortage was that in many instances, African American families preferred to send children to school, if that was available, and to have wives attend to the home and to the family's crops. The rhetoric of labor scarcity in states like Virginia, then, often implied a fear not that a labor force no longer existed, but that it could no longer be controlled.

Perhaps this helps to explain why, despite her complaints to the contrary, Dorinda does manage to secure black laborers and, once she does, why her problem becomes how to oversee those workers who, like her, stand midway between an economy based upon slavery and one based upon industrial capitalism. Dorinda meets the economic challenges posed to her by African American freedom by incorporating new technology and, more critically, by drawing on the "patient discipline" she inherits from her slave-owning ancestors, because "if she were once weak enough to compromise with the natural carelessness of the Negroes," the narrator tells us, "she knew that the pails and pans would not be properly scalded, and the milk would begin to lose its quality" (380, 310). Repeatedly plagued with the shortcomings of her farmhands, she nonetheless fares better than any of her neighbors because of her "faculty for 'getting on,' as she would have called it, with the Negroes. Unlike James Ellgood, who was inclined to truculence, she had preserved her mother's friendly relations with the established colored families at Pedlar's Mill" (463). Facing her workers with "an intuitive understanding of . . . how to keep on friendly terms with that immature but not ungenerous race," Dorinda can take her black employees for granted at the same time that she complains of not having enough of them and of having to deal with the shortcomings of those she does have (281). Her ability to master black labor coexists with, but also masks, her dependence on that labor: "without laborers, the farms she had reclaimed with incalculable effort would sink again into waste land" (469). So if part of Dorinda's success comes from her skills in managing her problematic black workers, another part comes from her assumption that however troublesome that labor is, it is still a resource she can master as her family had in the past. In fact, Dorinda's complaints about her workers *and* her supposition that acquiring black labor is her right stem from the same belief: that free African Americans should serve a similar role in the white South as slaves did.

Nevertheless, Dorinda's "faculty for getting along" with African Americans, hereditary as it may be, must be adjusted to accommodate the changing nature of race relations in the twentieth-century South. In particular, Glasgow describes the African Americans of Pedlar's Mill as a people on the verge of—but not yet through—the transition from dependence to citizenship: "As for the negroes themselves, they lived contentedly enough as inferiors though not dependents. In spite of the influence of Aunt Mehitable Green, they had not yet learned to think as a race, and the individual negro still attached himself instinctually to the superior powers" (282). The tentative language here suggests that however much Dorinda continues to benefit from the family black and white, Glasgow recognizes that such a system is inherently and inescapably hierarchical. Yet it is Mehitable's relationships to whites—she is "good stock" because of the white "family," namely Dorinda's, that once owned her—that explain why she is the black community's matriarch, and why her children are the most evolved and successful African Americans in Pedlar's Mill. The farm of Micajah Moody, Mehitable's son, is so thriving that he is a sore spot for Pedlar's Mill's poor whites, while Fluvanna, Mehitable's daughter and a valued servant and friend to Dorinda, is held up as the "best" example of African American progress in the novel. But the novel upholds Fluvanna as exemplary because she attaches herself "instinctually to superior powers," and thus she functions, most of all, as the proverbial sidekick, possessing enough good qualities to justify Dorinda's faith in her, but not so many that she can be seen as Dorinda's equal or as someone who thinks "as a race." Hale argues about Mitchell's *Gone with the Wind* a paradigm also at work in Glasgow's novel: in the post–Civil War farm where white men are absent, a black female servant "plays the woman," allowing the white woman to play the master.[42] Asking herself "how she could have managed the farm without Fluvanna," Dorinda responds by taking credit for the black woman's good qualities: "Heaven knows what I should have done if I had not had a pleasant disposition about me" (469). More than employer and servant, but less than equals, their long relationship is, like African Americans themselves, still in an in-between stage: "The affection between the two women had outgrown the slender tie of mistress and maid, and had become as strong and elastic as the bond that holds relatives together . . . Fluvanna respected and adored her mistress; and Dorinda, with an inherited feeling of condescension, was sincerely attached to her servant" (349). As Pamela Matthews suggests, the passage above describes Dorinda and Fluvanna's relationship as a process: if they have already "outgrown" mere employer-employee relations, perhaps Dorinda can outgrow her "inherited feeling of condescension."[43]

But doing so would compromise the more explicit aims of the text, for Dorinda's relation to Fluvanna is of a piece with her "faculty" for getting along with inferiors, and both are indispensable to her success and to the novel's feminist agenda. Glasgow uses the supposed shortcomings of her black characters in order to reinforce the virtues of her white heroine. At one point in the novel, for instance, Dorinda wonders if her need to closely supervise her employees is merely "woman's fussiness" or the "nervous mania that afflicted even the most successful farmer" (337). It is both; Glasgow uses the flaws supposedly natural to African Americans to combat ones supposedly natural to white women, asserting that such "fussiness" is a gender-neutral, but race-inscribed, mark of success. In other words, the claims the novel makes about racial equality or about African Americans themselves really serve to illuminate the white southern self, and in particular the "racial structure" of Dorinda's "vein of iron," her "saving fibre of instinct" (152, 184). This "vein of iron"—and Glasgow uses the phrase repeatedly in her fiction—aligns Dorinda with perceived notions of Anglo-Saxonism; in *The Voice of the People*'s terms, it is "the inborn Anglo-Saxon love of 'the man [or woman] who dares'" (396). For Dorinda's triumph in making Old Farm new again requires "not only perseverance," a quality Fluvanna likewise has, "but audacity as well" (348). While almost every white heroine of Glasgow's creation is endowed with such a "vein of iron"—a phrase encompassing qualities of strength, endurance, daring, and good judgment—nowhere in Glasgow's canon is there an African American character endowed with such qualities.

In manifesting her "vein of iron," Dorinda redeems the failed hopes of her family generally and her mother, Eudora Oakley, in particular. Eudora's wish to become an African missionary, which ended when the man to whom she was engaged died, haunts her for the rest of her life, driving her into periods of suicidal mania precipitated by a recurring dream of "coral strands and palm trees and ancient rivers and naked black babies thrown to crocodiles" (124). Popular in the late nineteenth and early twentieth centuries, this iconography of Africans and crocodiles found its way into cultural texts as diverse as Eugene O'Neill's *The Emperor Jones* and advertisements for Little Africa cigars. The touristic sacrifice of babies, like beautiful beaches and exotic trees, represents the sense of importance Eudora would have achieved had she been able to save Africans from the seemingly unending ritual of their sacrifice. As both a voyeur and a savior—eye and I—she would have been endowed with a kind of authority she doesn't have as a Virginian wife, especially one who has married a man lower in class status than she is. Giving in to "sordid actuality," Eudora loses interest in the "heathen" altogether: "bright coloured girls, even when they helped in the hen-house, left her indifferent" (284, 342). Although Eudora doesn't live long enough to see her daughter's triumph, the narrator tells us that the memory of her banished imperialist hopes is vindicated by Dorinda's success, that "in a changed form her mother's frustrated passion to redeem the world" finds "concrete expression" in the Virginian rather than the African landscape (346).

Dorinda vindicates Virginia's legacy in other ways as well, for in addition to rescuing Old Farm, she also rescues Five Oaks, the ancestral estate of the fiancé who jilts her at the beginning of the novel. To Dorinda, Five Oaks represents male prerogative at its worst; to the novel, it also represents a family black and white in the worst sense. The place where Jason's father produces children with his mulatto servant, Five Oaks is a metonym for miscegenation. While Glasgow vilifies Dr. Greylock for his sexual abandon (just as she does *Virginia*'s Cryrus Treadwell), she also uses the servant Idabella and her "anonymous brood of mulatto offspring" as metaphors for his flaws, for what, as we have seen, she labels in *Virginia* "the problem of the South" (7). Furthermore, while Dr. Greylock's terrible authority is symbolized by the mixed-race "swarm" he produces, that same brood also explains his deteriorating drinking habit, and by extension, the same habit in his son. Dr. Greylock spends a good portion of his day "wander[ing] about with a horsewhip, looking . . . for something to flog," but he also claims to be "afraid of being left with the negroes" (111, 92). This contradiction—he fears the same children whom he beats—represents one instance of Glasgow's deft handling of racism, in which unfounded fear is used to justify violence against the other. But the novel contradicts its own indictment of racism on a white man's part by justifying it on Dorinda's, for she sees how "several mulatto babies crawling like small, sly animals, over the logs at the woodpile" is sufficient reason for Jason to hate Five Oaks (134). At first, Dorinda's plan for restoring the Greylock plantation involves replacing Idabella and her "anonymous brood" with herself and her racially pure children: "Yes, things would be different when she and Jason lived here together and little children played under the great oaks in the grove" (145). Just as she adjusts herself to the economic imperatives of the end of "free labour," Dorinda amends her desire to possess Five Oaks as a mistress to possessing it as a master, proving that "[i]n the matter of sex, [Jason] had won; [but] matched merely as human beings, as man to man, . . . she was the stronger" (401). The prominence Dorinda achieves over white men like Jason hinges upon both her harnessing of the skills passed down to her by the ancestors who peopled the region's past and upon her ability to meet the racial-economic conditions of the new century.

In looking to aspects of the southern past in order to scrutinize the perceived turmoil of the nation's present, Cather and Glasgow use African Americans to build both their female characters and their own sense of themselves as writers. Their works register the ways a family that is structured around patriarchy—and nowhere was this more the case than in the South—denies white women's autonomy and authority, and they provide an alternative to this structure in their assessments of the roles served by slave mistresses and their more independent daughters, both of whom augment their place in part by keeping African Americans in their place. But the ostensibly feminist agenda of their works of the South become caught in the same dilemma Baldwin attributes to southern white men, for all "masters," male or female, kind or cruel, are indebted to those over whom they rule for their own sense of purpose.

4

A House Divided

The Interracial Family and the White Supremacist Community

I. SERVANTS AND STRANGERS

In *The Voice of the People,* as in many of her novels, Glasgow tempers her satire of southern society in the "age of evasive idealism" by linking Virginia's plantation elite to America's founding. However much they are the object of the narrator's ridicule, then, the aristocracy of the novel's setting, Kingsborough, can still take pride in the fact that "long ago theirs had been the first part in Virginia" (14). While Glasgow thus highlights the role her state played in shaping democracy in the past, many outside observers stressed the threat the whole region posed to democracy in the twentieth century. One of the most prominent commentators on modern democracy, Eleanor Roosevelt, did much to popularize this latter view. Like many Americans of her day, Roosevelt drew upon regional distinctions to characterize citizenship and its relation to race, chiding the anti-Semitism of many northerners, for instance, but nonetheless insisting that white southerners' discrimination against African Americans was far more damaging to the nation. At times, Roosevelt tempered her annoyance with the South for the sake of political expediency. Nevertheless, she was an early supporter of groups such as CORE (the Congress of Racial Equality), and had alliances with leaders in the African American community, like the NAACP's Walter White, that would prove to be critical to the downfall of segregation. And with friends like White she was more direct in her disdain of segregation than she was in public statements. In a letter to White written during World War II, for instance, she characterized the pro-segregationist stance of Oveta Culp Hobby, first director of the Women's Auxiliary Army Corp, as "completely . . . Texan," and a decade earlier she leaked to White state gossip concerning the "ridiculous" plans of Herman Talmadge to appeal to what she termed "'Georgia Rednecks'" by running "one of the dirtiest anti-Negro campaigns . . . in the South."[1] An ardent promoter of democracy and of the Democratic Party, Roosevelt was also a political realist who minced no words about the extent to which she thought the Solid South endangered the party's more progressive agendas.[2] "In a very real sense," Roosevelt wrote in her late work *Tomorrow Is Now,* "the United States is the world's show window of the democratic processes in action. We know, too well, what people see when they look in that window. They see Little Rock and Baton Rouge and New Orleans. They see Albany, Georgia. They see the deep-rooted prejudice, the stubborn ignorance of large groups of our citizens, which have led to injustice, inequality, and, sometimes, even brutality."[3] Although she often hedged on the issue of so-called social equality, on other occasions she was far more explicit than most white Americans, north or south, about the true nature of U.S. race relations: "A great many people believe that there should be no intermingling of races," Roosevelt wrote during the war, "Hitler has proved with bloody massacres that he holds this belief" (139–40). "Nevertheless," she continued, "it has been proved over and over again that this is one of the questions which people settle for themselves, and no amount of legislation will keep them from doing so. We would not have so many different shades of color in this country today if this were not so."

Roosevelt's responses to the South—often ambivalent, sometimes downright hostile—exemplify the ways assumptions about region have shaped assumptions about democracy. While the First Lady and later UN representative thought that the presence of legal segregation made the South the least democratic region in the nation, many southerners, defining democracy as applicable only to whites, posited that the opposite was true: it all depended upon the racial makeup of one's notion of a citizen. For her part, Roosevelt consistently maintained that democracy guaranteed equal rights regardless of race. In her *Moral Basis of Democracy* (1940), an attack on the definition of citizenship that many southerners (and others) held, Roosevelt claimed that democracy is "not a method devised to keep some particular group that is stronger than other groups in power," but rather "a method of government conceived for the development of human beings as a whole" (50). Contradicting those who argued that democracy was the by-product of white or Anglo-Saxon status, Roosevelt nonetheless understood the historical significance race played in shaping citizenship. In an essay originally published in *New Republic,* she argued, as James Baldwin would, that African Americans held a unique role in determining the future of democracy: "Perhaps because the Negroes are our largest minority, our attitude towards them will have to be faced first of all. . . . We cannot force people to accept friends for whom they have no liking, but living in a democracy it is entirely reasonable to demand that every citizen of that democracy enjoy the fundamental rights of a citizen" (135–36).

Not surprisingly, Roosevelt drew criticism for a variety of reasons during almost four decades in the national spotlight, but according to historian Allida Black, nothing so provoked her considerable number of detractors, from average citizens to powerful men such as FBI director J. Edgar Hoover, as did her efforts on behalf of civil rights.[4] Precisely because she was a white woman, Roosevelt's very public relationships with figures like White prompted many to question her own racial identity, in spite (or perhaps because) of her membership in an elite family: "I don't mean to be rude," one woman wrote to her in the early 1940s, "but do you have colored blood in your family, as you seem to derive so much pleasure from associating with colored folks?"[5] And nowhere in America did Roosevelt arouse as much censure and her racial status generate as much scrutiny as in the South. The *Alabama Sun,* for instance, devoted the entire April 1944 issue to Roosevelt's work for civil rights, an issue that included a front-page headline reading "Eleanor demands Equality for Negroes in Address," a photo caption featuring "Eleanor and Some . . . Niggers," and a byline claiming that the First Lady "Seems to Enjoy Talking to Negroes And Making Them Think They Are As Good Or Better Than White Women And Men."[6] Even some self-proclaimed liberal southerners, Allida Black contends, thought Roosevelt's associations with African Americans and her stance on the race question went too far.[7] Tenacious rumors of so-called "Eleanor Clubs," groups of African American domestic workers plotting the demise of segregation, proliferated throughout the 1930s and '40s South, despite the fact that no evidence of the clubs' existence could ever be mustered.[8] Whether in regard to the First Lady's influence on African American southerners or to her own racial heritage, such gossip reflected some of the most significant anxieties of the Jim Crow era. Members of "Eleanor Clubs," had such clubs actually existed, would have been using their places as servants in white homes—their places, that is, in the family black and white—to destroy segregation of the region's public institutions.

Such a threat also marks Cather's portrayal in *Sapphira* of the reappearance of Nancy Till in the novel's epilogue, which, as we have seen, depicts an important moment in Cather's development as a writer. The epilogue is set just after the first Reconstruction, and the novel was composed during Roosevelt's tenure as First Lady and during a time when segregation was beginning to garner the wide-ranging criticism that would culminate in the civil rights movement, also known as the Second Reconstruction. As we saw in the last chapter, Nancy's function as a slave is to define whites, and she herself has no definition other than what those white characters provide her. She is the object of Sapphira's jealousy and the proof of her power as well as its limitations. She is an outlet for Rachel's abolitionist zeal and the means by which the daughter challenges the authority of her mother. She is the object of Martin's (and Henry's) lust and a symbol of Henry's Christian worldview. As a character without a strong and discernable character, Nancy is a "blank space," as Naomi Morgenstern writes, but insofar as she embodies the power dynamics between white characters, she functions as a matrix of contradictory meanings, a "textual knot."[9] But when she returns to postwar Virginia, Nancy threatens to alter this, for she returns a freedwoman and a stranger from another place, more solidified, but far less readable, than she was when she was a native enslaved. As a young slave, Nancy's opacity is also rooted in her typicality, what the novel refers to as her "dreamy nigger side," but her ambiguity at the end of the text cannot be so easily attributed to her ostensible inferiority (178). This redefinition of Nancy's character complicates the otherwise nostalgic tone with which Cather imagines her own past. While the young Cather figure eagerly awaits Nancy's return to the family, she is disappointed when Nancy arrives because she is not the "*yaller gal*" of the nursery rhyme that her would-be rapist sings, but a refined woman whose appearance and demeanor—rather than her rape—blur racial boundaries. Also surprising to the girl are Nancy's fur-lined coat, silk dress, and gold watch chain, marks of her ascension from a slave to an aspiring member of the middle class. Poised and comfortable in such attire, Nancy is a far cry from her slave women ancestors, one of whom lit herself on fire trying to dress up for a servants' party (70).

Of all the signs of Nancy's transformation, though, none so bother the Cather figure as her manner of speaking. "Her words seemed to me too precise," the narrator tells us, "rather cutting in their unfailing distinctness. Whereas Mrs. Blake used to ask me if she should read to me from my 'hist'ry book' . . . Nancy spoke of the his-to-ry of Canada. I didn't like that pronunciation. Even my father said 'hist'ry.' Wasn't that the right and easy way to say it? Nancy put into many words syllables I had never heard sounded in them before. That repelled me" (284). While the Nancy of the novel proper testifies to the "hist'ry" of slavery and its justification in the black and white family, the Nancy of the epilogue suggests that in post-emancipation "his-to-ry," race relations have become strained because the power dynamics between groups are no longer fixed. No longer speaking like a southerner, Nancy has become a stranger (a fact that Cather's work emphasizes by having her end up a Canadian, not an American, citizen), and therefore she must be domesticated anew, reinitiated into the interracial family from which she had escaped. Her reunion with her white and black family and her belated recognition of her subjugated place there, made manifest by the "shade of deference" (284) with which she addresses the narrator's mother, for instance, precipitate a return of the Cather figure's fondness in remembering a childhood associated with "a regional longing for racial harmony."[10] Just as the issues evoked by slavery and the sexual exploitation of black women are assuaged rather than confronted by Nancy's removal from Back Creek, as I argued earlier, the issues evoked by African American freedom are subsumed, in the postwar era of the epilogue, by a white-woman-centered image of (segregated) domestic harmony that serves as an initiation rite for the Cather figure. As Lisa Marcus points out, "white femininity gets consolidated through the service of blackness," and racial injustice morphs into cause for feminist celebration.[11]

Yet the Cather figure's reminiscence of her own coming of age fails to resolve entirely the anxieties generated by Nancy's freedom and by African Americans' assumption of citizenship, for even as Nancy herself once again resumes the roles of servant and family member, if only temporarily, she is being told the tales of other former slaves like "Poor Tap," who "hadn't been able to stand his freedom" (290). As we have seen, Tap is unable to make the transition from slave to citizen and turns to violence. But the "real harm" his murder of another black man represents, as his former masters and mistresses understand it, is in the system that tempts him away from their "protection." Emancipation frees the guilty consciences of whites like Henry, then, more than it frees the bodies or the minds of African Americans like Tap. Like the rumors of Eleanor Clubs, the ambivalence created by Nancy's and Tap's divergent fates reflects a dichotomy at the heart of the Jim Crow era: emancipation had turned servants into citizens and made black "family" members also seem like strangers. Running counter to the hierarchal harmony of the interracial family reunion that Nancy's return implies, images of African Americans like Tap as inadequate citizens express the anxieties generated by the presence of African Americans—independent of whites—in public spaces, such as the tavern where Tap commits his crime. Segregation was designed to address those anxieties by circumscribing African Americans' claims to public spaces. Thus the integrated white home, on the one hand, and the segregated public realm, on the other, often worked together to bolster white supremacy. Yet this Janus-like approach to the suppression of African Americans in all areas of life was not without consequences for the whites who in so many ways benefited from it. Continuing relationships with African Americans in private while occupying explicitly whites-only spaces in public, white southerners often exhibited a schizoid view of African Americans as both servants and strangers that affected their views of themselves and other whites. These confused images of themselves create competing loyalties and codes of behavior that fueled many literary portrayals of the South before the civil rights movement.

II. WHITE SUPREMACY AND THE MAKING OF SOUTHERN REGIONALISM

To many southerners, the contradictions between private integration and public segregation were preferable to the social conditions of the North, with its different approach to race and the public/private divide. According to these southern critics of northern life, white northerners were integrationists so far as the public realm went (democracy having proliferated far beyond the boundaries of whiteness there). But in part because it was less common to count nonwhite servants as "family," northerners supposedly lacked the knowledge of their own minority groups that many white southerners thought they possessed of African Americans. Tennessee-born intellectual Joshua Caldwell, for instance, in suggesting that mob violence was the exception to otherwise friendly race relations in the South, insisted to an audience of northerners in 1902: "I tell you that not only do we get along fairly well with our colored citizens, but we are the only people that can get along with them."[12] Elsewhere, Caldwell favorably compared his region's "colored citizens" to the "Italian beggars and Hungarian serfs" he believed were plaguing cities above the Mason-Dixon Line (20). But Caldwell also asserted that what defined the South's greatness had little to do with African Americans, but rather with the white community itself. "For the Anglo-Saxon of the South," he wrote, "no life but one of freedom is possible and I can never believe that the hybrid population . . . which fills so many Northern cities and states, has the same love for our country, the same love of liberty, as have the Anglo-Saxon Southerners, whose fathers have always been free."[13] This linkage between racial purity and citizenship, the South's version of *herrenvolk* democracy, preserved a sense of southerners' civic distinctiveness by limiting African Americans' political rights, justifying such limitations in the interests of maintaining a homogeneous community. In dividing the interracial harmony they imagined to exist in their homes from the segregation that marked the public realm, white southern leaders established a culture that, as Caldwell pointed out, they thought to be at once the most regionalized and the most typically American. And in forcibly denying blacks the roles of citizens, they also created a new vision of southern society located not in the plantation, but in a more public arena in which all whites, regardless of class status, were welcome and from which all African Americans, regardless of their membership in a white family, were excluded. As Nell Painter writes, segregation assured that "all whites could share in the maintenance of all sorts of power, including the economic and political," even though these conditions "disproportionately benefited the better-off."[14]

Reflecting on these complex conditions, Glasgow's fiction examines the coexistence of two distinct regional communities, one private, interracial, and steeped in traditional class boundaries, and the other public, white supremacist, and more democratic insofar as class status goes. *The Voice of the People* is typical in this respect, and it shares with other works of its time, especially Charles Chesnutt's *The Marrow of Tradition,* published just one year later (in 1901), an interest in scrutinizing two competing definitions of southern regionalism: one that explores the local-color-like residuals of the family black and white, and one that investigates the tense relations between groups of natives on different sides of the color line that, on the basis of race alone, were increasingly being made strangers to each other. In neither text is the transition from one model of regional culture to another imagined to be swift, easy, or complete. But Chesnutt's and Glasgow's works differ in the ways they call for the South to respond to the crises that ensue from such alterations in southern society. In Glasgow's novel the break with the region's past is represented by a change of setting, from the colonial town of Kingsborough, where the former aristocracy and the family black and white hold sway, to Richmond, a more racially segregated space that facilitates class mobility among whites. As both a testament to the patriotism of Virginia's founding fathers and a nostalgic memorial to the Old South, Kingsborough reads like a town out of the local-color text of earlier decades, a place that "dozed through the present to dream of the past and found the future a nightmare" (13). Maintaining the boundaries that Glasgow associates with the era of "evasive idealism," the town is built around three institutions—an elite boys school, the royal governor's palace, and an insane asylum—that suggest lasting divisions among its white population. Life in Richmond, by contrast, is set to "the undignified music of the march of progress" (13). *Voice of the People,* much like Wharton's *Age of Innocence* and Cather's *Sapphira,* both revisits the nineteenth century and scrutinizes the threat to that past that modernity poses.

Rather than using setting to explore retentions of the old order, as *The Voice of the People* does, *The Marrow of Tradition* employs character types similar to those in earlier works, especially Uncle Julius of "The Goophered

Grapevine," to revisit the local-color world. Dependent on a fallen plantation to make his living, Julius attempts to dissuade the narrator, a northern carpetbagger, from buying the land by telling him that it is cursed. It is also possible, of course, that Julius's attempt is not meant to be successful, that he is pretending to be an ineffectual, harmless trickster to confirm the narrator's preconceived notions of him, which makes the white man, not Julius himself, look foolish. Still, Julius's act of storytelling indicates a necessary reliance upon whites, for his tale is shaped by the power the white man can exercise over him. *Marrow of Tradition*'s Aunt Jane and Jerry, servants of Olivia and Major Carteret, use many of the same methods to maneuver within the racial terrain of the Jim Crow era as Julius does within that of Reconstruction. In all cases, these characters play the fools, making their living by flattering whites' vanities. But where Julius appears to do so knowingly and, further, succeeds in his attempt, at least in so far as he is able to stay on the plantation, Jerry and Aunt Jane fail. Like many African American characters in southern literature of the period (*Voice*'s Verbeny and *Sapphira*'s Till, to name a few examples already discussed), Aunt Jane functions as the keeper of whites' historical memory, and because she "knows all 'bout de fam'ly," she feels her rightful place is as mammy to the accident-prone Carteret heir, Dodie.[15] And just like Till and Verbeny, Aunt Jane has a sense of entitlement tempered by a staunch loyalty to her white family. Far more than Uncle Julius, in fact, Aunt Jane resembles a Glasgow character in her devotion to whites, for whereas Julius uses a kind of rhetorical conjure to outsmart the narrator and thereby circumvent a white supremacist system, as Fetterley and Pryse have argued, Aunt Jane uses conjure to "ward off evil from the little grandson of her dear mistress," an effort that can only serve to perpetuate the same racist system under which she now lives (475).[16] While Chesnutt's narrator concedes that Aunt Jane's position gives her a certain expertise in the "undercurrents in the lives of the old families," such knowledge does her little good (472). Julius, Till, and most of Glasgow's servant characters profit from their continued association with whites, but Jane's loyalty to Olivia is responsible for her violent death: as she makes her way to the Carteret home to help Olivia during the riot that Carteret himself incites, Jane is attacked by the mob, and "not all her reverence for her old mistress, nor all her deference to the whites, nor all their friendship for her" can save her from the mob's indiscriminate wrath (720). Carteret's servant Jerry resembles Uncle Julius perhaps more so than Jane does: like that of Chesnutt's earlier character, Jerry's loyalty to whites is primarily mercenary. There are, however, strong indications that Julius is just pretending to be obsequious and stupid (his references to stereotypes involving watermelon, for instance, are conspicuously over the top), but the third-person narrator of *Marrow* points out that Jerry really *is* obsequious and stupid. Further, Jerry dies in much the same manner Aunt Jane does, at the hands of members of the race upon which he depends for "protection."

Not all white masters fall short of reciprocating the loyalty of their servants, however. The close-knit relationship between *Voice*'s Judge Battle and Cæsar that I discussed in the last chapter bears a strong resemblance to the relationship between old Mr. Delamere, an "ideal gentleman of an ideal past," and his faithful servant, Sandy (648). In both texts, master and servant are portrayed at times like parent and child (the white men take pride in having "raised" their black servants), and at other times like husband and wife (the servants spoil and fret over their masters much like a woman might). Even more than Judge Bassett does, Mr. Delamere views Sandy almost as an equal, a "gentleman in ebony," as he puts it, and Chesnutt's novel itself portrays these two men not as if one is merely a cheap imitation of the other, but as if they are two sides of the same coin (487): "Sandy, no less than his master, was a survival of an interesting type. He had inherited the feudal deference for his superiors in position, joined to a certain self-respect which saved him from sycophancy. His manners had been formed upon those of old Mr. Delamere, and were not a bad imitation; for in the man, as in the master, they were the harmonious reflection of a mental state" (576–77). Because he considers himself to be a sort of parent to the African American man, Mr. Delamere takes any condemnation of Sandy's character as a denunciation of his own, insisting, when his servant is arrested for the robbery and murder of Miss Polly, that Sandy cannot be guilty because he "has the family honor of the Delamere quite as much at heart" as he himself does (635). Mr. Delamere's loyalty to Sandy never wavers, and the novel makes plain that it need not, for Sandy does uphold the "family honor," so much so that he refuses to reveal that the real murderer is Tom Delamere, Mr. Delamere's debauched grandson, who gets away with his crime by disguising himself as Sandy. In fact, Chesnutt names the chapter in which Mr. Delamere visits Sandy in jail "Two Southern Gentlemen," as if to emphasize the parity of the two men and their old-fashioned values. Just as Mr. Delamere resists the characterization of African Americans that the more ardently racist Carteret makes throughout the novel, so does Sandy resist the characterization of himself by Tom as a "darky." As Sandy puts it, "dere's w'ite folks an' black folks,—but dere's manners, suh, . . . an' gent'emen oughter be de ones ter use 'em" (605).

Mr. Delamere, it is clear, agrees with Sandy, for according to the code by which they both live, African American family members should be differentiated from African American strangers. Horrified that his white counterparts could believe Sandy guilty of Miss Polly's murder, Mr. Delamere is equally stunned that his word as a gentleman testifying to Sandy's innocence is not taken at face value. In fact, the master's paternalistic loyalty to Sandy, a remnant of the Old South that is out of step with the Jim Crow era, places him at odds with much of the white community of Wellington (just as Sandy's reciprocal loyalty to him stands in opposition to his own interests). Chesnutt's narrator highlights this conflict by having Mr. Delamere remain so woefully ignorant of it for much of the novel. Both Delamere and Sandy consider the servant to be part of the master's family, and as much as the novel leaves unquestioned the sincerity of their beliefs, Chesnutt illustrates how inappropriate they are in the new era, when familiarity can just as easily breed contempt. Tom's ability to masquerade as Sandy, a testament to the familiarity engendered by continued family ties between black and white, is an ironic and destructive inversion of African American servants' abilities to imitate their masters. In the New South, the fidelities Mr. Delamere and Sandy uphold—Delamere's in his efforts to prevent Sandy's lynching and prove him innocent and Sandy's in refusing to give Tom away for fear of injuring Mr. Delamere—harm both master and servant because it is Carteret and McBane who now define race relations. Mr. Delamere's frequent comparisons of his faith in Sandy to his faith in Tom further suggest that the conflicts between himself and whites like Carteret and between past and present are irreconcilable: segregation necessitates that one choose between black and white family members. We see this sense of old giving way to new most forcefully in a chapter called "The Honor of a Family," in which Mr. Delamere visits Carteret to solicit his help in saving Sandy from prosecution. The two white men cannot agree on the proper course of action in the aftermath of Miss Polly's murder because they operate under contradictory constructions of family honor: for Delamere, the claims of family loyalty beckon back to the Old South's interracial notion of family and therefore shield Sandy as a Delamere, whereas for Carteret, "the old ties have been ruptured" and "family honor" now invokes the banner of white supremacy, which condemns Sandy regardless of his guilt or innocence (502).

So while the relationship between Sandy and Mr. Delamere closely resembles that of Cæsar and Bassett, they have different consequences: in *Marrow* the old southern values harm those who adhere to them; in *Voice* they continue to stunt the growth of the third "race" that, according to Glasgow's work, populated the Old South: poor whites. While former slave owners feel some disdain for poor whites, especially when, as in the case of the novel's rags-to-riches protagonist, Nicholas Burr, they elevate themselves beyond their station, the novel's African Americans are far more class-conscious than the elite. Further, the antagonism between former slaves and the white working class is far more trenchant. Glasgow attributes this antagonism to the plantation system's family black and white, wherein African Americans borrowed the prestige of their owners and poor whites were kept poor because they could not afford "free" labor. This class consciousness on the part of the formerly enslaved continues long after the war, even as divisions between whites are beginning to break down: Uncle Ish, much like his former master, General Battle, views Nick Burr merely as a "little no 'count white trash dat ain' never own er nigger un dere life" (28). Ish's frequent complaints about the lack of class boundaries between whites, coupled with his total lack of understanding of his own place in southern society (about which I will have more to say below), suggest that somehow emancipation freed whites like Nick at least as much as, and perhaps more than, it freed slaves (28). Ish's and other black servant characters' condescension toward working-class whites is used here, as it was used in the larger cultural discourse, to soften the elite's class prejudice and to justify their own continued authority, another benefit for former slave owners of maintaining family ties to African Americans. Indeed, according to the narrator, the "shrewd, childish race" understands that distinguishing between whites flatters the vanity of the upper class and that it concentrates their charity (and the charity of its aspiring members, like Nick) upon themselves (176). Members of the "poor white trash" have similarly low opinions of African Americans: Nick's stepmother, Marthy, for instance, prefers to tend to chores herself, refusing to establish the kind of integrated household that marks the aristocracy even when Nick can afford to provide her with a servant (319).[17]

Marthy Burr's disdain for African Americans is meant to be characteristic of working-class whites who stay in their places, while those who move above it, as Nick does, adopt the same charitable, paternalistic attitude toward servants that genteel whites display. As a working-class trailblazer, a figure common in Glasgow's works, Nick is meant to be a bit representative and, as Mark Graves points out, a bit exceptional.[18] Inheriting his father's capacity for hard work, Nick nonetheless is free of the elder man's penchant for failure. More importantly, our hero is free from the attitudes about citizenship displayed by Amos Burr, who understands his "rights" as being akin to getting handouts and who feels that the government's neglect of farmers justifies his own lack of initiative. Although the narrator attributes qualities to Nick reminiscent of those that Michael Akershem possesses (both are naturally intelligent and physically powerful), *Voice* never threatens to subject Nick to the naturalist fall that Michael experiences in *The Descendant*, for

Glasgow's aim in her third novel, unlike that of her first one, is to document triumphant and righteous social transformation. Furthermore, for the most part *The Voice of the People* positively portrays the new southern society that emerges once antebellum class divisions no longer separate whites. Through Nick's journey from a "barefooted boy" on an unproductive farm in Kingsborough to a "triumphant politician" occupying the governor's mansion in Richmond, the novel offers a reinvigorated version of white community, infused with the blood of poor whites, for the New South (313).

What is most interesting in *Voice*'s exploration of the rise of the plain man, though, is that Nick combines the best of what Kingsborough and Richmond have to offer: possessing "an old-fashioned democracy about him—a pioneer simplicity—as one who had walked from the great days of Virginia into her lesser ones," he combines the best of the Old and the New South (217). Once Nick and Eugenia Battle break their youthful engagement because the class barrier between them is, for her, yet too formidable, Nick replaces his love for her—a personal one—with the more public love for Virginia's democracy. Even as a struggling young lawyer in Kingsborough, Nick is acknowledged to be "the brainiest man these parts have seen since before the war," and because "the people want their own men," his path to the governor's mansion seems clear (266). Like David Blackburn of *The Builders* (1919) and Gideon Vetch of *One Man in His Time* (1922), also politicians, Nick cares more about a democracy of the people (at least the white ones) than he does about a Solid South for the Democrats. And because "the great, free people, the beginning and the end of all democracies," repeatedly "rall[y] to his standard," Nick repeatedly succeeds over the genteel politician Eugenia does marry, Dudley Webb (262).[19] As the ambivalence of the language here hints, Nick's association with an "old-fashioned democracy" sometimes places him at odds with the democracy of "the people" because that amorphous mass is so easily swayed; as Tom Bassett puts it, he is "a statesman that came a century too late" (308). The divide between past and present manifestations of democracy is particularly curious here, insofar as it is only the present moment and the rise of "the people" that allow Nick to transcend his humble origins at all. Nick is not the only political figure in the novel to come from the working class; his powerful and unscrupulous enemy, Rann, also hails from a less than genteel background, and as Eugenia observes, those who want to succeed in politics cannot afford to be "exclusive" in the New South (375).

This last point may well explain how Nick can effectively embody the class-stratified democracy associated with the past and yet be representative of the modern people. Eugenia's brother, Bernard, and, to a lesser extent,

Dudley Webb are the decadent products of the "age of evasive idealism"—that pastoral moment between the building of Virginia's antebellum democracy by genteel white men and the chaotic extension of rights to others associated with emancipation and the rise of "the people." It is a moment that the type Nick represents—non–slave owners—had little part in, and because of that fact, he symbolizes something Glasgow characterizes as more timeless and fundamental, as the following description of the Virginia Democratic Convention suggests: "A composite photograph of the faces would have resulted in a type at once . . . alarming to the student of individual endeavor, [and] reassuring to the historian of impersonal issues. It would have presented a countenance that was unerringly Anglo-Saxon, though modified by the conditions of centuries of changes. One would have recognised instinctually the tiller of the soil—the single class which has refused concessions to the making of a racial cast of feature" (299). Having sprung from tillers of the soil and risen to a station beyond theirs, Nick exemplifies the racial purity that Joshua Caldwell and others thought to be the hope of the New South. With "the inborn Anglo-Saxon love of 'the man who dares,' a regard for daring for its own heroic sake," Nick provides Virginia with a sort of missing link back to its Revolutionary past, bypassing the interracial family connections with which the elite justified slavery (396). By contrast, men like Webb, nurtured on those very connections, express "the softening influences of society," an "additional shadow" that obscures "the steadfast qualities of the race." Nick's rise to prominence begins to mend the gap between a racially pure but degraded working class and a genteel but decadent former aristocracy. As Walter Benn Michaels writes, *The Voice of the People* documents a "process through which white people cease thinking of themselves as belonging first of all to a family," which is both genteel and interracial, "and begin thinking of themselves as having first of all a color."[20] Indeed, part of the reason why Nick and his class have remained so pure is that they have steered clear of connections to and dependence on African Americans.

The Marrow of Tradition also attributes the rise of the plain man to the end of slavery: "No longer overshadowed by a slaveholding caste, some of this class had rapidly pushed themselves forward. Some had made honorable records. Others, foremost in negro-baiting and election frauds, had done the dirty work of politics, as their fathers had done the dirty work of slavery" (494). One interesting similarity between Glasgow's and Chesnutt's novels is the association of the rags-to-riches plain man with southern politics, even though, in reality, class mobility was more a result of new economic opportunities than political ones. This focus on politics, though, allows both novels to directly intervene in debates about race and citizenship in the Jim Crow era. *Voice* accentuates Nick's heroic qualities over the ruthlessness of other plain men like Rann. *Marrow,* on the other hand, highlights both the mostly honorable example of class transcendence that Lee Ellis embodies and the altogether negative example of upward mobility that the politically ambitious McBane represents. More astute and less swayed by racism than most of the white characters, Ellis is one of the first people in the novel to see that Sandy is innocent of Miss Polly's murder, and unlike Mr. Delamere's defense of a family servant, Ellis's efforts on Sandy's behalf are motivated by impersonal concerns. But even when he helps Miller to reach home during the riot, using his own whiteness to shield Miller's blackness, Ellis feels pressure to remain loyal to his race, for he cannot "approve the acts of his own people; neither could he, to a negro, condemn them" (715). His openmindedness as well as his reluctance to outwardly criticize other whites seem to be grounded equally in his lack of familiarity with African Americans, his place, coming from a non-slave-owning family, outside the structure of the family black and white: "Ellis had never pretended to that intimate knowledge of negro thought and character by which some of his acquaintances claimed the ability to fathom every motive of a negro's conduct" (567–68).[21] The riot poses an epistemological struggle to Ellis that threatens to overturn his notions of whiteness and blackness: "He would not have believed that a white man could possess two so widely varying phases of character" as that which he sees displayed before and after the riot, but neither can he bring himself to accurately judge African Americans based on the same set of events, for despite all evidence to the contrary, he tries to maintain the fiction that "No one could tell at what moment the thin veneer of civilization might peel off [African Americans] and reveal the underlying savage" (568). While Nick's lack of family connections to African Americans preserves his "Anglo-Saxon love of 'the man who dares,'" the same lack in Ellis simply makes him more likable than other white men, particularly his romantic rival, Tom Delamere.[22]

Although the novel shows the flaws in Ellis's views, it also makes clear that these are relatively harmless compared to those of the other plain-man-made-good, McBane. The descendant of an overseer from whom he inherits his talent for "negro-baiting," McBane is hateful of African Americans and spiteful of the genteel whites he colludes with to suppress them. Belonging to the "offensive element among the white people of the New South," he possesses a capacity for violence against African Americans that is matched only by the ferocity of his social aspirations (513). The narrator tells us that in the social world of Wellington (much like those of Glasgow's, Cather's, and Wharton's works), elite status is granted to those who possess at least two of three criteria, "birth, wealth, and breeding," and that because McBane has wealth but lacks both birth and breeding, he occupies an unclear place in the town's hierarchy. On the one hand, together with the more genteel Carteret and Belmont, he is one of the "Big Three" who plot to overtake the local government and destroy African American citizenship. On the other hand, men like Tom Delamere find the idea of McBane's joining their ranks offensive, and his own coconspirator, Carteret, thinks that McBane is "an upstart, a product of the democratic idea operating upon the poor white man, the descendant of the indentured bondservant and the socially unfit" (539). Carteret seems to think that he can bend McBane's "wealth and energy" to his own purposes, which would ultimately lead not just to the suppression of African Americans' rights, but also to the curtailment of McBane's authority. Indeed, McBane's augmented place in southern society is but "a strong incentive to Carteret in his campaign against the negro," for it is "distasteful enough to rub elbows with an illiterate and vulgar white man of no ancestry,—the risk of similar contact with negroes was to be avoided at any cost." Interestingly, what provokes Carteret's annoyance is that McBane, barking commands at Jerry, has violated the customs of the family black and white, for "a gentleman did not order his own servants around offensively, to say nothing of another's."

All of the events in the novel that are most threatening to African Americans and to civic order in general, especially the riot, result in part from Carteret's misguided assumption that he can use McBane to exert authority over African Americans and still maintain authority over McBane himself, for "those who set in motion the forces of evil cannot always control them afterwards" (725). First, McBane attempts to gain entrance into the gentlemen's club by blackmailing Tom, thus he is indirectly responsible for Miss Polly's murder, Sandy's arrest and near lynching, and old Mr. Delamere's death. Lacking Carteret's and Belmont's hypocrisy, McBane never sugarcoats his violent motives, assuming leadership of the race riot even as Carteret grows sickened by the extent of the bloodshed. His association with what Belmont calls the "age of crowds" indicates that "the people" here, as in *Voice of the People,* are devoid of individuality, lacking the good judgment and impartiality that Delamere, Ellis, and Miller often display (534). As Watson argues, in the South the modern mob is fomented by the color line, and when that is drawn, "if [whites] choose to stand together with the rest of their race against us, or to remain passive and let the others work their will, we are helpless" (630). Although the race riot hinges upon the power of mob mentality, Watson's comment here suggests that Chesnutt's work still invests some faith in the power of an individual citizen's choice—and therefore their duty—in and to a democracy. Indeed, Chesnutt's point seems to be that whites, possessing more rights, have more responsibilities, ones that, because of their unjust racial privilege, every white character (with the possible exception of Mr. Delamere) fails to assume completely. In spite of his success as a lawyer, Watson understands that he and his fellow African Americans are not wanted in the public realm, that "the white people would be good to them so long as they behaved themselves and kept their place" in the domestic one (671).

Glasgow's novel also ends in racial violence when Nick returns to Kingsborough to visit the dying Judge Bassett only to be forced to face down a lynch mob. The crime supposed to have been committed by the unnamed African American who is the mob's intended victim is never explicitly stated, but is called "the usual thing," Glasgow assuming, apparently, that readers will understand that what he is referring to is the rape of a white woman.[23] In keeping with his air of "old-fashioned democracy," Nick single-handedly confronts the mob armed only with his pride that no lynching has taken place during his term as governor, and as a result of his loyalty to civic order, he dies at the hands of other plain men in an attempt to save a "damned brute," as an onlooker puts it (217, 442).[24] While a governor's intervention in an attempted lynching may strike readers as an odd, melodramatic plot twist, Glasgow had good reason to insert Nick in this scene. Virginia's relatively few lynchings (compared to other southern states) can be explained in part by a strong public consensus that vigilante justice compromised economic progress and that, as W. Fitzhugh Brundage writes, "governors had a personal responsibility to prevent lynching."[25] Nick's death is the final proof the novel gives that he is an ideal democratic leader. Curiously, though, Nick sympathizes with the motives of the "country people" who attack him, as does the narrator, who attributes an orderliness to the men's actions not associated with the other descriptions of mobs we have seen: they move as "quiet as a congregation at prayer" to deliver a "vengeance so . . . determined that it was as sure as the hand of God" (440, 439). According to Nick, in fact, the men who gather at the jail to capture and lynch the unknown black man are not a "mob" at all, but a racially pure "incarnate vengeance" (440). Because both the would-be lynchers (poor whites) and their victim (alleged black rapist) are uncivilized, Nicholas appears all the more so, but the novel makes a distinction between the poor white's savagery and that of the black rapist. If it is his nature ("the usual thing") to rape white women, it is theirs to punish him for it, to reestablish white male rule over black and white female bodies. Because most lynching victims were strangers to the areas in which they were murdered, lynch-mob violence likewise made it clear to African

Americans that they had no claim on communal, public spaces, that whites need respect, and that their roles in the private realm were confined to those of servants, not equals. As a customary means of dealing with racial and geographical strangers, lynching is disturbingly relevant to a discussion of southern regionalism (as Walter White remarked, African Americans often considered the South "the lynching region") and, therefore, to debates about the political underpinnings of white women's regionalism.[26] In Glasgow's novel the lynch mob functions as a vivid illustration of white unity and of communal principles, for even as he falls victim to the crowd, Nick sees faces in it that "were as familiar as his own" (440). While I am not arguing that Glasgow justifies this lynching—if that were the case, Nick's death would be empty—I am arguing that she locates it within a natural response that is particular to whiteness, just as rape is taken to be particular to blackness. Although the men who try to lynch the black man but instead end up killing their beloved governor are insufficiently civilized, they are so in ways that provide the raw material for Anglo-Saxon greatness, the raw material, in fact, for Nick.

In both Glasgow's and Chesnutt's novels, the mob represents one southern community forged by violent resistance to another, interracial one. Nick is first inspired to become a political leader when he hears Judge Bassett speak passionately of his love for Virginia's founding fathers and of his disdain for the interracial coalition party, the Readjusters, then in power, whom he faults for the state's current troubles (it's not dead but "sleepeth" [162]). Nick's rise from being the son of an obscure, "land-poor" farmer to governor, then, is part of Virginia's "redemption," one that requires the implementation of public segregation as well as the defeat of the Readjusters and of black citizenship itself.[27] In the end, Nick dies not to protect a "damned brute" but to preserve the ideals of Judge Bassett and his illustrious forefathers, the founders of Virginian democracy. Although the actions of the mob that attacks Nick seem to betray those ideals, they share the same white-supremacist motives as the Readjusters' critics, who argued that integrating political institutions would lead to amalgamation in private relationships. Likewise, in Chesnutt's novel the "Big Three" incite the Wellington riot by tapping into whites' hysteria about black rapists, but their true object is to overturn the results of a recent election in which a fusion ticket is victorious. In doing so, they hope to rid their state of black citizenship and relegate African Americans to their former status as domestic servants, for "Negro citizenship was a grotesque farce—Sambo and Dinah raised from the kitchen to the cabinet were a spectacle to make the gods laugh" (533). In both novels the fear that African Americans will use whatever civic rights they possess to overturn the hierarchy of the family black and white is used to justify taking those rights away. But it is made plain in *Marrow* in a way it is not in *Voice* that such fear is based not on blacks' sexual impulses but on whites' racist ones.

Furthermore, if Carteret thinks that black citizenship makes "the gods" laugh, it is the reader who is meant to laugh at black citizenship in Glasgow's novel. *Voice of the People*'s farcical depiction of African American independence manifests itself in Ish's failure to understand history, for instance, as his description of the Civil War indicates: "Dar wan't much sense in dat ar war, nohow, an' I ain' never knowed yit what 'twuz dey fit about. . . . but Ise heered Marse Tom 'low hit wuz a civil war, en dat's what it wuz. When de Yankees come a-ridin' up en a-reinin' in dere hosses befo' de front po'ch, en Miss Chris come out a-smilin' en a-axin' howdy, en den dey stan' dar a-bowing en a-scrapin', hit wuz des es civil es ef dey'd come a-co'tin'" (29). Ish's retelling of the region's past is, of course, meant to be ridiculous, and we may even say that he is being a trickster here, deliberately playing the fool as Chesnutt's Julius does. But his inability to distinguish between public events with broad implications (war) and private matters (courting) suggests that his understanding of his own emancipation is limited. So, too, is his understanding of the rights and responsibilities that citizenship places upon him, for on the one hand, he moves off Battle land, away from the family black and white, but on the other, he only does so when "Some idiots," General Battle tells his sister, convince him "that if he went on living on my land he'd go back to slavery" (60). Further, Ish's self-sufficiency turns out to be mere pretense, for he continues to expect his white family to feed him, even though, as Eugie tells Nick, "we have to bring him things secretly, and he pretends the Lord feeds him" (189). Ish seems to feel that his own status as a ward to whites is simply in the natural order of things, and he is far from the only example the novel gives of racially ascribed dependence. Claudius, another former Battle slave, returns to the plantation decades after being freed, assuming that his old master will support the large family he has accrued in the interval (58). African Americans' failure to function autonomously throws into question not only the wisdom of the Fifteenth Amendment but also whether the war was worth the destruction it caused in the first place.

That is not to say that African Americans do not exercise their rights as citizens, although they seldom do so in ways meant to inspire confidence in their civic acumen. Voting the "correct" way (for Nick) in imitation of Judge Bassett, Cæsar (the servant who remains closest to his master) is used as a contrast to Ish, who votes "just to spite" his former master (271–72). In Battle's diatribe against Ish's voting, we learn that resentment toward African Americans is hardly confined to himself: "I told the fool," he tells the Judge, "he didn't know any more about voting than the old mule Sairy did, and he said he didn't have to know 'nothin' cep'n his name.' He forgot that when they challenged him at the polls, but he voted all the same—voted in my face, sir" (272). As ridiculous as Battle's complaints are, so, too, are Ish's politics: at once conservative (he upholds outdated class divisions, voting for Webb instead of Nick simply because Nick wasn't born into the elite) and misguidedly revolutionary (he moves off Battle land only to continue to accept Battle charity), Ish is clearly meant to be read as unfit to assume the responsibilities of a citizen. Besides, both his and Cæsar's examples of black suffrage hinge on an essentially reactive politics: Cæsar votes out of loyalty to the Judge, and Ish against his master. Historian Peter Rachleff demonstrates that until they were prevented from voting in the 1890s, African Americans in Virginia were highly politically organized, with churches and kinship groups fostering a sense of political consensus and with community leaders chosen in part because of their independence from whites.[28] Yet as Glasgow's novel would have it, when they are not using the ballot to react personally to the white men who used to own them, African Americans use it to fool other African Americans, as Carter does. A janitor at the state capitol, Carter plans to attend a church gathering where he will pretend to speak about a tariff. As he tells Nick's friend Galt, he will cover up his insufficient understanding of the tariff by putting on airs, repeatedly waving his handkerchief and forestalling his "splainin' er de tariff" until his coconspirator tells him his time to speak is up (422). Drawn from minstrel-like humor, these instances of African Americans' political actions become the butt of many jokes in the novel, even as we know that those actions are being curtailed, which is also part of the joke. One white character, telling an ostensibly funny anecdote about how he and other politicos used to destroy ballots cast by black citizens, observes that honest elections are now the norm because "the negroes have stopped voting in large numbers" (400). If African Americans have stopped voting "in large numbers" in the novel, as they had in the real Virginia of the period, why does Glasgow spend so much time narrating humorous incidents of black suffrage or its repression? The humor allows the novel to have it both ways, for both black citizenship and whites' fear of it are meant to look foolish—until, that is, Nick's violent death reminds us that both have tragic consequences.

In Chesnutt's novel, unlike in Glasgow's, citizenship is antithetical to service to whites. Rather than integrating the races as "social-equality" alarmists like Carteret and his cronies claim it will (and the sincerity of this belief is made suspect in the novel), the breakup of the family black and white and the emergence of an independent black citizenry further divide the races in Chesnutt's work, as Dodie Carteret's nurse indicates when she compares herself to Jane: "These old-time negroes . . . made her sick with their slavering over the white folks. . . . For her own part, they gave her nothing but wages, . . . and she owed them nothing more than equivalent service. . . . There was no question of love between them" (501). While the narrator tells us that this young nurse has a "chip on the shoulder," the "old-time negroes" to whom she contrasts herself certainly make the novel's worst citizens, along with the whites whom they serve. Chesnutt emphasizes Jerry's civic incompetence, for example, in one of the scenes in which the servant eavesdrops on a conference of the Big Three: "Jerry could hear the words 'vote,' 'franchise,' 'eliminate,' 'constitution,' and other expressions which marked the general tenor of the talk, though he could not follow it all,—partly because he could not hear everything distinctively, and partly because of certain limitations which nature had placed in the way of Jerry's understanding anything difficult or abstruse" (496). So incomprehensible are the responsibilities of a citizen to Jerry that he offers to abstain from voting to please Carteret, forgoing his public duty for a private assurance from his master that he will not be fired (675). Although he is just as uneducated, Josh Green understands the responsibilities of democracy that confound Jerry, signifying hope for what the novel calls the "democratic ideal" in his refusal to be a "w'ite folks' nigger" (563). It is Josh, not the more educated and refined Miller, who first tries to rally the black community in Sandy's defense, and it is Josh, not Miller, who attempts to defend his community's public institutions (including Miller's hospital) from the white mob at the end of the novel. Quite the opposite of Josh's, Miller's response to Sandy's arrest places the blame on his own people: "Try as we may to build up the race in the essentials of good citizenship and win the good opinion of the best [white] people, some black scoundrel comes along, and by a single criminal act, . . . neutralizes the effect of a whole year's work" (629). As Miller himself acknowledges, even Josh's desire to kill McBane in retaliation for his father's death is rooted in a sort of protodemocratic impulse: "When his race had reached the point where they would resent a wrong, there was hope that they might soon attain the stage where they would try, and, if need be, die, to defend a right" (562). What Miller does not see is that Josh *does* die defending a right, giving his life in an attempt to protect the institutions that symbolize his people's emergence as citizens.

The problem with Miller's accommodationalist stance, as the narrator sees it, is that it confines his dealings with whites to personal or professional rather than political encounters, and therefore offers little immediate remedy to the status quo. He believes that racist whites can be influenced to acknowledge African American citizenship if only members of the "talented tenth" like himself continue to make professional and economic strides: "when a colored man should demonstrate to the community in which he lived that he possessed character and power, that community would find a way in which to enlist his services for the public good" (521). But he overestimates the extent to which African Americans are a part of the southern community and, in turn, underestimates how whites can be swayed, against reason and even against their own interests, by what the narrator terms "local customs" to betray the ideals of democracy (704). As Fetterley and Pryse argue, works like "The Goophered Grapevine" use the terms of regionalism to pit the local values of Uncle Julius against both those of the plantation tradition and those of the white nation.[29] Chesnutt does something quite different in *Marrow of Tradition,* for here the "local customs" of Wellington (including mob violence and the threat of lynching) are far more racist than those of the northern narrator of "Goophered" or the northerners in the novel itself. No longer strictly servants, African Americans can no longer be counted as members of the community, for segregation has established "a lack of spontaneous friendliness between the people of these two races, as though each felt that it had no part or lot in the other's life" (587).

In the case of both *Marrow* and *Voice,* images of the family black and white serve as questionable antidotes to the violence and chaos of a public realm occupied by two hostile communities. The end of *Voice* alternates between narrating the events that lead to Nick's death and a less tense, but by no means less ambiguous, reinstatement of interracial domestic hierarchy. In a chapter that appears shortly before the one in which Nick dies, we learn that Eugenia, rather than redefining class boundaries by marrying Nick, as she meant to do when she was younger, redefines them by refusing to hire a black mammy to raise her infant son. Worried that his own social position is in jeopardy by Eugie's refusal, Dudley hires Delphy, an old Battle slave, to care for the child, thereby reinstating the black and white family. Despite Delphy's probable incompetence (she objects to Eugenia's employing "real doctahs"), Eugenia caves to the pressures that Dudley, Delphy, and the past exert over her, for "the training of her slave-holding ancestors was strong upon her, and she regarded Delphy's liberty of speech as an inherent right of her position. The Battle servants had always spoken their minds to their mistresses in a manner which caused them to become hopeless failures when they entered into strange families, where the devotion of their lives could not be offered in extenuation of the freedom of their tongues" (410, 411). In taking her place among women of her class—and that place is, as the novel acknowledges, a circumscribed one—Eugie successfully puts Delphy in her place within the family.

The Marrow of Tradition offers another interpretation of the role that the family black and white can take in the New South. In her insistence that her master marry her, Janet Miller's mother, Julia, had attempted to redefine the black and white family, at least in secret. But like other relationships rooted in the past, Julia's effort to create a family born out of the ashes of slavery cannot withstand the pressures that ensue from an "imperfect blending of old with new, of race with race, of slavery with freedom" (501). Despite Julia's failure, family connections remain central in the novel, for as Eric Sundquist has argued, Chesnutt's interracial family serves as a "means of delineating the racial crisis of American history."[30] In the parallels Chesnutt draws between the Millers and the Carterets—Janet and Olivia are half sisters, and Miller's father purchased the old Carteret home after the war—readers are reminded that total segregation of the races was never possible, and that interracial family connections exist beneath the surface of segregation. The denial of those connections in the interests of a southern community based upon white supremacy end up hurting whites and blacks alike, for in *Marrow* Chesnutt insists, as Eleanor Roosevelt would decades later, that whites' "attitude towards [African Americans] will have to be faced first of all" (Roosevelt, *Moral Basis,* 135–36). Olivia's hatred for Janet and for the familial relationship between them, for example, is far more self-destructive than Janet's longing for recognition from Olivia is. In getting rid of the evidence of Julia's marriage and thus of Janet's claim to legitimacy, Olivia inadvertently threatens to destroy Dodie, a threat that she eventually must meet by throwing herself at "the feet of" the family she has scorned (742). Even the most viciously racist whites, like Carteret, end up needing their black family, for it is Miller alone who, at the end of the novel, can save the white male heir. Unlike in Glasgow's novel, which ends in Nick's death, the violence that closes Chesnutt's work suggests that segregation, if allowed to continue, would destroy the race it was designed to protect. It also suggests that the only hope—distant as it might be—for both the southern community and for democracy itself is in the personal, familial connections between the races that run afoul of so many of the region's "local customs."

III. SEEING THE FAMILY BLACK AND WHITE THROUGH THE "DARK THICKNESS OF RACE"

In *The Voice of the People* and other early novels, Glasgow sentimentalizes African Americans' place within the integrated white home, but she portrays their activities in the public realm as dangerous, ineffectual, and comical. By the twenties, however, as we saw in *Barren Ground,* she was creating black characters like Fluvanna Moody, who are more hardworking and self-sufficient than their cohorts in previous works, and more so than many white characters. And by the time she published her last few novels, in the late thirties and early forties, Glasgow displayed open dissatisfaction with segregation and the region's status quo, insisting that her fellow southerners heed the call made by Roosevelt and others to evaluate their own racial attitudes and their assumptions about what constitutes southern community. She was not alone in doing so. A growing trend toward liberalism (the nostalgia of *I'll Take My Stand* notwithstanding) among white southern intellectuals began to develop at the same time that nationwide economic hardship prompted many to question the extent to which democracy had been achieved. "Either the Negro must attain full citizenship status with all the rights and obligations thereby involved, even in the most remote sections of Mississippi," Walter White argued, "or the democratic process for all Americans will be made meaningless."[31] Claiming that northerners largely remained ignorant of this until the 1930s, White called the 1932 election—FDR's first—"the emergence of the Negro as a force which no political party could longer ignore or flout" (139). While it is true that many white southerners were becoming, according to White, "pathologically sensitive" to criticisms of segregation, it was also true, as he acknowledged, that such sensitivity was sparked by the increasing support other whites began to show for civil rights (102). White's assessment of the thirties as a watershed time for civil rights is in keeping with much of the recent historical work on the decade. In her study of groups such as the Association of Southern Women for the Prevention of Lynching (ASWPL, 1930) and the Writers' League Against Lynching (1933), Mary Jane Brown shows that many southerners were growing tired of the South's reputation as "the lynching region" (59).[32] Some white southerners, Brown contends, became frustrated not only with mob violence but also with Jim Crow itself, leaving segregated groups like Jessie Daniel Ames's ASWPL for interracial ones.[33] Simultaneously, the influence of some of the most successful proponents of scientific racism, such as Lothrop Stoddard and Madison Grant, began to wane, while the theories of cultural anthropologists like Franz Boas were becoming more popular.[34] "[T]he emergent race politics of the 1930s," writes Matthew Frye Jacobson, "dramatically heightened the salience of 'Caucasian' identity by imploring whites to dwell upon their whiteness and to work toward the eradication of its unjust privileges."[35]

In her second-to-last novel, *In This Our Life* (1941), Glasgow dwells upon whiteness in ways that she does not in previous works. Set in Queenborough, a fictionalized Richmond, *In This Our Life* sounds the death knell for the family black and white, portraying two families, the white Timberlakes and the black Clays, that are connected to each other biologically, economically, and emotionally, but by ties that bear the stress of decades of segregation. Family relations between the Timberlakes and the Clays are less comfortable than those between the Oakleys and the Moodys in *Barren Ground*, and the two sides lack the easy familiarity with each other that we see *Voice of the People*'s Eugenia and Delphy display. This distance seems to be a good thing for the Clays, at least at first. Despite the fact that young Parry Clay's ambitions to become a lawyer are fraught with stumbling blocks from the start, overall, the Clays appear more content than the Timberlakes do precisely because they have no part in the New South's white community, one forged not by the high ideals of democracy but by a blasé consumerism. The dissatisfaction, disease, and death that pervade the novel from beginning to end are imagined to be the result of the fact that the Timberlakes are the modern remnants of the old, all-but-defunct aristocracy. Asa Timberlake, unhappy with his marriage, cannot bring himself to break with the conventions that keep him with his wife, Lavinia. We are told that growing up, Asa faced the same kind of financial barriers to education that Nick does, but Asa, repeatedly described as "panting" like "a man who has run a hard race and lost," lacked Nick's energy and drive and thus was unable to improve his situation.[36] Lavinia, a hypochondriac who confines herself to her room, lacks the energy even *The Deliverance*'s Mrs. Blake, also an invalid, has. Even more energetic characters suggest racial collapse. Lavinia's uncle, William Fitzroy, has made a fortune overpowering others, but he is heading for a painful death by the end of the novel, while his wife, Charlotte, lives with an irrational fear of cancer. The younger generation are either satisfied with mediocrity (Andrew Timberlake) or, worse, suffer from impossibly contradictory values and desires: Roy Timberlake Kingsmill believes in personal freedom, but is desperate to keep her husband, Peter, with her; Craig Fleming is supposedly dedicated to social justice, but fails in his commitment because of his love for Stanley Timberlake; and Stanley, although engaged to Craig, seduces and runs away with Peter.

As the scandal Stanley causes suggests, what Asa characterizes as the "nonsense about freedom" associated with the younger generation implies "some obscure inner decay" and an attendant return to primitive, base impulses (69, 24). Although democracy's promotion of "modern iconoclasts . . . without culture" is partly responsible for such decay, the southern traditions of the "age of evasive idealism" are also linked here to the white characters' degeneration.[37] Beneath the old plantation traditions that he wears as a garment—and perhaps this is why he is so often described as shabbily dressed—Asa as much as the rest of his family possesses "a bottomless abyss of dark impulses," and the only thing that separates Asa's generation from that of his children is that the young feel justified in acting on these impulses (153). As Wharton's *Twilight Sleep* does, *In This Our Life* uses the family as a metaphor for the dissolution of the race, but unlike Wharton's novel, Glasgow's work suggests that it is not the breakup of the family but the family itself that is the problem. Despite the fact that "family feeling had stood in the way of everything he had ever wanted to do," Asa continually puts off leaving his wife, and his loyalty to conventions out of step with modernity is described as a sort of masochism, as if the family is "draining every drop of his blood" (16, 301). Family ties only serve the family member who feels the least responsible for others, Stanley. A kind of Scarlett O'Hara for the Jazz Age, Stanley is a cross between the rapacious vamp and the vapid southern belle. Roy, on the other hand, is giving and independent, possessing "all the qualities . . . that men have missed and wanted in women," or at least all that "men have *thought* they . . . wanted" (21). Similarly, the lovers they end up swapping (Roy and Craig pair up after Stanley and Peter run away) embody opposing masculinities: Craig is genteel, well-meaning, and ineffectual, and Peter is domineering and undisciplined. While the characters are seemingly unable to escape from the family bonds that hold them together, the novel itself highlights the Timberlakes' incompatibility, which, as it does in the case of *Twilight Sleep*'s Manford-Wyant clan, suggests a larger racial collapse.

Although in earlier novels, as we have seen, Glasgow faults modern democratization for such cultural disintegration, here she blames the southern pieties that transcend historical eras, especially those associated with an idealization of white womanhood. It is the vivacious, beautiful Stanley, with an outward appearance that belies her inner character, who represents the surest proof of racial decline in the novel, for as Asa puts it, there is no "hope of making a civilized world" as long as she is protected as a model of innocence and grace (366). While the other characters mistake her for a racial paradigm, shielding her from the ramifications of her own actions, the narrator makes plain that the whiteness she represents is not only diseased, but contagiously so. Glasgow's work suggests this from the start in the incestlike relationship Stanley has with her great-uncle William Fitzroy, which hints at a dangerous exaggeration of racial purity. So, too, does Stanley's relationship with her sister's husband, which ends in Peter's suicide. Having "no real existence apart from her effect upon other people," Stanley uses her status as a symbol of southern womanhood to escape punishment after she drunkenly runs down a little girl in the street, blaming the accident on Parry in an act of scapegoating meant to hint at the truth behind the myth that black men posed a danger to white southern women (243).

So while *The Voice of the People* depends upon the veracity of that myth to prove Nick's civic greatness and the existence of an all-white community, here Glasgow does something quite different, exposing how the white community is formed only through the terrorizing of African Americans. As the Timberlakes discuss the accident, all pretending to believe that Parry is guilty, their "divided personalities, which had seemed to rush apart and away, were united in a single unbroken front of opinion" (384). Facing the rest of them armed only with the truth, Asa judges that their weapons—white supremacy and an attendant access to African American "family"—may be stronger than his, forming an "intangible but wholly firm barrier" that he tries to penetrate (412). "Held together by a single wave of emotion," even the most well-meaning whites are tempted to conspire against Parry to protect Stanley (414). Charlotte, previously so wise about Parry's predicament and seemingly sincere in her desire to help him, completely falls back on racism, prevaricating that "colored people don't feel things the way we do" (415). Despite his stated commitment to helping Parry to become a lawyer and despite being one himself, Craig won't commit to defending Parry, confessing, when William forces his hand, "I suppose I am one of you" (417). And even Asa, who refuses to go along with the family's lies, has trouble transcending his assumptions about white women and his racial loyalties, dreaming that the little girl Stanley has killed is Stanley herself. In betraying his race, Asa must stumble down an unfamiliar path: "I do not know where I am going," he thinks at the moment he decides to stand up to his family, "I cannot see a step before me; but I must go on" (399). This disloyalty is the turning point for Asa, for as he confronts the power of whiteness that the rest of his family is content to wield to Parry's demise, he not only loses his "sense of inferiority" but he also finds himself: "They are all against me, . . . but I can see my way" (413, 418).

Still, Asa's choice, as he understands it, is not between defending Parry's rights or Stanley's wrongs, but between "a force he hated and yet could not resist" and the need to shelter an ideal he knows to be false (414). In his failure to empathize with Parry, Asa himself forgets what the novel takes pains to prove all along: Parry *is* family, the product of the Timberlakes and their slaves on his mother's side, and, on his father's, of the Fitzroys and their slaves. While much is made of the lightness of Parry's skin, the miscegenation that produced him remains unspeakable to both white family members (the one time it is discussed, by Charlotte, Lavinia gets angry and Asa changes the subject) and African American ones, as his mother, Minerva, recalls:

> Parry had always been the lightest of her children and the smartest too. . . . Indian blood, Grandpappy had said . . . But Granny had made out . . . it wasn't Indian blood in Parry, but white blood coming out, as sure as you're born. Then her mammy had asked right sharp, "Where'd he git hold of that white blood, Granny?" But Granny she didn't say nothing a-tall. . . . All the answer she gave was to sort of sing aloud, the way she did when she made believe she was seeing things: "I knows what I knows, an' I sees what I sees. *Dar's a long run an' a short turn, an' de wind has full sweep.*" (317)

Although Minerva conflates intelligence with whiteness, she is troubled by the other signs (like ambition) of her son's mixed racial heritage and its confluence of supposedly immutable differences. Granny's cryptic remark suggests that Parry is payback for interracial sex (or rape), but whom his existence is meant to punish or to vindicate remains unclear. The white characters recognize their black family only when it is convenient for them to do so, such as when William justifies the scheme to shift Stanley's guilt onto Parry by promising, "he could have the best counsel. It would be kept close in the family" (416). For the most part, though, the white characters respond to Parry as Asa does, with "an obscure and illogical sense of contrition, as if he himself were to blame for some act of injustice in which he had taken no part" (214). Their view of Parry is obscured not by his unintelligibility (for Parry is quite articulate about his ambitions) but by their own inability to reconcile the two sides of his mixed racial makeup. As an ambitious African American, Parry appears to be an anomalous combination of native and stranger; as Charlotte and Asa see it, the young man's very familiarity makes him a "foreigner," or even the member of "another species" altogether (123, 27). Suffering from what Hale calls a "shock of racial sameness," Asa cannot view Parry through what he calls "the dark thickness of race": "All he really knew of Parry was a neat blue suit of clothes, outgrown, no doubt, by the son of one of Minerva's patrons, a well-laundered blue shirt, also a hand-me-down, . . . and black hair, without a kink. . . . But beyond these external details . . . he felt the thick silence, not of mystery, but of a vast emptiness" (30).[38] These external details, should Asa choose to interpret them, could tell him much about Parry, but Asa is searching for a way to see Parry as a metonym of blackness (just as Stanley is taken to be one of whiteness) or apart from race altogether, rather than through it, which is why he lapses into racist characterizations about the young man (that he will be lured away from his professional goals by "some light-colored wench," for instance) that miss the mark (30).

Emphasizing Asa's literal inability to see Parry, the novel always presents the African American man through the white man's perspective, which is just as troubled by Parry's wish to carve a role for himself outside of the family black and white as it is by Parry's belonging to that family. This is why Parry is so mysterious to him, while with Parry's grandmother, Asa "felt as much at ease . . . as with his own grandmother" (27). Asa's level of comfort with the black family decreases with each generation as they "had improved [their] stinted lot in life" (28). His vision of Parry, or lack thereof, constructs the racial oppression of his own time as inescapable, and by assuming his own powerlessness, he absolves himself of responsibility. However uncomfortable Asa may be with the new generations of Clays, his likeness to and connections with Minerva, Parry's mother, are especially strong. Thinking of his mother, Asa remembers that she "prided herself on her walk and on what used to be called her noble bearing; but his mother had been dead now for nearly thirty years, and only Minerva, their washerwoman, had retained a noble bearing" (47). Asa may define Minerva only as a "washerwoman," but the familial traits she shares with his mother are unmistakable, as are the similarities between Minerva and himself. Both characters frequently complain about fatigue in their legs, which indicates similar lives of hard work as well as a shared background, as Asa's father, also related to Minerva in some way, committed suicide when he became paralyzed. Chapters narrated from Asa's point of view alternate with two chapters narrated from Minerva's, which enforces a reading of the characters as sharing a siblinglike relationship grounded in common experiences. Despite the aims of segregation, the family black and white ties its members to one another in ways that transcend law.

Asa rightly understands, however, that it is his own racial privilege that blinds him, so if his knowledge of the Clays diminishes with each generation, this process does not work in reverse: "Our servants know all about us, while we know nothing of them. They are bound up in our daily lives; they are present in every intimate crisis; they are aware of, or suspect, our secret motives. Yet we are complete strangers to the way they live, to what they really think or feel about us, or about anything else" (27). This realization on Glasgow's own part, perhaps, led her to write, for the first time in her career, from the perspective of an African American. The author's only stab at an African American point of view, the two chapters narrated from Minerva's perspective vacillate between statements that insist on racial equality and ones that rely on a kind of Uncle Tom-like acquiescence to racial hierarchy. On the one hand, Minerva is proud of her connections to "quality" whites and honors her relationship to the Timberlakes by caring for the "odds and ends her white friends had discarded" (just as Till in Cather's *Sapphira* does) (80). Further, Minerva worries that Parry is too demanding, too complex, and therefore too much like whites, and she mourns for the time when "all you had to do was to settle down in your place and be thankful if [the Lord Almighty] hadn't made it a tight squeeze" (319). Embodying the stereotype that African Americans are "naturally" happy, Minerva complains that whites and New Negroes like her son "had never really learned how to have fun" (75). These chapters therefore echo the segregationist argument that African Americans are happier when kept in their place. On the other hand, they reinforce the similarities between Minerva and Asa and, because Minerva rightly predicts all of the crises of the Timberlake family before they happen, show that Asa is right in his suspicion that African Americans hold a sophisticated knowledge of whites that is not matched by whites' knowledge of themselves.

This last point stands in contradiction to Minerva's musings about the virtues of her humble, happy-go-lucky approach to her place in life. Indeed, her knowledge, like the knowledge Chesnutt's Jane possesses of her white family, does her little good, nor can Minerva help it when the Timberlakes' problems become her own. Perhaps it is in part her son's ambition, prompting his association with the Timberlakes as possible benefactors of his education, that makes him vulnerable to being used as Stanley's scapegoat, but the tradition of the family black and white is also to blame for Stanley's ability to accuse Parry of the crime Stanley herself commits. The automatic response all the Clays have to Parry's arrest suggests that whites' victimization of young black men is far more random, and more pervasive, than Minerva's justifications of racial hierarchy indicate. After Parry's arrest, the Clays must focus their actions on one thing—self-protection—and even that gets misinterpreted by whites like Asa. While he feels for Minerva and her family, he also knows that "a whole universe, not of life but of custom, not of reason but of psychology, divided him . . . from these . . . alien people to whom he was sincerely attached" (391). But knowing about race's constructedness and being able to see through the "dark thickness" with which it obscures one's perspective are two different things, as Asa demonstrates. Visiting Parry in jail, Asa compares "the rank odors of Africa" he thinks he smells there to the smell of the segregated public realm outside the jail, "the blessed smell of the sky, or of nothing" (399, 406). Asa wonders how "an incident like that, barely twenty-four hours in jail, [could] have completely knocked the spirit out of a boy who was so nearly white," and concludes that, after all, Parry isn't white enough (464). While Asa cannot see beyond one night in jail to the collective history of oppression of which his confinement is a part, the novel's African American characters cannot see anything else. Rather than speak the truth, they prevaricate, mumble, and look away, pretending to confirm whites' expectations of them as ignorant, just as Chesnutt's Julius does. Living in a culture in which "back talk," the "momentary sneer," and the "averted look" were all interpreted as "grievous wrongs," the Clays, open and talkative before Parry's arrest, react immediately out of fear.[39]

At the end of *In This Our Life,* Parry seems without hope, and he never appears in *Beyond Defeat,* the novel's unfinished sequel. This omission suggests, perhaps, a dawning awareness on Glasgow's part that she did not know African Americans like her mammy, Lizzie, as much as she thought she had. Having followed Roosevelt's advice to face her racial attitudes, Glasgow was led to conclude that her own gendered and racial identity was a source of terror for African Americans, and no vestige of a plantation myth about "family" could change that.

PART III

"Fortunate Country": Old Immigrants and New Women in Cather's and Wharton's West

American social development has been continually beginning over again on the frontier. This perennial rebirth, this fluidity of American life, this expansion westward with its new opportunities, its continuous touch with the simplicity of primitive society, furnish the forces dominating American character.

—Frederick Jackson Turner,
The Frontier in American History (1920)

The West is purely a railroad enterprise . . . We started it in our publicity department.

—Transcontinental railroad executive, quoted in Robert Hine and John Mack Faragher's *The American West*

5

How the West Was Whitened

I. THE SIGNIFICANCE OF FEMALE FRONTIER HISTORY

In the final sentence of *O Pioneers!* Willa Cather calls the Nebraskan prairie a "fortunate country" that, receiving the hearts of the great pioneers "into its bosom," will give those hearts "out again in the yellow wheat, in the rustling corn, in the shining eyes of youth."[1] Linking the land to "the people who own" it, "who love it and understand it," this exchange memorializes transient pioneers who transform the blank landscape into "fortunate" country (272–73). In portraying such a symbiosis, Cather engages here, as she does elsewhere, in what Dorothee Kocks calls a "geographical embrace," a belief that the "soil has its own agenda to which human beings submit."[2] And it is the soil's agenda that a woman, Alexandra Bergson, rather than a man become one of the great pioneers who, having owned and loved it, will be received unto the land and made one with it. In looking to the environment to reenvision frontier history—Alexandra is a superior pioneer—Cather's "geographical embrace" articulates a feminist version of the Jeffersonian yeoman, confirming a set of values that are seemingly written quite plainly on the landscape itself. Those values, of course, serve as a corrective to others associated with the West: rather than gun-toting cowpunchers riding past an endless series of mesas, or even an empty prairie that made it "possible for the largely male, wage-earning work force to improve its circumstances and condition in life," Cather imagines a landscape made fruitful largely by the efforts of women, many of whom are immigrants from Europe considered by others to be too foreign to qualify as Americans.[3]

Notwithstanding the Hollywood-generated images of the region, Cather was not alone in stressing the importance of women to westward expansion.

Because communities were understood to be aggregates of home and family, women were considered to be fundamental to the establishment of lasting cultural and social networks in a newly settled region. William Fowler's 1880 *Woman on the Frontier* called women to the West as wives of pioneers, agents of civilization, and even "founders of the republic," an idea echoed decades later by the eugenicists, who warned of the effects of foreign colonization without female settlement.[4] Since women were ostensible representatives—if not arbiters—of civilization, the eugenicists claimed, their absence in a new territory would impede long-term conquest or, worse, lead to racial amalgamation (as supposedly was the case in South America). Even the most stereotypically masculine narratives of the region tap into the belief that women create permanent communities; in Owen Wister's *The Virginian* (1902), an early Western that helped to establish the conventions of the genre, the transition of the title character from a wandering cowboy to the "bridegroom husband" of Molly Stark Wood, a teacher from the East, seems inevitable, a process to be welcomed even as it creates nostalgia for lost freedoms.[5] As Jane Tompkins argues in *West of Everything,* "what makes *The Virginian* so interesting from the standpoint of the history of the Western is that it states so openly the counterargument to its own point of view," ending with its manly hero transfigured, Wister writes, into an "important man, with a strong grip on many various enterprises, and able to give his wife all and more than she asked or desired."[6] The vision of a male-centered West, so pervasive in *The Virginian* and in the popular American imagination, tells only part of the story, representing just one step in the evolution from a supposedly empty landscape to a thriving regional community.

Indeed, while recent work on the region has striven to paint a fuller picture of its gendered history, there are many indications—including the works of Willa Cather—that we have overemphasized the extent to which the West was, early in the last century, associated with men. If it is true, as Tompkins and others argue, that the region popularized by Wister and Turner was associated with masculine freedoms because of the early scarcity of white women, it is also true that, not much later, those women enjoyed their own sorts of freedom there. For instance, the mobility of the "new" region brought by railroad travel "broadened the geographical scope" of women's social and economic options. So did the fact that in the first decades of the twentieth century, western women obtained more university degrees than women in other regions (and of the three women I examine here, Cather alone attended college).[7] The West's developing urban centers, to which, by the 1880s, women moved in greater numbers than men, also augmented women's social and economic prospects. In both urban and rural environments, western women took active roles in shaping many of the most important debates of the Progressive Era: prohibition, women's suffrage, and conservation, three movements associated with women, were especially popular in the West.[8] Similarly, the relatively strong support of Populism in the region gave women frequent opportunities to engage in the political process, a fact that, for historians Robert Hine and John Mack Faragher, helps to account for the relative success of women's suffrage there. Of the fifteen states to grant women the right to vote before federal ratification of the Nineteenth Amendment, thirteen were in the West.[9]

Such opportunities allowed women to add their voices to debates about citizenship in the region. What all "geographical embraces" of the West, from Wister's to Cather's, have in common is "the illusion that the landscape before you is free of politics" even as it seems to bolster one's own political positions.[10] One example of this dichotomy that is central to Cather's works is this notion of women as essential to settlement. At once feminist and racist, the portrayal of women as western community builders, as Peggy Pascoe rightly asserts, assumes that "the West only became 'civilized' when white women entered it."[11] In opening up new social, economic, and political opportunities for white women, immigrants, and the working class, the West became the region most "synonymous with the American dream," but the region is only west of earlier Euro-American settlement, a geographical designation oriented by assumptions of white racial supremacy.[12] On the same day (January 1, 1863) that the Emancipation Proclamation was signed, freeing enslaved African Americans in the occupied South, Abraham Lincoln also signed the Homestead Act into law. One document gave an unprecedented number of white Americans and European immigrants the opportunity to possess private property—a crucial marker of citizenship—and the other granted slaves the promise of citizenship but, as it would turn out, no land. As Theodore Allen writes, "By shaping the homestead policy as a white-skin privilege, the ruling class had secured the acquiescence of laboring-class whites" in a way that helped to destroy the aims of Reconstruction in the South and to render the working class itself "powerless to shape land policy" in the West.[13] Appealing to "the acquisitive values of subject populations," the Homestead Act provided two possible scenarios for obtaining land: settlers could gain title to property if they improved it by building a home and residing there for five years, or they could purchase title to the land at a low price after six months.[14] Its very name suggesting the sphere traditionally associated with women, the Homestead Act held gendered as well as socioeconomic and racial implications, for at least the first of these provisions—to build a home on the land—attached an importance to women settlers, many of whom, as Cather's novels show, were European immigrants. By the U.S. Census of 1890 (the same one that announced that the frontier was "closed"), the region had the largest foreign-born population in the nation, and by the time the homestead program closed in 1935, it had provided farms (mostly in Kansas, the Dakotas, and Nebraska) for four hundred thousand families, the overwhelming majority of whom were European or European American in origin.[15] Set in such a context, Cather's "geographical embrace" reaches in two directions simultaneously: toward one that supports women in both the domestic realm and in more public ones, and toward another that welcomes the contributions to the West made by European immigrants.

II. EUGENICS, CULTURAL PLURALISM, AND IMMIGRATION ON CATHER'S PRAIRIE

When Cather wrote novels of a prairie teeming with diverse immigrant communities, she entered a debate about the relative whiteness of various European groups we now call "ethnic." Competing notions of white racial identity had been in circulation long before Cather created immigrants like Alexandra Bergson of *O Pioneers!* and Ántonia Shimerda of *My Ántonia,* of course, but among Americans of the early twentieth century "the general tendency," writes Reginald Horsman, "was for greater and greater refinement of racial divisions, both among the white and colored races."[16] This greater refinement of racial divisions included a separation of Europeans into superior and inferior white races, a trend that coincided with the arrival into the United States of new immigrants like Slavs and Mediterraneans. These new immigrant groups were viewed as being biologically, psychologically, and intellectually distinct from "old" immigrant groups like Anglos and Scandinavians. As Lothrop Stoddard put it in his 1924 *Racial Realities in Europe,* "although the European races are unquestionably closer to one another in origin than they are to more remote human stocks like the yellow Mongolians of Eastern Asia or the African negroes, they nevertheless separated ages ago, and for ages thereafter remain separate."[17] The notion of distinct European races, espoused especially by eugenicists like Stoddard, oftentimes refuted prejudice against immigrant groups like the Irish, as well as nativist prejudice toward all immigrants per se. Claiming for itself the patina of "science," the eugenics movement also tried to refute the Progressive Era faith in assimilation, eventually garnering enough political clout to influence the restrictions on new immigration passed in 1924.[18] Until that time, all European immigrants, no matter what their country of origin, benefited from their status as members of one or more "white race(s)" in that, unlike Asians, they were permitted entry into the United States at all. And once they became American citizens, all European immigrants enjoyed privileges denied to all "nonwhites." But as Matthew Frye Jacobson contends, immigrants from southern and eastern Europe became part of a singular Caucasian "race" only over time, and "all of them . . . faced certain challenges to their racial pedigree along the way." These challenges, Jacobson continues, often amounted to "a contest over political 'fitness' among a now fragmented, hierarchically arranged series of distinct 'white races.'"[19]

The "fitness" of new immigrants from southern and eastern Europe was challenged on the basis of their religion (Catholicism, Judaism) and their European class positions in addition to their racial status. And their presence in the West was particularly troubling to some Americans; writing in 1891 about the "perils" of immigration, Josiah Strong argued that "in the East, institutions have been long established and are therefore less easily modified by foreign influence, but in the West, where institutions are formative, that influence is far more powerful. We may well ask—and with special reference to the West—whether this in-sweeping immigration is to foreignize us, or we are to Americanize it."[20] While Bohemians like Cather's Ántonia Shimerda were sometimes defined as the "most advanced" of the Slavs (a race supposedly notable for their moodiness and their heavy brains),[21] they were also spoken of as being feudal throwbacks, constitutionally incapable of democratic citizenship. And they were blamed for a host of social ills, from labor unrest to the so-called differential birth rate between higher and lower elements of American society. In *Racial Hygiene* (1929) Thurman Rice argued that "[m]embers of the Slavic or Alpine sub-race should be allowed to enter [the United States] only in exceptional cases, since we now have all of this blood that we can absorb, and probably more than is good for us."[22] For Stoddard, Rice, and others who advocated a eugenics approach to immigration, newcomers from eastern Europe threatened to pollute the "excellent stock" of northern and western European immigrants who had created the American body politic (243–44). In *Racial Realities* Stoddard asserted that if the Alpine race "has contributed little that is strictly great to politics, art or ideas," "its tenacity, endurance, and vitality favor its steady growth, and wherever it has a foothold it appears to be increasing at the expense of the Nordic and Mediterranean elements" (16).

At the same time that reactions to new immigration contributed to a fractured whiteness and called into question the racial credentials of the Slavs, such responses cultivated a sense of racial solidarity between Anglo-Americans and northern European immigrants, like the Swedish Alexandra

Bergson. In fact, northern European immigrant groups participated in the heightened anti-immigration rhetoric of the World War I years, which was specifically targeted at new immigrants.[23] Stoddard defined northern European Nordics as a race of "warriors, sailors, pioneers, and explorers" endowed with "high political ability," democratic among themselves and aristocratic toward others (17). While American democracy, according to the eugenicists, was said to be as foreign to eastern Europeans as they were to it, Scandinavians supposedly came predisposed to life in the New World; recall Stoddard's insistence, quoted earlier, that "democratic parliamentary institutions have been a real success only among peoples largely Nordic in blood" (112). Countering other definitions of democracy that linked it to diversity, the mid-twenties United States Committee on Selective Immigration—which greatly influenced the eugenics-based restrictions on new immigrants passed in 1924—found that Europeans from northern nations, along with their racial counterparts from western Europe, were "the best material for American Citizenship."[24]

During the years she was writing and publishing *O Pioneers!* and *My Ántonia,* Cather often spoke of her deep interest in the immigrants she had met as a youth in Nebraska, and, as she claimed in a 1913 interview, she was particularly interested in "Scandinavian and Bohemian pioneers."[25] Cather was exposed to popular derogatory images of Bohemian immigrants at least by 1910 when, as editor of *McClure's,* she oversaw the publication of Elizabeth Shepley Sergeant's essay on new immigration, which praised the contributions of old immigrant groups, which she called "Northern races," and disparaged the new immigrant races who "differ fundamentally" from them.[26] While scholars such as Katrina Irving and Ann Moseley have illustrated the extent to which Cather adhered to Horace Kallen's notion of cultural pluralism, it is also true that several aspects of the eugenics theory of racial differences among Europeans dovetail with Cather's sense of European diversity. As both Guy Reynolds and Marilee Lindemann have argued, Cather's immigrants bring qualities with them that indicate their typicality.[27] Indeed, Cather's novels draw upon the eugenics construction of racial distinctions between "Scandinavian and Bohemian pioneers" in order to discount nativist anxiety concerning all foreigners, such as that the residents of Black Hawk display in *My Ántonia.* Whereas Black Hawk's nativists lump all immigrants together, Cather herself saw the racial and class distinctions between Europeans—between Alexandra Bergson and Ántonia Shimerda, for example—as more salient. The notion of white racial diversity also provided Cather a way to critique assimilation, the other side of the nativist coin: both nativism and faith in an American melting pot fail to differentiate among foreigners, and both depend on a construction of American identity rooted in homogeneity. Cather makes this connection in her frequently quoted interview statement decrying assimilation European immigrants: "have come here to live in the sense that they lived in the Old World, and if they were left alone their lives might turn into the beautiful ways of their homeland. But they are not left alone. Social workers, missionaries—call them what you will—go after them, hound them[,] pursue them and devote their days and nights toward the great task of turning them into stupid replicas of smug American citizens. This passion for Americanizing everything and everybody is a deadly disease with us."[28]

The passion for assimilating immigrants was one that was openly espoused by some of the most influential commentators on the American frontier, men like Edward Ross and Frederick Jackson Turner. While Ross and Turner expressed reservations about new immigrants, they also minimized the kind of white racial differences the eugenicists found so important to safeguard. Both men located America's greatness in its ability to unify distinct national, class, and religious groups from the Old World, and both argued that such unification produced a better racial stock than any to be found in Europe. Although Ross shared eugenicists' distaste for Slavs as well as their fears about granting citizenship to new immigrants "who have not yet passed the civic kindergarten," he also trusted in America's powers to assimilate them more than Stoddard and his ilk, who regarded assimilation of new immigrants as part impossible and part dangerous. In *Changing America* (1912) Ross even went so far as to claim that "race is no barrier to" what he calls the "worldwide and tidal" "movement toward democracy."[29] Because he, like Turner, often saw immigration issues through a particularly regional lens, he was more apt to praise than to disparage racial fusion; the West, he contended, is the "meeting place of men from everywhere," where "elements of the greatest diversity were blending into a common American type" that surpassed its various European parent stocks.[30] In "The Significance of the Frontier" (1893) Turner similarly argued that "too exclusive attention has been paid . . . to the Germanic origins, too little to the American factors" of white racial greatness.[31] To Turner, the frontier had been the most significant site for such racial development, "the line of most rapid and effective Americanization" and its corresponding "movement away from the influence of Europe" (3–4). Disputing eugenicists and other critics of open-door immigration policies who charged that Italians and Slavs come to America in order to satisfy a "dull and blind materialism," Turner claimed that all European immigrants have "hopes which they have formed for a newer and freer life across the seas" (264). But if their hopes are similar, their destinies are not. It is "almost pathetic," he lamented, "when one considers how far" the new immigrants' American dreams are from becoming reality. Yet it was as much the closing of the frontier as it was racial difference that would deny new immigrants the frontier opportunities enjoyed by old immigrants from western and northern nations.

Cather uses the notion of racial difference among Europeans to counter opinions like those of Ross and Turner that the success of the West (and of the nation) rests upon producing a "common American type." She also rejects the negative valuation of new immigrant races made by the eugenicists and their followers, like Sergeant, who argued that Slavic Alpines or "roundheads," as Stoddard called them, were unsuitable for American citizenship. To be sure, her old and new immigrant characters suggest that she may have agreed with Stoddard that "the Northern European comes to us predisposed by his heredity to understand and to sympathize with the civilization that his kinsfolk have built up in America," and that groups like the Slavs "are thus not predisposed" (*Racial Realities,* 241). But for her, this is not a negative but a positive, for the introduction of eastern European traditions enriches the New World and its frontier. And while the eugenicists' hostility toward new immigrant races manifested itself particularly in the realm of democratic citizenship, Cather refocuses the debate about new immigrants upon culture. In other words, her positive stance on new immigrants' contributions to the cultural diversity of the prairie, and to the nation more generally, relies on the same rhetoric of racial difference between Europeans that eugenicists used to disparage these same groups.

That is because "culture" for Cather is a manifestation of each European group's distinct traits. Writing to Connecticut governor Wilbur Cross about her presentation of French immigrants in *Shadows on the Rock,* Cather commented upon her commitment to old-world retentions:

> An orderly little French household that went on trying to live decently . . . interests me more than Indian raids or the wild life in the forests. And . . . once having adopted a tone so definite, once having taken your seat in the close air by the apothecary's fire, you can't explode into military glory, any more than you can pour champagne into a salad dressing. (I don't believe much in rules, but Stevenson laid down a good one when he said: *You can't mix kinds.*) And really, a new society begins with the salad dressing more than with the destruction of Indian villages. Those people brought a kind of French culture there and somehow kept it alive on that rock . . . and all this temperately and shrewdly, with emotion always tempered by good sense.

> It's very hard for an American to catch that rhythm—it's so unlike us.[32]

As her generalizations about French immigrants' qualities (temperance, shrewdness, good sense) suggest, Cather roots cultural distinctiveness in the kind of racial difference many believed made eastern Europeans differ from northern and western Europeans. Furthermore, these traits and the differing cultures they engender are associated with traditionally feminine rather than traditionally masculine pursuits: salad dressing rather than war both preserves a group's distinctiveness and begins new societies. Cather's insistence on the roles women play in maintaining and transmitting cultural distinctiveness helps to explain why her immigrant pioneers are so often women, and her reliance upon European racial differences works to clarify how those women differ from one another. Her novels explore the distinctions between European races by assigning two very different versions of womanhood to them. Her Slav or Alpine immigrant women are tied to home, hearth, and ultimately to the past, while her northern European, Nordic immigrants become independent, professionally minded New Women who transcend traditional gender roles and succeed in widening the scope of acceptable spheres for women.

Unfettered by the gaze of "natives" like *My Ántonia*'s Jim Burden (except the author's own gaze), the immigrant pioneers of Cather's first novel of the West, *O Pioneers!* (1913), translate old-world differences onto the empty landscape of Hanover, Nebraska. In many pioneer accounts the supposed threat of Native Americans looms large, creating, according to Glenda Riley, a "frontier psychology" intent on testifying to the hardships of western life.[33] But in Cather's novel the challenges confronting immigrant pioneers are displaced from wrestling the land from Natives to wrestling with the land itself. By glossing over Native removal, Cather is able to use "nature as umpire" or mediator in disputes about new immigrants and racial difference among Europeans, for her, "frontier" is not so much a site of conflict between "savage" Indians and advancing "civilization" as it is a site of old-world survivals and their place in the New World.[34] These survivals are exemplified most forcefully in the contrast between the Swedish Alexandra Bergson and the Bohemian Marie Shabata. Unlike Alexandra, Marie is often excessively emotional, "incapable of being lukewarm about anything that pleases her," a trait associated both with traditional notions of femininity and with the supposedly "yielding" temperament of Slavs (*O Pioneers!* 194; Ross, *Old World,* 120). Marie's hyper-femininity, in fact, is embroiled in her violent death in ways that assign the gender construction she embodies to the past.

As Carl observes, she is one example of women who "spread ruin around them through no fault of theirs, just by being too beautiful, too full of life and love" (270). And it is Marie's identity as a Bohemian that marks her as overtly feminine: "not a woman who could live without loving," she is characterized by her difference from Alexandra and her tragic associations with men (222). In both her unhappy marriage to Frank Shabata and her affair with Emil Bergson, we see how the novel draws upon constructions of old-world racial and class distinctions and suggests their connection to assimilation. In *Changing America* Ross observed that "to-day two ideas of the family are struggling for mastery—the old despotic family, of Roman origin and ecclesiastical sanction, based on the authority of the husband and the merging of the wife's legal personality in his, and the democratic family, of Germanic origin based on the consenting and harmonious wills of two equals" (58–59). Marie's marriage to Frank certainly exemplifies the "old despotic family," while her relationship with Emil gestures toward a more "democratic family." The daughter of "one of the more intelligent Bohemians who came West in the early seventies," Marie is part of a group of Bohemian immigrants who were widely considered to be more genteel than the mass of their poorer countrymen who came at the turn of the century (131). In "Nebraska: The End of the First Cycle," Cather makes this distinction between early and later Czech immigrants explicit: "the political emigration resulting from the revolutionary disturbances of 1848" brought "people of a very superior type" to Nebraska, a group "distinctly different" from those who came later for "economic causes" (4). These early Czech arrivals, according to Ross, were among the few Slavs who had experienced a "great intellectual awakening," allowing them to advance beyond their feudalistic past and develop skills that made them valuable additions to America, unlike the more recent Bohemian arrivals (*Old World,* 124). Theorists like Stoddard and Rice argued that in their own country these enlightened Slavs were being destroyed by the significantly less advanced but more numerous peasant classes, just as Marie is destroyed by Frank on Cather's prairie. For Frank embodies all of the worst qualities attributed to the peasant-turned-new-immigrant: despite his upper-class pretensions, he is an atavistic primitive who resents his betters and abuses his wife, as Slav peasant men were said to do.[35] But since Marie is not of "Germanic origin," her miscegenational relationship with Emil is equally doomed. Her gender type as well as her class and racial status as a genteel Slav all suggest the inevitability of her demise.

The ways in which Cather combines eugenics and its seeming opposite, cultural pluralism, to explore western womanhood become clear when we compare *O Pioneers!* to another novel of prairie diversity, O. E. Rölvaag's

Their Fathers' God (1931). Rölvaag's novel, like Cather's, features immigrant settlers struggling to build a new regional society even as they try to remain true to their religious and cultural beliefs, and both works explore the extent to which a western community can be forged of disparate racial elements. Despite Rölvaag's title, both *O Pioneers!* and *Their Fathers' God* are marked by an absence of fathers: John Bergson dies early in Cather's novel, and Peder's father has already died before the start of Rölvaag's work. In both cases, then, it is the figure of the mother that connects the pioneering children of immigrants to the old country. Both novels feature relationships between northern Europeans and members of other races (Emil and Marie in Cather's work and Peder and Susie in Rölvaag's) that are destined to fail because the racial distinctions between the characters are too great. While both Cather and Rölvaag denounce the ethnic chauvinism with which members of one European race often treat others (Tom McDougal's anti-Norwegian speech at the end of *Their Fathers' God* is a particularly dramatic example), the "geographical embrace" of both novels reads the land as making plain the importance of remaining loyal to one's racial heritage. As Beret Holm in Rölvaag's work puts it, "we don't keep wheat and potatoes in the same bin."[36] Like the Bohemian Catholic Marie, the Irish Catholic Susie is intensely passionate (Rölvaag's work being much more sexually explicit than Cather's), feminine, and superstitious, while the Nordic characters, Peder and Alexandra, are enterprising freethinkers. In both novels forbidden love is associated with the fecundity of the land: orchards are the settings both for the consummation of Emil and Marie's affair and for Peder and Nikoline's romantic exchange. Significantly, though, Cather's orchard scene—one of interracial liaison—ends in violence, while Rölvaag's, a meeting of like and like, seems tragic only because it is clear that the two Nordics are a more suitable match than Peder and Susie are. Absent from *Their Fathers' God* are the class divisions between members of the same European race that are so significant to *O Pioneers!*, for Marie and Frank's marriage—one of racial sameness, but class difference—is just as unhappy as Peder and Susie's is. Both novels extol the virtues of old-world retentions and decry what the Lutheran minister in Rölvaag's work calls a "perfect democracy of barrenness" that makes "everybody alike by blotting out all racial traits" (210). But both works also attribute a greater penchant for the duties of citizenship (open-mindedness, a sense of responsibility to the greater good) to Nordics than they do to members of other European races (210).[37] Echoing the eugenicists, the minister argues that "the spirit of democracy" was a particular gift of the Norseman, making them superior pioneers with the strongest "desire for liberty and individualism" (207, 211).

But in Cather's novel it is a Norsewoman rather than a Norseman who makes the best citizen pioneer. Alexandra's fate, like Marie's, is inexorable, for it is her particular manifestation of Swedishness that accounts for the certainty of her agricultural success in America. As she herself defines it, as a Swede she is "terribly practical," while Marie, as a Bohemian, is "high-strung" (204). Alexandra's practicality and her lack of those qualities Marie possesses in excess, such as "women's intuition," serve to make her an ideal American. While Marie thrives on personal connections, Alexandra is capable of enjoying "the idea of things more than the things themselves," a quality necessary, Cather tells us, in a pioneer, and one that was linked by theorists like Stoddard to the Nordic's racial predisposition for democracy (50). The typical Scandinavian man, according to Stoddard, possesses "creative energy, political ability, self-reliance, self-control, and common sense," and is naturally fitted for life as a "prosperous yeoman" and property owner (*Racial Realities,* 57, 60). While Cather draws upon these racialisms, she also regenders them, and in doing so, she links traditional Nordic qualities to a pioneering American womanhood.[38]

For as Marie is associated with darkness (dark skin, kisses in the dark), Alexandra is overwhelmingly associated with whiteness. Despite her farmer's tan, she elsewhere maintains "the skin . . . of such smoothness and whiteness as none but Swedish women ever possess," and she is also most often described as dressing in white (85). As Ivar observes, Alexandra is a "white figure" (249), but she is also figuratively white: "Her mind was a white book, with clear writing about weather and beasts and growing things. Not many people would care to read it; only a happy few. She had never been in love, she had never indulged in sentimental reveries. Even as a girl she had looked upon men as work-fellows. She had grown up in serious times" (185). As the novel defines it, her "white" mind marks her departure from gender convention. Unlike Marie, Alexandra doesn't define herself exclusively, or even primarily, through personal relationships, nor through her emotions for men. Instead, her embodiment of whiteness is associated with hard work and "serious" considerations. Such qualities give her a rarity, and make her a particularly fine example of Nordicism; as Edward Ross observed, "the goodness of these people is from the head rather than the heart" (*Old World,* 91). The Nordic qualities Alexandra imports from the old country become the reason for her career-oriented identity in the new country.

Unlike Rölvaag's novel, which predicts dire results for a prairie melting pot, Cather's Divide accommodates and celebrates both traditional Bohemian femininity and independent Swedish womanhood, as well as a democracy rooted in Nordicism and one that promotes European racial diversity.

Indeed, the friendship between Alexandra and Marie thrives, at least until the end of the novel, on their differences from each other. Marie's emotional nature enlivens Alexandra's often lonely life, and gives her a friend who, unlike the members of her own family, intuits and supports her feelings for Carl. In turn, Alexandra's practicality provides Marie, who is prone to moody protests against past mistakes, an example of calm resignation. Cather's "geographical embrace" praises the European racial diversity these two women represent especially against the backdrop of the western landscape:

> Carl sat at a little distance from the two women, his back to the wheatfield, and watched them. Alexandra took off her shade-hat and threw it on the ground. Marie picked it up and played with the white ribbons, twisting them about her brown fingers as she talked. They made a pretty picture in the strong sunlight, the leafy pattern surrounding them like a net; the Swedish woman so white and gold, kindly and amused, but armored in calm, and the alert brown one, her full lips parted, points of yellow light dancing in her eyes as she laughed and chattered. (124–25)

While Marie is dark, restless, and chatty, Alexandra is white, calm, and self-assured. As Langdon Elsbree points out, nature in the West is often used, as it is here, as a way to harmonize difference.[39] Yet it is Alexandra more than Marie who possesses the authority to preserve such racial and cultural distinctions, who, armed with the power of a successful landowner, protects both Ivar and Mrs. Lee from Lou and Oscar Bergsons' attempts to homogenize them. Her relationships with other immigrants prove that she has learned the region's lessons, that the land has taught her "how to achieve democracy" based on a sense of "obligation of the strong to the weak."[40]

Yet the "pretty picture" of Alexandra and Marie's racialized gender differences becomes implicated in what Melissa Ryan calls the novel's "deep anxiety" about "the process of civilization," a process that, with Marie and Emil's liaison, hints at the threat of relationships between members of differing European races.[41] Alexandra's disapproval of this relationship is one the text shares, for the site of Carl's happy contrast between Alexandra's whiteness and Marie's darkness—the apple orchard—is, of course, the same one where Frank Shabata murders Emil and Marie in mindless, primitive rage. Once an idyllic setting for communication between racially diverse expressions of womanhood, it becomes a warning against impurity: white mulberries fall upon the two dead bodies, leaving dark stains to match the stains of blood; white butterflies flutter around the shadows the bodies cast (240–41).

Lindemann asserts that while Emil's body "remains reticent," Marie's death is "long and excruciatingly detailed,"[42] a narrative device that is consistent with Marie's Bohemian emotional displays in life. So while white racial diversity provides the novel's Divide with its cultural richness, and provides a varied presentation of the roles of women, the violent turn taken by the plot of the novel suggests that such diversity must be maintained and contained simultaneously.

Like *O Pioneers!*, *My Ántonia* (1918) refutes prejudice against new immigrants by integrating eastern European Slavs into its prairie community. It also draws from the construction of racial distinctions between eastern and northern European groups, employing these differences in order to explore differences in womanhood, for the Bohemian woman, Ántonia, becomes a mother of Americans while Lena Lingard, a Norwegian, becomes an American herself. Unlike Cather's earlier novel, though, *My Ántonia* explores these issues of gender and race against a backdrop of Anglo-American nativism. Also unlike *O Pioneers!* this novel introduces, with the appearance of Blind d'Arnault, a white-black binary to mitigate the "crisis of overinclusive whiteness" that new immigrants were thought to pose.[43]

As Mike Fischer has written, *My Ántonia* tells a story of western settlement "for whites only."[44] But it also tells a story about the distinctions between whites, for although the novel ends with the sense that "natives" and immigrants alike belong to the West, the first section of the novel, "The Shimerdas," highlights the racial distinctions between Slavs and the Anglo-American Burdens. It is the overwhelming sense of the Bohemians' foreignness—made manifest in their poverty, their helplessness, their linguistic difference, and the slow pace at which they adapt to American ways—that creates the ritualistic structure of book 1, whereby the tranquil monotony of life on the Anglo-Americans' farm is repeatedly disrupted by the Shimerdas. Jim is presented with diverse ways of reacting to eastern European racial difference, from Jake's nativism and Mrs. Burden's Darwinian angst to Mr. Burden's patrician noblesse oblige. The novel often presents these popular views of new immigrants with irony, even while it simultaneously insists upon the Shimerdas' foreignness. And however much the novel exposes the Burdens' hypocrisies, it also renders them the wise and kindly benefactors of hapless foreigners. Mr. Burden, for instance, tolerates all of the Shimerdas' shenanigans; he allows them to keep a cow for which they fail to pay him, he says nothing when Ambrosch breaks his horse collar, and he gallantly acquiesces to Mrs. Shimerda's folksy, misguided insistence on her husband's being buried at a crossroads. Mrs. Burden, despite often being annoyed by the Shimerdas' seeming lack of initiative, becomes angry when she learns that the Norwegian community of Black Hawk refuses to allow Mr. Shimerda to be buried there, vowing that when spring comes, she will have a "liberal-minded" graveyard built to offset the foreigners' clannishness.[45] In these ways, Anglo-Americans, instead of being nativist, surface as less prejudiced against new immigrants than other European immigrants are.

As a young southern boy who is inexperienced in racial distinctions *between whites* (as opposed to those between whites and blacks), Jim alternates between these responses and his admiration for Ántonia. For example, among his fondest memories of their childhood friendship are their visits to the prairie-dog town, where the two children would go to "watch the brown earth-owls fly home in the late afternoon and go down to their nests with the dogs" (29). Although, as Jim tells us, he and Ántonia "felt sorry for the owls," they also agree that "winged things who would live like that must be rather degraded." While this judgment is attributed to both Jim and Ántonia, immediately after this scene Jim compares the owls to the Shimerdas in what Merrill Skaggs rightly calls an "evocative juxtaposition."[46] Recalling how their cousin Krajiek swindled the family, Jim tells us: "[The Shimerdas] hated Krajiek, but they clung to him because he was the only human being with whom they could talk. . . . They kept him in their hole and fed him for the same reason that the prairie-dogs and the brown owls housed the rattlesnakes—because they did not know how to get rid of him" (31). On the one hand, Jim understands that Krajiek's deception depends on the family's not speaking English; on the other, this comparison, following so closely on Jim's description of the owls in the prairie-dog town, not only makes the Shimerdas, like the snakes' prey, "quite defenseless," but it also makes them "rather degraded" (29). According to Anne Hyde, prairie-dog towns were an integral part of the "well-crafted panorama" created by western guidebooks, which encouraged train travelers to look for them as an exciting "feature" of an otherwise monotonous prairie.[47] The novel uses this popular image to manifest the ambiguity surrounding new immigrants' capacity to acquire the American value of "self-government."

Yet *My Ántonia* also deploys class as a way for Anglo-Americans to read and assimilate new immigrants. Despite their ignorance about the Bohemians' customs, food preparation, and religion, the Burdens immediately understand that Mr. Shimerda, with his "dignified manner," is middle class and Mrs. Shimerda is not (just as Marie Shabata is and Frank is not) (23). Although most Slav immigrants were said to come from a degraded, neo-feudal peasantry, even racial theorists like Stoddard, as we've seen, acknowledged that some possessed gentility, although he argued that Czechs who did had an infusion of Nordic blood (*Racial Realities*, 174). When Jim and

Mrs. Burden pay their winter visit and find the Shimerdas in need, Mrs. Shimerda laughs "scornfully" at the Americans' surprise and shakes an empty coffee pot at them with "a look positively vindictive" (71). Mr. Shimerda, on the other hand, sits Mrs. Burden down and calmly explains that he is from a respected Bohemian family, that their present need is circumstantial (73). Mr. Shimerda, in other words, satisfies the Burdens' social sensibilities in several ways: he is genteel, he is grateful for their charity, and he recognizes their respectability. Like Frank Shabata, Mrs. Shimerda embodies many of the worst qualities associated with new immigrants: she is tactless, ungrateful, and contemptuous of the Burdens' social advantages.[48]

Just as Jim's responses to Ántonia alternate between respect of and disdain for her foreignness, Ántonia herself alternates between exhibiting her father's old-world gentility and her mother's new-immigrant crassness. At times Ántonia is gracious, sensitive, and attuned to high "culture," like her father; at other times she is boastful and contemptuous, like her mother. After Mr. Shimerda's suicide, her mother's and brother Ambrosch's new immigrant qualities threaten to subsume the finer characteristics of Cather's title character, and Ántonia becomes less genteel both by becoming more "masculine," doing farmwork that "a girl ought not to do," and by becoming darker skinned, her body morphing into one resembling "peasant women in all old countries" (121, 117). "The Shimerdas," then, reverses Cather's more common attribution of traditional femininity as a Bohemian racial trait. Instead, this section of the book draws upon conceptions that "'peasant' is in fact the term which best describes the typical Alpine" and that, more generally, "lower" races and classes "suffered" from a lack of gender differentiation, from their men and their women being too similar.[49] Just as Ántonia is in danger of becoming her brother's "drudge" twice in the novel—after her father's death and after she returns home pregnant and unmarried in "A Pioneer Woman's Story"—Slav women of the peasant classes were believed to be the drudges of their tyrannical husbands: "Engaging in . . . masculine work," according to Ross, "not only prevents immigrant women from rising to the American woman's sense of self-respect, but it hinders their men from developing the American man's spirit of chivalry" (*Old World,* 219).[50] Ántonia's spiteful attitude toward Jim at this point in the novel suggests that Mrs. Burden is correct when she observes that Ántonia was better off when she "had that genteel man," her father, to protect her from her mother's and brother's influence (149).

Book 1 of *My Ántonia* is unique in that it spotlights Anglo-Bohemian differences; book 2, "The Hired Girls," shifts the novel's focus to an exploration of immigrants against the backdrop of a nativism more forceful than that which the Burdens display in the first section. In using a small town instead of the farm hinterland as her setting, Cather widens the scope of her immigrants from the Shimerdas to the hired girls, who include Ántonia and the three Bohemian Marys but also Lena Lingard (Norwegian), Tiny Soderball (Swedish), and other eastern and northern Europeans. What links the hired girls together in the townspeople's minds is their perceived difference from Americans, not their European "racial" similarity. "The Hired Girls" explores the ways American nativism, defining all newcomers as "ignorant people who couldn't speak English," masses immigrants together regardless of national origin and automatically assigns even the most genteel of them working-class status (151). Furthermore, whereas "The Shimerdas" section explores Anglo and Bohemian family life, this focus on family gives way in "The Hired Girls" to an investigation of how working-class, immigrant status affects womanhood, making immigrant girls "physically . . . almost a race apart" from Anglo-American femininity (192). Unlike the rest of Black Hawk's Anglo-Americans, Jim and the novel itself celebrate the unconventional gender roles the immigrant girls' working-class status thrusts upon them, for it allows them to succeed in such a way that their children will be "better off than the children of the town women" they serve (194).[51]

Yet the mixing of this "race apart" with Black Hawk's Anglo-Americans leads to what Jim calls a "curious social situation," placing the immigrant girls in competition with the Anglo "native" girls (191). Most of the adults in Black Hawk view the hired girls as "a menace to the social order," but their sons are tempted by the girls' foreign eroticism, and thus "the specter of assimilation through marriage," as Blythe Tellefsen writes, "hovers over the entire town" (195).[52] And because Jim seems the most enthralled, his social position is in the greatest jeopardy, for "people said there must be something queer about a boy who showed no interest in girls of his own age, but who could be lively enough when he was with Tony or Lena or the three Marys" (209). Refusing to join the Anglo, middle-class youth group, the owls (an interesting reversal of the metaphor for the Shimerdas in book 1), Jim disappoints his grandparents and alienates Mrs. Harling by furtively going to the less genteel firemen's hall dances, where he can dance with Ántonia "against and around the hard-and-fast beat of the music" (216).[53] The anxiety the hired girls create among Black Hawk's middle class gestures toward one of the central tensions of immigration. On the one hand, American capitalism demanded a steady supply of cheap labor, and where better to get such labor than from the "lower orders" of Europe?[54] On the other hand, the eugenicists and others warned that bestowing citizenship to new immigrants was a misguided extension of democratic rights to the civically unfit.

Jim's nonconformist defense of the hired girls is not simply a matter of unfettered admiration, based as it is on defining them exotically/erotically as bodily free, natural, and quite a "race apart" from social convention. Nothing makes this clearer than his attitude toward the town girls. As Jim describes them, these Anglo-American girls are conspicuous for their absolute lack of conspicuousness: "Some of the high-school girls were jolly and pretty, but they stayed indoors in winter because of the cold, and in summer because of the heat. When one danced with them, their bodies never moved inside their clothes; their muscles seemed to ask but one thing—not to be disturbed. I remember those girls merely as faces in the schoolroom, gay and rosy, or listless and dull, cut off below the shoulders, like cherubs, by the ink-smeared tops of the high desks" (192–93). The inflexible bodies of the town girls, accentuated as they are by new dancing styles that do not require such rigidity, are meant to contrast the hired girls' suppleness. The picture of young Anglo womanhood here is distinctly cerebral: Jim remembers the town girls as students, cut off at the neck. So even as he tries to flout convention and revalue hierarchy, he relies on a racist paradigm—the mind as white, the body as othered—to do so.[55] And he relies on immigrant women to mark his own rejection of mainstream values, to distinguish himself from the "Black Hawk boys" who "looked forward to marrying Black Hawk girls, and living in a brand-new little house with best chairs that must not be sat upon" (195). Jim's epithet for such boys—"white-handed, high collared"—makes plain the racialized and class-inflected nature of the gendered imperatives of respectability from which he tries to separate himself (198).

The three chapters that lead to Jim's description of the "curious social situation"—from Ántonia's story of a homeless man's suicide, to the chapter on Blind d'Arnault, to the arrival in Black Hawk of the Vannis—allow readers to frame the tensions between the novel's Anglo "natives" and immigrant girls not in terms of carte blanche nativism, as the bourgeois citizens of Black Hawk do, but in a critique of it. For this sequence insists upon both the value of old-world retentions and the absolutism of black-white binaries. First, Ántonia's recalling the suicide of a nativist tramp serves to allay the threat her immigrant status poses to the townspeople, for while she and the other hired girls ultimately display the value of "self-government" by working themselves out of poverty, Cather's nativist tramp, it seems, cannot do likewise.[56] Instead, he resents immigrants ("I thought this was Americy" [172]), believing his being native-born trumps his working-class status. Nativism—whether the working-class man's or middle-class Black Hawk's—thus becomes a denial of how vital class differences are, in the novel's terms, to making life in a new homeland successful.

The next chapter presents the hired girls in the context of another stranger, Blind d'Arnault. Janis Stout maintains that the novel's "domestic racism" is marked in two ways: by d'Arnault's presence in the text, his rather random appearance in Black Hawk, and by the absence of Native Americans in the same space.[57] Indeed, although the novel itself provides readers with multiple ways to question Jim's more erroneous assumptions about the hired girls, it does not do likewise in its presentation of a black man. With the exception of his uncharacteristically proud refusal to be led, Blind d'Arnault's character is rooted in stereotype: Jim defines his "soft, amiable" voice, with its "note of docile subservience," as essentially "Negro" (177–78). "He had a Negro head, too," Jim informs us, which amounts to "almost no head at all." We should recall here Jim's characterization of Black Hawk's young white women: all heads. In this way, d'Arnault as a black man from the South is the white western woman's Ur-other. It is not surprising, then, that Blind d'Arnault can perform only "barbarously and wonderfully," nor that Jim would ascribe the black man's musical talents to blind instinct, not intellectual engagement (he has almost no head, after all) (183). Because of its physical nature, d'Arnault's music tells us something about his race, not his artistry: "[T]o hear him, to watch him, was to see a Negro enjoying himself as only a Negro can."[58] We learn in the introduction of the novel that Jim's writing of his memories is, like d'Arnault's playing, unpolished and unrevised. Yet the similarities between d'Arnault's artistic practice and Jim's have their origins in very different aspects of their (raced) characters. Jim's authorship, romantically conceived (he makes no notes [6]), springs from a life of the mind. In contrast, d'Arnault's art, "definite as animal desire" (182), is embroiled in Cather's version of negritude as well as in his excessive physicality, as we see when Jim describes the African American man's first experience with a piano:

> Through the dark he found his way to the Thing, to its mouth. He touched it softly, and it answered softly, kindly. He shivered and stood still. Then he began to feel it all over, ran his finger tips along the slippery sides, embraced the carved legs, tried to get some conception of its shape and size, of the space it occupied in primeval night. It was cold and hard, and like nothing else in his black universe. . . . He seemed to know that it must be done with the fingers, not with the fists or the

> feet. He approached this highly artificial instrument through a mere instinct, and coupled himself to it, as if he knew it was to piece him out and make a whole creature out of him. (181–82)

D'Arnault's relationship to the piano at once draws from the stereotype of the oversexed black man (oversexed indeed, since he is supposedly a child here) and diffuses the threat it usually implies by making a piano, not a white woman, its object. The piano is both black and white, at once yieldingly feminine and stiffly masculine, drawing d'Arnault's sexuality, by extension, way beyond the bounds of anything easily categorized, and it is this unbounded sexuality that perhaps accounts for the nervous tic of his body. But Jim, Ántonia, and the rest of his nonblack audience enjoy the spectacle of his playing "as if all the agreeable sensations possible to creatures of flesh and blood were heaped upon those black and white keys" without challenges to white authority, however relative it may be (183). Set in the context of his blackness, nativism surfaces as absurd: there are, Blind d'Arnault makes us see, more "foreign" bodies than those of the hired girls.

Although Blind d'Arnault is "the other against whom all the other others are juxtaposed and rendered equal," his appearance in Black Hawk also serves the additional function of setting in motion the "curious social situation" between the hired girls and the town's Anglos.[59] His impromptu performance in the town's hotel, during which the hired girls dance for the first time in the novel, directly precedes "the enthusiasm for the dance" created when the Italian Vannis arrive and set up their dance tent, the site of Black Hawk's "curious social situation" (209). As we saw in chapter 2, popular dancing (unlike fancy ball dancing) was linked in the American imagination both to a growing consumer culture and to anxieties about an erosion of boundaries between different genders, classes, and races. The Vannis are wise enough not to challenge these boundaries outright, but they are partly responsible for the "curious social situation" because it is in their dance tent that "the town boys" and "the country girls" are placed on what Jim calls "neutral ground" (197). Although respectable Anglo dance clubs are formed, Jim tells us that "the young men who belonged to the Progressive Euchre Club used to drop in late [to the Vannis' tent] and risk a tiff with their sweethearts and general condemnation for a waltz with 'the hired girls'" (192).

Although the novel clearly makes light of the seriousness with which Anglo Black Hawk views the "curious social situation," its effects on the hired girls differ according to their racial membership, and they are particularly harsh for Ántonia. It is at the Vannis' tent that she is "discovered" by Black Hawk's young men, and her "success" as a dancer has "its consequences" (198, 199). From this point on in the novel, Ántonia is repeatedly subject to a native-born/immigrant, Anglo/Bohemian, male/female double standard. Her "enthusiasm for the dance" results in her losing her job at the Harlings', and thus her nominal claim to respectability, and places her in Wick Cutter's grasp, which, in turn, precipitates her getting "fooled" by Larry Donovan and having to return to the family farm an unwed mother and once more her brother's "drudge." The threat of the hired girls is rendered "stupid" by the tramp and Blind d'Arnault, then, but the fact remains that Ántonia does get "fooled." So, too, did at least two of the three Bohemian Marys (196) and Mrs. Shimerda, a former servant in her husband's home whom, Ántonia tells Jim, Mr. Shimerda could have paid off instead of marrying (229). Female sexual vulnerability thus surfaces as a distinctly Bohemian trait.

It is this trait that forces the town's Anglo natives—especially Jim—to reevaluate their attitudes toward the hired girls' differences from themselves and from one another. This reevaluation is due to the fact that in the remaining three sections of *My Ántonia,* "A Pioneer Woman's Story," "Lena Lingard," and "Cuzak's Boys," we see that the northern European Lena Lingard—whose reputation in Black Hawk is worse than Ántonia's—doesn't get "fooled." The "curious social situation" and the sequence of chapters that lead to it result in a curious fragmentation of the hired girls, particularly Ántonia and Lena, which shifts the novel's focus once again from an exploration of the differences between European immigrant and Anglo-American womanhood to the contrast between Slav and Nordic womanhood. What Jim perceives to be Ántonia's restlessness in town, her fall from respectability, and her engagement to a man with an Irish name all point to her straying away from the expected, traditional life of a Bohemian woman. Ántonia redeems herself in Jim's eyes—and indeed in her own—only when she once again begins to embody the aspects of Bohemian life Cather most values: a marriage to another Bohemian followed by the raising of a large, energetic family according to values that blend American ways with those of the Old World.

By contrast, Lena, embodying the traits of a Nordic, fulfills her destiny by turning away from all that Ántonia finds most satisfying. Lena's ambitions, not unlike Alexandra Bergson's, are to achieve independence and economic self-sufficiency; as Edward Ross observed, "among the Scandinavians the spirit of improvement is very strong" (*Old World,* 76). Although Jim finds Lena's accomplishments all the more impressive because of her lowly origins, her New Woman, newly middle-class status gives her the same privileges. As Jim informs an old neighbor who scolds him for attempting to "compromise" Lena, "a girl who makes her own living can ask a college boy to supper without being talked about. We take some things for granted" (278). The same is not true, of course, before Lena becomes a financially independent, urban professional—indeed, as a hired girl she is so gossiped about that Ántonia fears being too closely associated with her. Lena's New Womanhood aligns her with many of the most valued qualities commonly associated with white racial identity, in particular its Nordic variety. She displays the individuality and open-mindedness said to define the so-called best whites (usually men); and like them, she relies on no one else to take care of her. She is, indeed, the definitive white American citizen: self-governing. Like the "best" whites, she works hard and takes responsibility for her family, and, like them, she is ambitious in her work but never greedy for excessive wealth or its gaudy display. In contrast to Ántonia, she also possesses (as Alexandra Bergson does) the ability to be practical in matters of the heart; when she and Jim discuss Ántonia's engagement to Larry Donovan, Lena remarks, "[S]ome of us could tell her things, but it wouldn't do any good. She'd always believe him. That's Ántonia's failure, you know" (260). Like Alexandra, Lena does not define her fate in terms of romantic relationships with men, opting instead for personal independence and professional success. Despite her (undeserved) reputation in Black Hawk as oversexed, and despite Jim's assumptions that she will eventually marry, Lena remains determined to live out the goals she sets for herself as a young girl. In this way, she does not really change throughout the course of the novel so much as others' perceptions of her do; early on, for example, we can see Lena's belief in personal sovereignty in the way she suggests to her brother to have her mother's initial and not "M" (for "mother") embroidered on the handkerchiefs he purchases as Christmas presents (166).

It is perhaps Lena's self-governing qualities, moreover, that explain why her move to town is the beginning of the achievement of her goals, while Ántonia's time in Black Hawk precipitates her fall from respectability. As Frances Donovan, a Chicago social worker, observed in 1919, the urban West held special significance for the farmer's-daughter-turned-New-Woman: "It is her frontier, and in it she is the pioneer."[60] Lena becomes more American by becoming less traditionally feminine, while Ántonia, at once more foreign and more traditional, moves in the opposite direction, a contrast Jim notes when he compares Lena's "American" speech to Ántonia's "impulsive and foreign" speech after she has had children, or that the novel does when it compares the "untiring interest" Lena shows in fashion to the hard work Ántonia puts into making her trousseau during her engagement to Donovan

(272–73, 270, 300).[61] Important to note in this regard is that Ántonia's "passionate" "Gypsy nature," praised by critics like Susan Rosowski, could also mark her and other Slav immigrants as unworthy citizens, just as the government's 1911 *Dictionary of Races or Peoples* did when it defined them as "inequable or changeable in mood and in effort—now exalted, now depressed, melancholy, and fatalistic."[62] For unlike Lena's steady desire to remain independent, Ántonia's goals frequently change because she is most often seen through her relationships with others—she is her father's darling and her brother's "drudge," the Harlings' Tony, Jim's Ántonia, the mother of Cuzak's boys. Debatable (perhaps endlessly so) is the extent to which Jim's point of view misrepresents Ántonia, but what is less ambiguous is that the sections of the novel themselves link Ántonia to others—to "The Shimerdas," "The Hired Girls," the pioneer past, and to "Cuzak's Boys"—while book 3, "Lena Lingard," names the northern European woman in such a way as to recognize her individuality.

Above all, Ántonia is a "natural-born mother," and as such she is destined to nurture rather than to directly participate in the future. Kathleen Conzen illustrates that pioneers like Ántonia who were steeped in traditional family structures were seen as "preserving for the nation its body of independent freedom-loving householders and, not coincidentally, preserving the West for the nation."[63] That Cather bestows this role on a Slav woman is significant indeed; for she uses the language of fragmentary whitenesses to refute those who linked this fragmentation to the capacity for democratic citizenship and hence to political rights, those, like Stoddard, who argued that "'America' means not only certain ideals and institutions but also a racial stock, which must be preserved if the ideals and institutions which that stock has created are to endure" (*Racial Realities,* 243). As Irving writes, in confining Ántonia's racial difference to "private habits and domestic practices only," Cather nullifies the charge made by Stoddard and others that immigration has "punitive political and economic effects."[64] Indeed, Ántonia's ultimate pride in her family and their ownership of the land proves her capability for citizenship (no matter what language she speaks) and, in a larger sense, the capacity for citizenship of new immigrants. This link between private property ownership and citizenship was, of course, part of the logic underpinning Native American removal, a logic reflected in the way the novel duplicates the removal west—to Nebraska—of Black Hawk, the dissident Native American whose tribe was located in Illinois. Chief Black Hawk was resistant to coexisting with white settlers and assimilating their values in large part because, like many of his people, he disagreed with the very concept of private property. So on the one hand, Ántonia's realized pioneer dream proves Black Hawk—both the Native chief and the nativist town—wrong, and thus proves her worthy of citizenship.

But Ántonia remains fixed by her racially inscribed, traditional femininity, and because she does so, she is constantly defined as someone else's (mostly Jim's) inspiration. As Jim tells her, "I'd have liked to have you for a sweetheart, or a wife, or my mother or my sister—anything that a woman can be to a man," and his lack of specificity serves to make Ántonia seem more like a myth (eternal woman) than a woman of flesh and blood (312). As a mythic mother Ántonia is meant to shape others: "It was no wonder," Jim observes, "that her sons stood tall and straight. She was a rich mine of life, like the founders of early races" (342). Nurturing her children on "the incommunicable past" that she shares with Jim, Ántonia seems to matter less as an individual than as a symbol, which perhaps explains why at the end of the novel Jim looks forward to seeing her boys and her husband in the future, but makes no mention of seeing Ántonia herself (360). So just as Cather draws upon the rhetoric of fragmented white races, as did the eugenicists, to refute both nativism and prejudice against new immigration, she likewise taps into the largely male-dominated mythos of a heroic pioneer past to place women squarely within it. In Cather's revisionist history, the new-immigrant woman becomes a testament to old-world retentions and to their importance to the pioneer past. And it is the novel's two New Women, Lena Lingard and Cather herself, who are most able to see Ántonia's value to regional history. "I owe it to Lena Lingard that I went to see Ántonia at last," Jim tells us (318). With characteristic open-mindedness, Lena is able to value Ántonia's choices even as they differ from her own: "I shouldn't care for a family of that size myself, but somehow it's just right for Tony" (319). Cather, Lena, and (with her help) Jim become linked with a future America that respects the past, while Ántonia becomes the past in need of memorialization. Melody Graulich asserts that the difficulty of enduring the West is commonly gendered female, while men's experiences of the region encapsulate a sense of unbounded freedom, of new possibilities.[65] For Cather, this opposition between endurance and freedom, as well as the opposition between being symbolic of the West's past and shaping its future, are instead manifested in the contrast between Bohemian and Nordic womanhood. On Cather's prairie, New Women from northern Europe both transcend and preserve the memory of new-immigrant women who enact traditional roles.

"American Progress" engraving by George A. Crofutt, c. 1873, after the painting by John Gast, 1872. Courtesy of the Library of Congress.

6
New Women and the World of Business

I. AMERICAN "PROGRESS"

John Gast's painting *American Progress,* reproduced widely in print form in the late nineteenth century, captures in microcosm many of the nation's deeply held beliefs about Manifest Destiny. Telling the story of a frontier dividing line between two worlds—one of which must make way for the other—the image is divided in half: on the left side, Indians and animals (including the paradigmatic buffalo) scurry toward the margins of the frame, fleeing in fear of the advance of trappers, cowboys, and homesteaders as well as the railroad and telegraph wire that follow in their wake. Evocative of the biblical creation myth, *American Progress* uses light to divide the worlds of the West before and during the establishment of "civilization." The shadowy landscape of the Native and the buffalo is dry and barren, while that of white settlement is fecund, irrigated, and filled with light, a "fortunate country," to use once again Cather's phrase from *O Pioneers!* Glorifying Indian conquest and the alteration of the natural environment in the name of "progress," the print also pays tribute to the pastoral, that stage between the existence of a wild, uncultivated landscape and the over-cultivated, exhausted one. Interestingly, the one extreme—that of an untouched landscape—that is visible in the print evokes the other extreme that is not, for the mountain peaks of the far West look something like the chimneys of factories, presumably the kind of eastern landscape the figures in the middle are attempting to leave behind. *American Progress* also lionizes the role of white women in the West, upholding the notion of them as civilizing agents that I discussed in the last chapter. The white female figure embodying America's Manifest Destiny defines the dividing line of the frontier; it is she who, godlike, brings light to the West, and thus it is she whom the Natives most fear. Wearing what a précis of a print version tells us is a "Star of Empire," she is "too much" for the Natives, one of whom throws up his arm to shield his eyes from the sight of her. An obvious metaphor for whites' construction of "civilization" and all that it entails (division and cultivation of land, literacy, technology), America's brightness comes not only from her imperial start but more so from her clothing and, especially, her skin color.

American Progress explicitly endorses the "legacy of conquest" about which Patricia Limerick and others have written and mythologizes white women's roles in such conquest, yet I want to argue that it is also possible to read this image ironically.[1] As the ambivalence of an untouched landscape being evocative of a polluted one suggests, some observers worried that the supposedly "new" region was being cultivated with the seeds of its own demise. We saw in the last chapter that some critics of the region worried about the effects of its racial diversity and its supposed lack of class boundaries, while many of the leading proponents of the West thought that the moving line of the frontier had forged, for these very reasons, a white American race distinct from and superior to what Edward Ross called its various "European parent stocks" (*Old World,* 24). The logic linking geographical movement to racial development begs a question I want to take up now: what happens to this new "race" once the movement stops? Given Frederick Jackson Turner's pivotal role in disseminating this logic, his frontier thesis, a lamentation of the "closing" of the frontier, can also be read for what it can tell us about the function the West was thought to assume in America's racial and social makeup. According to Turner and the like-minded, movement to a raw frontier destroyed the fixed class hierarchies that ruled Europe and the East, ushering in a new, superior white American race and the world's first democracy. Yet in its very novelty, the white race the frontier had supposedly spawned could be said to be in more danger of decline than its "parent stocks." As Barbara Will points out, Turner worried that the closing of the frontier would hinder white racial evolution, that the racial development of which he spoke would stagnate once the settlement process was complete and the pastoral moment had run its course.[2]

Further, many Americans began to voice serious reservations about what that process might mean for the rest of the nation, for the white American race that Turner and Ross praised for its freedom from class hierarchy was not necessarily free of class categorizations altogether. Instead, that "race" was overwhelmingly associated with a rising working class and the burgeoning corporate-based economy that supposedly had created it. While acknowledging that westerners are "rooted strongly in material prosperity" and that frontier conditions permitted "lax business honor," Turner was nonetheless rather defensive about the criticisms made of the region by outsiders. One such outsider whom Turner addressed in his writings was French political scientist Emile Boutmy, who in 1891 had claimed that America was "not so much a democracy as a huge commercial company for the discovery, cultivation, and capitalization of its enormous territory."[3] In "The Problem of the West," Turner admitted that westerners were primarily concerned with the "Titanic labor" of settlement and economic exploitation of the land, and that, as a result, they'd had had little time to devote to developing an artistic and cultural life in their region (211). For Turner, though, what they lacked was more than made up for by the fact that, as "the product[s] of . . . democratic conditions," westerners had "promoted equality . . . and reacted as a check to the aristocratic influences of the East" (226, 212). Turner's means of defense, then, was not so much to disagree with Boutmy as to justify the regional deficiencies he cited. But whether one was a critic of the region or its defender, the West was considered an "early staging ground for some of the central discursive mechanisms" of corporate and consumer capitalism, becoming the region most closely associated with what Woodrow Wilson in a 1911 speech called "the world of business."[4] For example, as the "first large corporate entities in America," the railroad companies that were so influential to western settlement also asserted great power over the form that settlement took.[5] Typical in this respect was the Burlington railroad, whose routes run through the Nebraskan towns of Cather's novels. Encouraging western settlement by advertising in the United States and Europe the sale of lands in Nebraska and elsewhere, the Burlington traded its transportation fees for homesteaders' future farm income, assuring its investment in the production of raw materials and using such economic influence to shape the region's politics.[6] This corporate dominance of the region—recall the claim of the railroad executive quoted earlier that the West was "purely a railroad enterprise" started in a publicity department—compromised the extent to which western life was free of class hierarchies. Yet despite evidence to the contrary, the myth remained that all westerners possessed a "relentless entrepreneurial drive," or, in the slang of day, "pep."[7]

This concern with having the "pep" to "get ahead" was seen as diametrically opposed to the attainment of culture, at least for those who defined culture as the "higher sphere of activity associated with class privilege and with the older Anglo-Saxon America."[8] In his acknowledgment of the region's cultural deficiency, Turner urged his fellow westerners to redirect their attention from accumulating wealth to nourishing the principles that made such accumulation possible: "It is to the realm of the spirit, to the domain of ideals and legislation, that we must look for Western influence upon democracy" (261). In *The Valley of Democracy* (1919), another western booster, Meredith Nicholson, echoed Turner in his recognition that "our preoccupations are mainly with the utilitarian," suggesting that the West's cultural contribution to the nation "will not be an efflorescence of literature or the fine arts," but a "perfected system of government that will assure the happiness, contentment, and peace of the great body of our citizenry."[9] Justifying the West's acquisitive values, Nicholson maintained that what he termed the region's "folksiness" constituted the largest advance in the nation's democratic experiment to date. But westerners' "folksiness" was problematic for those such as Randolph Bourne, who reviewed Nicholson's work in the essay "Mirror of the Middle West" and found the assertions Nicholson made in the book smug and self-satisfied. Bourne acknowledged that the region's claims to being the heart of the nation and synonymous with democracy were justified, but he also worried that westerners' "folksiness," their "genius for adaptability," placed "a premium on conformity" that made cultural advancement difficult.[10] The "warm social mixability" that democracy in the West had engendered, Bourne maintained, "goes so far to compensate for" westerners' "lack of intellectual nuances and spontaneous artistic sensibilities," but, he implied, not quite far enough (266). Concerned that the West made plain that "democracy may come to mean that the individual feels himself somehow expressed—his private tastes and intelligence—in whatever the crowd chooses to do," Bourne indicated that what made the region so impressive—its relatively swift establishment of uniformly thriving towns—also made it the most complacent and conformist (267).

In his review Bourne highlighted Nicholson's "enthusiasm . . . for the college-girl wife," a figure presumably common in the West who was the product of the educational, social, and political opportunities the region offered (267). When seen through the lens provided by Ross's and Turner's perspectives, such women were thought to represent the epitome of white femininity, but for those who doubted the frontier's ability to create a new race or who feared the effects that race might have on the rest of the nation, the "college-girl wife" was taken as a sign of the kind of dangerous uniformity that portended white racial degeneration. For the female figure at the center of *American Progress* could be interpreted as leading Americans away from their heritage as much as she is guiding them to their future. The "emancipated women" of the West, as Nicholson called them, enjoyed not only greater opportunities for political and social involvement in their communities, as I discussed in the last chapter, but they also benefited from less restrictive divorce laws than those of the East (38).[11] Traditionalists charged that such freedoms threatened both patriarchal prerogative and the fixed class status that was ostensibly required to maintain social and cultural stability. And it was here that the region's reputation for a lack of culture, on the one hand, and for "pep," on the other, had important ramifications for the construction of womanhood. No longer so removed from the "world of business," women, many feared, could now advance their own positions by parlaying business "pep" into the private realm, "getting ahead" by trading one man for another. As we shall see, depictions of western women often combined the characteristics of the New Woman—educated, active in the public realm, or at least no longer bound to the home—and the qualities most associated with capitalism, such as the "persistent drive toward accumulation" and the "inclination to repeated . . . change" for which the railroad companies also were known.[12]

As novels such as *A Lost Lady* (1923) indicate, Cather did not embrace the world of business as much as she did the world of immigrants in novels like *My Ántonia.* Her disdain for the former world was shared by Edith Wharton, who located in the region the same kinds of problems that Cather saw in the West after what she termed its "first cycle" had run its course. In their examinations of the world of business and "pep," both writers equate unscrupulous, newly wealthy businessmen with women who translate their traditional roles as guardians of culture into the new economic order. The alliance of these self-made men and women, both of whom value material greed and social conformity and often lack taste, foretell a less than glorious future for the West. And because for both Cather and Wharton the West represented American "progress," the sham culture it was creating threatened to subsume other, more valuable cultures such as those (for Cather) of the pioneers or (for both writers) of the East and Europe. This representation of the West reverses some of the basic assumptions we often make about regionalism, for certainly in neither author's characterizations of western "pep" can we say that a disempowered hinterland is being oppressed by the self-centered machinations of an urban, eastern elite. Quite the opposite, in fact, is true: it is just such an elite class that is being oppressed by westerners, as Cather, Wharton, and others imagined it. Thus Dale Bauer asks a question of Wharton's works that can also be asked of Cather's: "How does the culture [they] disparage . . . make explicit the changes in values [they], like many people, once associated with whiteness?"[13] In the case of both authors, this question can also be applied to their constructions of place, for the culture they disparage is unmistakably a culture of business that, following the bountiful crops, sprung up in the West. Employing the language of racial difference in order to undercut what they considered to be a dangerous homogeneity of class, Cather and Wharton examine how westerners, having conquered Natives and buffalo, turn their attention to other regional cultures they attempt both to duplicate and destroy.

II. HOW CATHER'S LADY GOT LOST

In her biography of Cather, Janis Stout illustrates how a regional opposition between the East and the West represents, in Cather's works, a more intangible conflict between "art and a philistine world," a conflict that is most pervasive in novels about the end of the pioneer era written after the war.[14] While the pioneers, as we have seen, respect differences in race, class, and culture, the prosperous townsfolk of the "consumerist orientated and homogenized" West, as Steven Trout remarks of Cather's *One of Ours,* stress conformity to the set of values associated with "pep."[15] I argued earlier that Cather critiques nativists like the residents of *My Ántonia*'s Black Hawk because they ignore immigrants' class status, and that for Cather herself the best members of a society are those who value gradations of taste and culture, not those, like the frontier settlers Turner praised or the prosperous townsfolk Nicholas did, who ignore them. In *A Lost Lady* Cather explores how the pioneers' social and economic control of the region is being usurped by Nicholas's townsfolk. This fact accounts for the comparison the novel makes between the Sweet Water of "thirty or forty years ago," when Captain Forrester and his wife, Marian, constitute recognized aristocracy, and the town of Ivy Peters, free of class distinctions and full of "pep."[16]

Marian herself functions to exemplify the changing symbolic roles that white women played, from civilizing agents to consumers, in the transition between the West of the pioneers and the West of the world of business. Endowed with "the power of suggesting things much lovelier than herself," Marian as an individual character matters less to the novel's contrast between the past and the present than her associations with others do, which is why the seedier aspects of her character (her drinking and her infidelity, for instance) that are present from the start fail to detract from the overall impression she makes on those around her (147). Symbolic of Sweet Water itself, Marian first personifies a town "of which great things were expected" and in which "two distinct social strata," the eastern "bankers and gentleman ranchers" and the workers, "there to make a living," coexist (8, 3).[17] When she brings cookies to a polyglot group of boys in the scene that opens the novel, each of them reacts to her, and she to them, in relation to their respective places in this social strata. For Niel Herbert and George Adams, she is "different from the other townswomen," Marian's inferiors in class and ethnicity (most are Irish) in ways that, as members of her own class, Niel and George can easily recognize (12). For the Blum brothers, sons of working-class German immigrants, she is "one of the rich and great of the world," part of a "fortunate and privileged class" they are content to regard "humbly," as the Germans were said to do (12–13).[18] So obvious is Marian Forrester's superiority that, the narrator tells us, many of the Irish townspeople, who are generally disdainful of class divisions, pay her due respect: "*even* rough little Thad Grimes . . . knew that Mrs. Forrester was a very special kind of person" (12; emphasis Cather's). The fact that Marian possesses the abilities to mark others' class and ethnic distinctions and to "easily and graciously [keep] everyone in his proper place" helps to explain why Niel repeatedly associates her with whiteness (131). Like Alexandra Bergson in *O Pioneers!,* Marian is often described as dressing in white, but unlike Alexandra's whiteness (recall the description quoted earlier of her "white mind"), Marian's seems extrinsic to her character, a point Cather's novel makes by having Niel remark that her complexion is not "one of her beauties" even as he describes it as having the "fragrant, crystalline whiteness of white lilacs" (11, 26). Later in the novel, as Marian comes to represent western "pep," her whiteness, as Niel sees it, wilts into "the ivory tint of gardenias that have just begun to fade" (94).

As a symbol of Sweet Water's democratization, Marian represents the shifting dynamics of white male authority over the town's economy as well as its social realm. At first Marian's beauty and charm are objective correlatives of her husband's power, partly derived from his position (he can "command" respect from his workers because he can "order them off his place, or dismiss them from his employ") and partly from his clear sense of noblesse oblige (102). So obvious is Captain Forrester's gentility to the working-class depositors of his bank, in fact, that they trust him to make compensations to them when the bank fails, and so natural is his status as an aristocrat that Cather can attribute humble origins to him. Part of a class of fortunate and deserving men who built "all our great West," the Captain is contrasted to unscrupulous men like Ivy Peters as well as to naturally unlucky ones "who get nothing in this world," an example of the American Dream meant to buttress a more fixed class system than that dream implies (44). Like his wife, Captain Forrester embodies Niel's nostalgia for "the road-making West" with an economy based upon entrepreneurship (144).[19] Conducted on a "paternal basis" with informal agreements made with the gentlemen who enjoy his wife's hospitality, Forrester's business practices must give way to a corporate system based upon up-front capital, formal contracts, and the use of lawyers like Ivy.[20] Just as Wharton's Old New Yorkers do, Cather's pioneers lose their economic and social influence because they cannot keep step with the business practices of a new era: "The Old West had been settled by dreamers, great-hearted adventurers who were unpractical to the point of magnificence; a courteous brotherhood, strong in attack but weak in defense, who could conquer but could not hold. Now all the vast territory they had won was to be at the mercy of men like Ivy Peters, who had never dared anything, never risked anything . . . The space, the colour, the princely carelessness of the pioneer they would destroy and cut up into profitable bits" (89–90). Captain Forrester's "princely carelessness" prompts him to return the bank depositors' money in full, rather than in part, as his younger partners do, and he loses most of his fortune. Despite the fact that their business success has made them "well thought of in the community," as Judge Pommeroy remarks, the other directors fail to "pay their losses like gentlemen" because, the Judge implies, they are not really gentlemen at all (77, 75). The fact that men like them possess a social status equal to Forrester and his cohorts, according to the Judge, robs white, upper-class status of its value: "In my day the difference between a business man and a scoundrel was bigger than the difference between a white man and a nigger" (76). Drawing on a logic similar to that which held that public rights would lead to "social equality" between blacks and whites in the South, Cather's work, as Tomoyuki Zettsu argues, transposes "the question of black-white boundaries" "into the rhetoric of class boundaries."[21]

Yet as its opening scene suggests, the novel also draws on a rhetoric of ethnic differences between whites, ones that Cather in large part celebrates in earlier novels but that, here, become symbolic of economic changes that threaten to destroy the cultural order established by the pioneers. In "this new business world that's coming up," as Judge Pommeroy calls it, Marian and Sweet Water are transformed from a wife and a town that confirm Captain Forrester's "princely carelessness" to a wife and a town through which the "lines of social demarcation are . . . obscure to the vanishing point" (Cather, *Lost Lady,* 56; Nicholson, 77). Ultimately, though, the contrast between Captain Forrester and Ivy Peters relies not so much on class, since both men build rather than inherit their money and position, but on internal characteristics, ones that in Ivy's case are linked to his being of Irish descent. We might wonder, for instance, how either the Captain or Ivy can "risk" anything when, presumably, they both start out by having little to risk. But here, as elsewhere in Cather's works, ambiguity is the purview of the culturally superior, for *A Lost Lady* attributes contradictory class markers to the Captain while keeping the qualities associated with working-class Irishness at the forefront of Ivy's character description even after he has made his money. Despite the trappings of respectability in which Ivy can increasingly afford to clothe himself, "a glance," as Niel tells Mr. Ogden, is sufficient to convince others of his essential baseness (130). Joseph Urgo argues that although we *know* Ivy is unscrupulous in his business dealings, we can't be sure the Captain is.[22] And we may even go further and say that the Captain's professional conduct, in comparison to Ivy's, is held up as an ideal, for instead of juxtaposing how both men gain wealth by taking land from Native Americans—although both do so—the novel compares how Ivy cheats Indians to how the Captain refuses to cheat his bank customers. Ivy's penchant for unscrupulous business practices is foreshadowed early in the novel not only by his violent streak but also by his unpleasant nickname, his unattractive appearance, and his singular disdain for the Forresters' position. Such traits draw on stereotypes of the Irish that we saw Glasgow employ in her description of Michael Akershem's followers in *The Descendant* and that Wharton uses in her characterization of Undine Spragg in *The Custom of the Country,* as we will see. In the works of all three authors, the Irish are often portrayed as "mushroom plutocrats," to use a phrase from Glasgow's *Life and Gabriella,* who lack taste, resent those who have it, and who attempt to push their way up by dirty dealing (160). Mere "stage-hands" in Marian's play, Ivy and his friends aspire to and destroy her gentility simultaneously (143). So, too, do the women to whom they are related, "the Mrs. Beasleys and the Molly Tuckers," who share Ivy's Irishness, his resentment of his betters, and his lack of cultivation (117). Described as insectlike in their conformity, these women descend on the Forrester home "like ants" who violate Marian's privacy simply to satisfy their own curiosity, gratified to find they can criticize a house they are supposed to admire: "the kitchen was inconvenient, the sink was smelly. The carpets were worn, the curtains faded, the clumsy, old-fashioned furniture they wouldn't have had for a gift, and the upstairs bedrooms were full of dust and cobwebs" (118).

The contrast between the Captain and Ivy, as well as the one between the Sweet Water of the pioneers and of the world of business, is reflected in the difference between the Marian we meet at the beginning of the novel and the character she later becomes. Merely disappointed—and temporarily at that—by Marian's liaisons with Frank Ellinger, Niel is exasperated by her increasing willingness to associate with Ivy, for "it was one thing to greet the president of the Colorado & Utah *en déshabille,* but it was another to chatter with a coarse-grained fellow like Ivy Peters in her wrapper and slippers, her sleeves rolled up and her throat bare to his cool, impudent eyes" (100). Marian justifies herself by claiming that she is simply fulfilling her duties as a genteel, cultivated white woman: "I've wanted for a long while to do something for the boys in this town . . . I hate to see them growing up like savages, when all they need is a civilized house to come to, and a woman to give them a few hints" (133). But it is clear that rather that lifting them up, she is pulled down by them. Once an agent of civilization who "easily and graciously" kept people in their places, Marian debases herself to a point at which none of her genteel acquaintances feel they can associate with her, her once-charming house becoming a place "where old friends . . . were betrayed and . . . where common fellows behaved after their kind and knew a common woman when they saw her" (146). In becoming a "common woman," Marian becomes increasingly synonymous with, rather than removed from, the world of business, accepting the fact that Ivy's professional "rascality" "succeeds faster than anything else" (106). Left to symbolize a dying era, Marian will come to regard her husband's code of ethics as foolish, advising Niel that "money is a very important thing. Realize that in the beginning; face it, and don't be ridiculous in the end, like so many of us" (96). Her refusal to "die with the pioneer period to which she belonged," to continue to symbolize a town that in reality no longer exists, suggests that Marian is lost long before she actually leaves Sweet Water and disappears from Niel's acquaintance (145). It is her removal from the town, in fact, that eventually allows Niel to remember his lost lady fondly, rather than with the resentment he feels toward her when he associates her with Ivy, whom he dislikes "blindly" and "instinctively" (89).

Niel's wish that Marian "die with the pioneer period" indicates his own inability to see her as anything but a symbol, his disregard of the fact that she must go on living beyond her husband's death and, in order to do so, must adjust herself to the economic conditions in which she lives. His instinctively antagonistic relationship with Ivy Peters suggests that Niel needs Marian to remain a static embodiment of the past in order to justify his own place in the present. Yet like Jim Burden and Lena Lingard in *My Ántonia*, Niel is a guardian of historical memory. So even as Cather employs him (as she employs Jim) to scrutinize the male gaze, she shares with both male narrators and with Lena an admiration for the West's "first cycle" and especially for the women in it. However much distance Cather places between the narrative and the authorial points of view in the novel, both she and Niel insist on telling "the splendid story of the pioneers," and both regret that that story has been replaced by one embroiled in the "new business world."[23]

III. WHARTON AND THE "LAND OF PANCAKES AND PANACEAS"

The "courteous brotherhood" of the pioneer era that Cather uses to critique the West's new business world is absent from Edith Wharton's comparative analysis of region, which is not to say she does not portray the West at all. Although scholarship on her has generally overlooked the fact, westerners are everywhere in Wharton's fiction, from the early novella *Sanctuary* (1902) to her final, incomplete novel, *The Buccaneers* (1938). Still, the only critic who has made Wharton's characterization of the region a central point of analysis is Frederick Hoffman, who in 1955 argued, "[T]he forces that, in [Wharton's] opinion, were destroying the society she respected seemed always to have come nakedly from the Midwest, where apparently all commercial drives, all cultural stupidity, existed in a pure, abstract form, waiting merely [for] the impetus to move them eastward."[24] Critics since Hoffman have expanded upon his observations regarding Wharton's critique of consumer culture, but they rarely place that critique geographically. Cynthia Griffin Wolff, for example, calls arrivistes like *The Custom of the Country*'s Undine Spragg "high-riding buccaneers" and "pioneers" with the energy of a "Western tornado," but she does not draw out the regional implications of these terms, while Elizabeth Ammons notes with little elaboration that the West both "alarmed and fascinated" Wharton. Similarly, Carol Wershoven remarks that the Midwest is "a vehicle for a considerable amount of satire" for Wharton, but, in general, that satire is treated only in passing or as being metaphorical for broader concerns.[25]

I think this scholarly omission exists in part because Wharton treats the West as a region that not only stands against regionalism but also seeks to destroy it. From *The House of Mirth* and *The Custom of the Country* to *Twilight Sleep* and *Hudson River Bracketed,* Wharton characterizes newly wealthy westerners as invaders who infiltrate and transform older, more coherent societies they fail to understand because, coming from a new region and changing their class status, they lack a cultural inheritance of their own. Their silly, unpleasant-sounding names (Abner Spragg, Elmer Moffatt), as well as the ridiculous names of the towns from which they hail—Exploit, Apex, and Euphoria, to name just a few obvious examples—announce an absence of taste and tradition.[26] Such names also indicate Wharton's hyperbolic treatment of what Kathleen Conzen identifies as the frontier's association with "a breed of restless wanderers, ever seeking elbow room or speculative profits over the next horizon," for her westerners do not care enough about any one place to name it well.[27] Wharton's western towns spring up overnight and just as quickly disappear because they are manifestations of the kinds of unethical business deals at which *Custom*'s Mr. Spragg and Elmer Moffatt excel rather than of organically developed local cultures. So pronounced is this aspect of western life in Wharton's works that natives of the region can almost not be considered natives, since they uniformly attach so little importance to home, local community, and ancestry. As *Custom*'s

Raymond de Chelles argues, Undine and Americans like her come from "hotels as big as towns, and from towns as flimsy as paper, where the streets haven't time to be named, and the buildings are demolished before they're dry," which, he also correctly asserts, means that his wife and her kind "are as proud of changing" as he and the French aristocracy are of maintaining tradition (341–42).

Yet this does not mean that Wharton's westerners possess nothing in common with one another, for unlike Meredith Nicholson, who insists that "one is struck by the remarkable individuality of the States, towns, and cities of the West," Wharton exaggerates the region's supposed uniformity, writing of an undifferentiated "West" that spans from Missouri to Minnesota and from California to Kansas without acknowledging much difference between them (15). In addition to a restless lack of loyalty to their homeland shared by characters of what Cecelia Tichi aptly calls the "Invader era," characters like Pauline Manford of *Twilight Sleep,* as we have already seen, consistently exhibit an openness to the latest fads, a susceptibility that led Nicholson, despite his praise of the region, to call the West a "land of pancakes and panaceas" (21).[28] Yet another shared characteristic, as the names of towns suggest, is westerners' mangling of language, or what the narrator of *The Custom of the Country* calls a "total inability to deal verbally with emotional crisis," an ineptness that elsewhere in the novel the narrator attributes to regional affiliation: "In the south, if you had a grudge against a man you tried to shoot him; in the West, you tried to do him a mean turn in business; but in neither region was the cut among the social weapons of offense" (276, 81). Even after her successful siege of New York and Paris, Undine often misconstrues what her aristocratic husbands say, although she is able to intuit Elmer Moffatt's meaning despite his inarticulateness because he "spoke her language" and "understood instinctively all the deep-seated wants" for which her "acquired vocabulary . . . had no terms" (336). As Candace Waid argues, this difference in language suggests that "the invaders have not only conquered a race; through their imitation of 'the speech of the conquered race' they have robbed language of meaning."[29]

What such characters lack in geographic fidelity and linguistic acumen, though, they more than make up for in a natural ability for wheeling and dealing, for like Cather's Ivy Peters, Mrs. Beasleys, and Molly Tuckers, Wharton's westerners are grasping members of a society that "joyously revolved about their central sun of gold" (121). Western men like Abner Spragg and Elmer Moffatt, both seemingly without a past or antecedents, amass large fortunes through shady business deals that translate a local environment to which they are strangers into a commodity. Western women, using their own "career" of marriage and divorce, turn themselves and other people into commodities, bringing "the excitement of the business deal into the drawing room" in what one *New York Times* article called a rage for American "Dollar Princesses."[30] Although she knows little about the world of business itself, Undine is motivated by the same sort of "business shrewdness" that makes her father successful, an instinct that endows her with the ability to end her marriage of the moment "like a business partnership" (222, 212). Having the same "patient skill with which her father had conducted the sale of his 'bad' real estate in the Pure Water Move days," Undine is apt at judging how and when to exchange one husband for the next, taking the same kind of risks, the narrator tells us, that men do who are successful in Wall Street (a region, as I argued in chapter 1, of strangers) (126). Even when Undine fails in her "bold move" of having an affair with Peter Van Degen, a move that might have led to a large payoff in the marital realm like "the happiest Wall Street 'stroke,'" she is still able to recuperate her hold on men and even capitalize on the failure, marrying de Chelles instead (229). Indeed, when she does not get what she wants, it is because she lets her emotions control her, as they do when her marriage to de Chelles begins to sour. As a "monstrously perfect" example of westerners' obsession with getting ahead at the expense of lasting personal ties, Undine lays "siege" to finer societies through marriage and divorce in the same way her father and Moffatt eat "salt" in the "enemy's tent" through business deals (131, 19, 164).

Sharing the regionalized distinction between "art and a philistine world" that Stout identifies in Cather's oeuvre, Wharton's depictions of the West highlight what she took to be the troubling social ramifications of the "world of business," a world that reverses the east-to-west movement of Manifest Destiny.[31] As novels such as *The Custom of the Country* suggest, Wharton likens this west-to-east movement of "the world of business" to an invasion of one race by another that is inferior to but more powerful than it, an assessment that echoes the eugenicists' anxiety about the threat posed by the supposedly lower races to Anglo-America. Like the reaction of the eugenicists to what they understood to be groups unfit for civic responsibility and the reaction of Niel to Ivy Peters, such a response underscores a fundamental incompatibility between westerners and easterners, "new" and "old" money, "mushroom plutocrats" and established elites. Despite the irreconcilable differences between them, Wharton imagines that westerners' "social mixability" leads to what amounts in *The Custom of the Country* to a combining of disparate populations through marriages conducted "like a business partnership," for "the daughters of his own race" sell "themselves to the Invaders" and "the daughters of the Invaders" buy "husbands as they bought an opera-box" (Bourne, "Mirror of the Middle West," 266; Wharton, *Custom,* 212, 50). Such groups may intermarry, in other words, but they remain largely incomprehensible to each other, as the novel illustrates in the contrast between Undine and Ralph's other love interest, Clare Van Degen. Although Clare has sold herself to the invaders, she ends up embracing the values of Old New York, as Ralph does after his own marriage, proving Elaine Showalter's point that "to cut your deal as a woman in Wharton's world and to emerge with dignity, it is necessary to be an aristocrat."[32] One means by which Wharton indicates the essential differences between westerners and Old New Yorkers is by making vague reference to Irish stereotypes in her description of characters like Undine, who shares with Glasgow's Mrs. Pletheridge an unsubtle and unrefined, even vulgar, beauty.[33] They also share with her and with Cather's Ivy Peters a simultaneous need to be accepted among the elite and a desire to destroy the lines that separate classes. As Jennie Kassanoff writes, *The Custom of the Country* "dramatizes America's racial dilemma" because Undine, "like the country whose initials she bears," is not "virgin wilderness" but a symbol of the nation's "contaminated costs of conquest and hybridity."[34] In Wharton's works the world of business is made up of both Jews like Rosedale and newly wealthy upstarts from the West with shady backgrounds (or no backgrounds at all) and unsavory ethnic affiliations.

Another way Wharton achieves this sense of innate regional distinction is by Ralph's likening of himself to the "vanishing denizens of the American continent doomed to rapid extinction with the advance of the invading race," a simile that is reiterated by the narrator of the novel as well as by the narrators of works such as *The Age of Innocence, The House of Mirth,* and *Twilight Sleep* (47). Ralph's analogy between Indians and Old New Yorkers, on the one hand, and the pioneers and "the new capitalist hegemony of speculators," on the other, underscores both the authenticity of Wharton's class and its doomed fate, as Christopher Gair has shown, much like *House*'s use of Rosedale's Jewishness does for Lily.[35] Ralph and Lily both meet their demise because they lack "pep" and possess scruples, both refusing to blackmail their enemies in order to secure their own survival. Because of his adherence to the code of professional and personal ethics that he has inherited, Ralph not only refuses to threaten Undine with the information sent to him by a Parisian private detective, but he also trusts Moffatt, Undine's coconspirator, to help him acquire the money he needs to pay Undine to keep their son, Paul, with him, a "hereditary failing" that leads him to commit suicide in the same sort of illness-induced haze in which Lily dies (274). As Tichi has written, while Undine is "totally self-interested," Ralph is her seeming opposite, "self-sacrificing to a fault" and to the death.[36] Like *A Lost Lady's* Niel, Ralph is a victim of his own adherence to an idealized vision of women, and like Lily, he is a victim of his own principles and others' lack thereof.

As Wharton's criticism of westerners suggests, one of the things that damn Old New Yorkers like Ralph and Lily is an assumption that the world of the home should be kept distinct from the world of business. In true western fashion, as Wharton understands it, Undine exchanges homes and geographies just as she does husbands, moving from an Apex home to an Apex hotel (believing that "fashionable people" live in hotels [11]), then to a midwestern lake area; a Virginian resort; Skog Harbor, Maine; New York; and finally to Paris. Hotels in Wharton's works often provide anonymity to those without elite origins and allow status to be determined by extrinsic makers of wealth—by the ability to reside in hotels—rather than by family or origin. The décor of the luxury hotels frequented by Undine and *The House of Mirth's* Mrs. Hatch, for instance, marked by "excesses of . . . upholstery" and "restless convolutions of . . . furniture," signify the worst in decorating taste as Wharton and Ogden Codman define it in their *Decoration of Houses* (*House of Mirth*, 212). Moreover, the excesses and convolutions apply equally well to these ladies themselves. While the narrator speculates that Mrs. Hatch must have "a real past," must be the product of "diversified contacts with the wholesome roughness of life," as a hotel dweller attempting to change her class status she possesses "no more real existence than a poet's shade in limbo" (213). Even more so than Mrs. Hatch, Undine's very physicality duplicates the décor of the luxurious hotel: her beauty, Wharton writes, is "as vivid, and almost as crude, as the brightness suffusing it" (*Custom*, 14–15). Where Mrs. Hatch's attempt to use her residence in hotels to lay marital siege to Old New York fails, Undine meets both of her aristocratic and unwitting husbands, Ralph and de Chelles, in hotels. In their inability to distinguish between public and private spaces, Undine and other westerners like Elmer Moffatt litter both their homes and hotel rooms, which don't look much different from one another, with an abundance of bric-a-brac, a decorating faux pas to which Wharton and Codman devote an entire chapter of their book. And while "privacy would seem to be one of the first requisites of civilized life," they write, "the planning and arrangement of the average house" displays "how little this need is recognized."[37] Wharton and Codman caution against making one's rooms visible to servants, for example, advising their readers to leave all doors of the home closed and to situate the fireplace away from view of the salon door. Inviting servants or merchants into one's salon, as Mrs. Spragg and Undine do, even when that salon is rented, thus constitutes both an invitation to invade one's privacy and a disregard for class boundaries. Just as hotels represent homes for now, families and communities forged by hotels represent kin for now. In having no past, no traditions, and no values, Undine and other westerners have no place, belonging, as Charles Bowen remarks, to "a phantom 'society,' with all the rules, smirks, gestures of its model, but evoked out of promiscuity and incoherence while the other had been the product of continuity and choice" (171). Here Bowen voices the argument that Wharton herself makes in *French Ways and Their Meaning* (1919) that while the American wife is a "parenthesis" to her husband, the European wife is "in the very middle of the picture" (*Custom,* 130). The differences between French society and that of the American West seem to stem not from the power women enjoy, but from the ways in which they are permitted to express it. Nicholson's observation that "young women seem everywhere to be in motion in the West" disturbed Wharton not necessarily because she was antifeminist, for if that were the case, she likewise would object to the position of authority assumed by French women like de Chelles's mother, who, unlike Undine, takes an intelligent interest in her son's agricultural plans for Saint Désert. The author's criticism has to do with the role she thought divorce played in increasing class fluidity, not with women's emancipation per se, for even as Wharton portrays Undine as more destructive than her father or Moffatt, as Jeanne Boydston has observed, she is so because she possesses the social equivalent of their finely honed business "pep."[38]

Thus while Wharton is not a "western writer" in the sense that Cather is, her interest in the region makes manifest the place-bound nature of her concerns about the democratization of culture in ways that function as important counterpoints to her portrayal of New York (and, for that matter, that of Europe). As I stated earlier, Wharton regrets "the sudden possession of money" among her fellow citizens because the newly wealthy lack "inherited obligations, or any traditional sense of solidarity between the classes," and what a comparative reading of region in her works reveals is that she overwhelmingly associates this phenomenon with the West, a fact suggested in her attributing to the vulgar "New American" a taste for "cowboys de chic."[39] The attempt Wharton makes in such comments to prove her own sophistication by assuming others' crassness is hardly rare; indeed, it might be said to be a national pastime. But her complaints about the taste of America's nouveau riche are inseparable from the oppositions between the East's culture and the West's democracy at work in Cather's novels as well as in Turner's and Nicholson's defenses of the region. When Wharton mourns, "all that I thought American in a true sense is gone, and I see nothing but vain-glory, crassness, and total ignorance," she is mourning a loss of cultural authority once possessed by the same Old New York and other genteel East Coast societies she at other times criticizes.[40] "You know how hard it is to make a good fire in a hearth from which all the ashes have been cleared away," Wharton tells Zona Gale in a 1927 letter, adding that "this is what America has done with all her great inheritance of culture and manners—and our fires do not burn long."[41]

Wharton's most extended treatment of how westerners stifle such cultural "fires" is in her late novels *Hudson River Bracketed* (1929) and its sequel, *The Gods Arrive* (1932), which follow a figure she characterizes as something of a contradiction in terms: the midwestern writer Advance Weston, whose first and last name both suggest his unsuitability for his chosen profession. Like Undine, Vance moves from place to place, going steadily eastward (from Pruneville, Nebraska; to Hallalujah, Missouri; Advance; and, most recently, to Euphoria, Illinois) and learning that "home" means only "a succession of new homes" that are "shells shed annually, almost, like a crab's."[42] "Ignorant of class distinctions" and "glad that no aristocratic blood clogged his own lively circulation," Vance's "pep" works against his yearnings to be a writer, and after two volumes of several hundred pages each, Wharton lets this tension stand (92, 51). Lacking, but striving to possess, taste, Vance symbolizes both the rawness and the promise of the western man as Frederick Jackson Turner described him, but while Turner emphasizes the promise, *Hudson River Bracketed* stresses the rawness. Taught that "success was the only criterion of beauty" and that "the real business of life was to keep going, to get there—and 'There' was where the money was, always and exclusively," Vance is even advised by another writer from his home region to "take up newspaper work" and "write pure manly stories about young fellows prospecting in the Yukon," Alaskan prospectors apparently being, according to Wharton, the new "cowboys de chic" (9–10, 15, 257). Dale Bauer rightly claims that both *Hudson River Bracketed* and *The Gods Arrive* are "animated by social questions about the abilities of working-class and uncultivated people" to "think beyond themselves," a situation Wharton found far more troubling in the West, where class boundaries, as we have seen, were thought by many to be "obscure to the vanishing point."[43]

As I discussed in regard to *Twilight Sleep*, critics have often found Wharton's later works to be too shrill in their satire, but in many ways her depiction of Vance's predicament is more sympathetic than her portrayal of Undine's situation, for Undine is incapable of the competing urges Vance feels between "art and a philistine world." In order for Vance even to half realize his potential as a writer, he must leave the West and travel east, where he is first introduced, through the Old New Yorker who becomes his lover,

Halo Tarrant, to the kind of authentic intellectual culture his grandmother, an untutored spiritual guru, can only poorly imitate. One of the things Vance first learns upon his arrival in New York is that his own culture is by definition imitative, and that easterners of all classes are far more settled in their long-established ways of life: "In the very part of his immense country which represented all that western wealth strove for and western ambition dreamed of, Vance found himself in a community apparently unaware that such strivings and ambitions existed" (42). Taught to display "'pep' and prosperity" through "almost annual turnovers in real estate, stocks, automobiles, wives and husbands," Vance is unprepared for the stability he encounters in the home of the Tracys, his poor eastern cousins, and he is especially ill-equipped for the refinement he encounters at the Willows, Halo's ancestral home (5).

Despite his "pep," something in Vance responds immediately to the atmosphere of the old estate, and it is only in such a milieu, and only with Halo's guidance, that he is able to write anything of value. But first he must struggle to assimilate something of Halo's taste and discrimination, a task at which he is only partially successful. It is Halo and her family who introduce the nomadic westerner to the very concepts of home, roots, and inheritance, which in turn expose Vance to the past apparently for the first time: as soon as he sees the Willows, Vance thinks, "Why wasn't I ever told about the Past before?" (59). Wharton's characterization of Vance's ignorance of the past makes plain that she would have found little to celebrate in Nicholson's boast that "if any one thing is quite definitely settled" among westerners, "it is that yesterday's leaves have been plucked from the calendar: this verily is the land of tomorrow" (20). In order to downplay their humble origins (the same ones that the Tracy family has maintained), westerners like Vance's parents and grandparents have had to promote the idea that the past has no bearing on the present, and in doing so they have also placed the future of the artist in serious jeopardy. Vance learns that the process of self-reinvention undertaken by his forefathers and foremothers necessitated a break with the past and its accumulation of knowledge, for unlike Upton Tracy and his sister, Laura Lou, whom Vance marries, Vance has been showered with every advantage—including a college education—his wealthy father can afford, but he nonetheless remains culturally illiterate in comparison to Halo: "the simplest things she said presupposed a familiarity with something or other he was ignorant of: allusions to people and books, associations of ideas, images and metaphors" (97). For this reason, Vance's talent may well be as impermanent as his hometowns have been: "The meagerness of his inherited experience, the way it had been torn off violently from everything which had gone before, again struck him with a pang of impoverishment.

On the Fourth of July, at Advance and then at Euphoria, the orators of the day (and Grandpa Scrimser foremost among them) had been much given to dilating of the priceless qualities the pioneers had brought with them into the wilderness. To Vance it sometimes seemed that they had left the rarest of all behind" (323). In preserving their inheritance, easterners like Halo actually end up being less provincial than Vance's rootless ancestors: "the language, the intonations, the allusions of Eaglewood did not belong particularly to Paul's Landing, were indeed hardly concerned with it, but embraced, though so lightly flitting, great areas extending not only to New York and beyond, but backward through this mysterious past which was so much newer to Vance than any present" (118).

Vance's novel "Instead" constitutes his only attempt to confront the past, to "see what we came out of" and to capture "that sense of continuity that we folks have missed out of our lives—out where I live, anyway" (325, 345). Although it is seen as a touch old-fashioned, much like, as Wharton characterized it, a local-color text, "Instead" is his only good novel, a fictional account of the Willows and of a Miss Lorburn, Halo's ancestor, who lived there. Because of the success of the invaders, even the New York cultural scene is now dominated by "cowboys de chic"—by literary periodicals named *Jerks and Jazzes* and novels titled *Egg-Omelette,* for instance—but despite that and despite his ambition, Vance finds himself "captivated" by his image of Miss Lorburn, a genteel "spinster" who spends her days with her extensive library (125). His vision of Alida Lorburn, a Jewett-like figure in her cultivation and independence, is motivated by an almost romantic "rhythm" that differs from that of writers working in the modernist vein, "a movement without jerks and breaks, flowing down from ever so far off in the hills, bearing the ships to sea" (345).[44] Such a movement, even he understands, requires an attention to particulars (such as the way a lady like Miss Lorburn might hold her handkerchief) that is characteristic of the self-consciously regional text. Yet unlike those regional works Wharton had faulted earlier in her career for being too "rose-coloured," "Instead" transcends the formulas of nineteenth-century regionalism because Halo insists that Vance refrain from making Miss Lorburn "a predestined old maid or a pious recluse" (344). Somehow, despite his obvious intellectual deficiencies, he is able to interpret a local culture to which he is a stranger and to make that culture resonate beyond geographical borders:

> Under his touch the familiar setting of the Willows became steeped in poetry. It was his embodiment of the Past: that strange and over-

> whelming element had entered into his imagination in the guise of these funny turrets and balconies, turgid upholsteries and dangling crystals. Suddenly lifted out of a boundless contiguity of Euphorias, his mind struck root deep down in accumulated layers of experience, in centuries of struggle, passion, and aspiration—so that his absurd house, the joke of Halo's childhood, was to him the very emblem of man's long effort, was Chartres, the Parthenon, the Pyramids. (338)

For much of *Hudson River Bracketed* and its sequel, though, Vance rejects the guidance of the culturally superior Halo, and in *The Gods Arrive* he betrays her for a western woman named Floss Delany. Like *Twilight Sleep*'s Dexter Manford, another westerner, Vance lacks control over his emotions and his sexual impulses, and these, combined with his western "pep," make him increasingly dismiss the value of Halo's intellectual and social credentials and embrace the "boundless contiguity of Euphorias" and the world of business through Floss, a successful real-estate speculator. Despite his claims of being dedicated to his art and removed from commerce, he finds Floss's fascination with wheeling and dealing and her indifference to all but business matters (including her indifference to himself) "exasperating and yet mysteriously stimulating."[45] Having completed "Instead" under Halo's guidance, Vance undertakes a novel about modern New York called "Loot," his wish to "see what we came out of" being overcome by his instinct to explore the process of getting ahead. Even the marks of his intellectual progress suggest his ultimate failure to fully assimilate Halo's values: while she remains loyal to her flighty family members both out of pride and sincere attachment, Vance becomes increasingly detached from his, justifying "how far he had traveled from Mapledale Avenue" by convincing himself that, as an artist, he is above the demands made upon him by others (478, 485). What he does not understand, of course, is that as much as he rejects his family members as individuals, it is entirely in keeping with their values for him to detach himself from his origins, and with the values of his region to move to New York to do so.

From the beginning of *Hudson* to the end of *Gods,* Vance remains an unsettled and unsettling mix of "instability and power," an artist whose paucity of inherited resources suggests a dim future for the American cultural scene (270). In leaving "the rarest of all behind" (*Hudson River Bracketed,* 323), the "pioneers" of Wharton's works produce a culture that destroys what she considered to be "American in a true sense"(quoted in Lewis, *Edith Wharton,* 424). Fearful, to paraphrase a title of one of Cather's essays, that the restlessness associated with the region did not make for beauty, both Wharton and Cather imagine the West as increasingly destroying the cultivation and stability they found in the admirable, if quaint, local societies of America's pastoral past. In its supposed absence of boundaries of all sorts, the West made all too clear the dangers to art and culture that supposedly existed in America's "progress."

Conclusion

"Always, Everywhere, Inferior": Regionalism as/and Minority Status

The price the white American paid for his ticket was to become white—: and, in the main, nothing more than that, or, as he was to insist, nothing less. This incredibly limited not to say dimwitted ambition has choked many a human being to death here: and this, I contend, is because the white American has never accepted the real reasons for his journey. I know very well that my ancestors had no desire to come to this place: but neither did the ancestors of the people who became white and who require of my captivity a song.

—James Baldwin, "The Price of the Ticket" (1985)

Throughout my examination of works by Cather, Glasgow, and Wharton, I have tried to show how these writers use regionalism, an accepted form of women's literary production, to explore and comment upon the changes they witnessed in social constructions of citizenship at the turn of the twentieth century. And I have argued that in order to do so, these women revised the ways in which regions were portrayed, disavowing any affiliation between their works and earlier regionalism and highlighting regional comparison and conflict in the process.[1] In closing, I would like to return briefly to a point I made at the beginning of my discussion: that the attractiveness of regionalism to white women writers like Wharton, Glasgow, and Cather partly lies in its being geographically equivalent to their own social position and to the social positions of their characters. Despite being marginalized, white women are considered members of a larger, national "imagined community," to use Benedict Anderson's phrase, just as regions themselves are.[2] The three women writers I've discussed in this study all employ multiple regional settings to explore their own marginalization and to claim their authority to speak on the marginalization of others, and their perspectives contributed to debates about democracy that were fundamental in shaping American culture in the first half of the twentieth century. Those debates are critical to the ongoing scholarly discussions concerning the supposedly progressive or retrograde nature of women's regional writing. As Fetterley and Pryse write, it is important to consider "how and whether race emerges as a concern within a movement defined primarily by gender" and "whether 'white' itself constitutes a racial marking in regionalism," which, I have argued, it does inescapably.[3] Indeed, in the final analysis, what my examination of women's regionalism suggests is that it is a literary mode that is more comfortable and fitting for white women than for writers of other oppressed groups. While Fetterley and Pryse, covering an earlier set of regionalists, conclude that "regionalism becomes a site where questions of race and questions of gender find mutual and dynamic articulation for both white writers and writers of color," my own comparisons between Glasgow, Wharton, and Cather and other writers reveal that such mutuality only goes so far.[4] The marginalization of white women shares several characteristics with that of other groups, but there exists one important difference between white women, on the one hand, and, on the other, men and women of racial and ethnic minorities (however racial and ethnic differences are defined in a given historical moment) that is critical to regionalism: at no time in the history of American patriarchy have white women been considered outsiders (or strangers, in regionalist parlance) in the same ways immigrants and people of color have.

For instance, Lily Bart, like many women characters I have discussed, longs for spatial transcendence and repeatedly attempts to leave New York for Europe, first by her brief engagement to a European and later in her sojourn there after being ejected from Bertha's yacht. Figuratively and literally homeless throughout *The House of Mirth,* Lily lacks the authority to control her place in her society. But her search for spatial and communal alternatives to New York—in Europe and among figures such as Selden, Gerty, and the Gormers—never negates her status as a New Yorker, even as she vacillates in her loyalties to her community. Likewise, Ellen Olenska's inability to live in New York (because it is too near Archer) is the surest indication that despite her exile she is an insider. For in making the sacrifice to leave Archer and New York and in refusing to return to the morally shady region occupied by her husband, as her New York relations would have her do, Ellen proves herself to be very much a New Yorker and an American, as M. Rivière discovers. These and other New York women, like Halo Tarrant, stand in sharp contrast to western women like Pauline Manford and Undine Spragg, who are incapable of finding their place. Dead or alive, in New York or elsewhere, Wharton's New York women have a place whether other natives, like May, or invaders, like Rosedale, recognize it or not. Recall Vance Weston's observation about Halo Tarrant and her family in *Hudson River Bracketed*: upper-class New Yorkers have a communal identity that allows them to transcend a myopic, limiting affiliation with only one place. But as much as Wharton praises cosmopolitanism, she also understands the importance of belongingness, and mocks characters such as Archer who think they can forgo regional affiliation. When, toward the end of *Age of Innocence,* Archer asks Ellen to leave New York with him and go to a place "where we shall be simply two human beings who love each other," Ellen articulates Wharton's central theme concerning communal identity: "Oh, my dear—where is that country? Have you ever been there? . . . I know so many who've tried to find it; and believe me, they all got out by mistake at wayside stations . . . and it wasn't at all different from the old world they'd left, but only rather smaller and dingier and more promiscuous" (293). While Wharton valorizes exile, it is an exile that proves one's native status.

Like so many female characters in turn-of-the-century southern writing, Glasgow's Dorinda Oakley spends her youth looking past home, which represents to her a kind of stagnation mired in the past. Alternatively, works like *Virginia* show what it meant for white women to remain stuck in both time and place, for the title character lacks that racialized "vein of iron" needed to develop the New South. Like Wharton, Glasgow locates an idealized cosmopolitanism in the best manifestations of regional identity, but both writers also locate it in a healthy balancing of past and present notions of that identity.[5] Glasgow's women usually return to the homeplace and redeem their family history, as Dorinda does with Old Farm, or succeed in establishing roots elsewhere, as her transplanted Virginians do in New York. Being a certain kind of southerner, like being a certain kind of New Yorker, assures that one can be at home wherever one may roam. Even the most homeless Glasgow characters—those of *In This Our Life*—eventually find themselves a home. Though Asa and Roy have lost forever the ancestral home (which is actually being destroyed at the beginning of the novel), both find an alternative one, in *Beyond Defeat,* at Kate's farm. By contrast—and it is a contrast of which Glasgow, despite regional stereotypes about white southerners necessarily upholding white supremacy, seems aware—Parry Clay cannot feel at home in the South, even among blood relatives, simply because he is an African American man. While Minerva begins the novel believing that her son would be happier if only he kept to his place, circumscribed as it is, Stanley's and the other Timberlakes' use of their racial privilege proves that no matter how humble or assertive African Americans are, there is no safe place for them in the Jim Crow South.

Indeed, while characters like Parry as well as Tap and Nancy of Cather's *Sapphira* experience their regional home as a place of danger, where the threat of actual violence looms large, Cather's immigrants to the midwestern prairie are able to make a new home even if that home gestures to another left behind. As if to refute the critics of immigration who charged that immigrants, having left one home, lack the ability to form ties altogether, Cather's characters harmoniously balance the ways of the old country and the new. Once they find their places—whether as a farm wife and mother or a New Woman in a city—they tend to stay in them. These immigrants are distinct from the largely Irish, working- and middle-class natives of Cather's settled West who, like Wharton's westerners, cannot conceive of home and therefore end up destroying regional distinctiveness. If characters like Blind d'Arnault establish the native status of characters like Ántonia (just as Nancy establishes Cather's southernness in *Sapphira*), characters like Ivy Peters, born and raised in one town, are repeatedly described as being out of place. Such native outsiders can only destroy the good that newcomers do to the regional environment and culture, just as Ivy drains the Captain's marsh and just as "the Mrs. Beasleys and the Molly Tuckers" destroy the graceful way of life in Sweet Water that Marian had once symbolized.

All three writers, then, uphold certain values and valorize certain kinds of characters by aligning both with a particular region and with membership in a place-specific but cosmopolitan community. Often, white women utilize regionalism to assert their status as natives (to varying conservative or progressive ends), whereas writers of color approach regionalism as strangers. For instance, critics such as Robert Russ and Roger Rosenblatt have located a "perpetual homelessness" and an attendant quest for belongingness in African American literature,[6] and we see this at work in all of the African American novels I have discussed here. Russ shows how *Home to Harlem* is more about homelessness than belonging, as none of the main characters are from Harlem and none end up staying there, and this characteristic is one that McKay's novel shares with many other works of the Harlem Renaissance, including Nella Larsen's *Passing*. While Irene appears to be almost too settled in her place in Harlem society, she is a Chicago native (as is Clare) who is motivated chiefly by fears that her place will be usurped. That sense of safety she longs for and that is perpetually just out of reach is the safety of knowing that she cannot be displaced. While she shares this longing with Lily, for instance, Wharton insists that Lily, in a way Larsen does not of Irene, belongs even as others succeed in effecting her exile. Similarly, the African American characters in *The Marrow of Tradition* struggle to claim their place in the South. Some, like Watson, leave Wellington during the riot, giving up the hope that they might belong to the community, while others, like Josh Green, maintain that they belong to the death. Watson understandably lacks regional loyalty, while Josh manages to possess an abundance of it only by insistently redefining the terms by which community is understood. For unlike Watson and, until the end of the novel, the Millers, Josh emphasizes membership in a racial community (regardless of class differences) rather than in an interracial, regional one. Indeed, Josh manifests his fitness for citizenship by refusing to let McBane and others displace him, by literally, vehemently standing his ground. Of course, Chesnutt does not fail to note that Josh's efforts end in his death, thus acknowledging how fraught with complications being rooted in place can be for racial and ethnic minorities.

Being so rooted often is fraught with complications for immigrant groups too. In Cahan's work, for instance, David associates women both with his memories of the Old World (in the form of his mother, whom he continually chides himself for failing to honor) and with the new, in the "fascinatingly American" women to whom he ardently but only temporarily attaches himself. For David, then, women are equated with geographical belonging, so it is significant, that despite his frequent lamentations that he is lonely, he never manages to form lasting ties to a woman. Rather, he seems to excel at sabotaging the very relationships he thinks will help him finally settle and find his place. Roaming from one woman to another, David likewise roams from one home to another, a wandering drummer even after his success frees him from having to make sales calls himself. Unlike the immigrants in Cather's work, whose immigration precedes their being rooted in place, David reenacts his initial journey over and over again. While Rölvaag's immigrants resemble Cather's in their rootedness, Peder Holm shares with David Levinsky the sense of belonging to two worlds, and therefore to no particular place. Peder imagines that he can contribute to his family's newly adopted home by getting involved in local politics, and despite the narrator's criticisms of him, the novel does not question the sincerity of his commitment to the public good. Peder's political ambitions are dashed, however, when Susie, his wife, betrays him in order to help her own people advance themselves in the election Peder hopes to win, an ironic conclusion that suggests that Peder's wish for an interethnic civic community cannot be fulfilled because competition between immigrant groups for local clout is too intense.

As these works suggest, the writing of region can be approached from a variety of vantage points, and oftentimes writers of racial and ethnic minorities have been compelled to write of the region from the outside, looking in. James Baldwin's remarks quoted above make this last point brilliantly: using metaphors of traveling and arrival, Baldwin defines racial privilege in terms of spatial belonging, wherein who journeyed here and why has been lost in a false sense of which of us belong and which of us do not. Thus in another essay Baldwin writes that his own people and other groups oppressed on the basis of race are forced into displacement: they are "always, everywhere inferior" to those who feel that only they belong.[7] What Baldwin's comments suggest is that the ability to claim a regional identity, to belong to a local culture, is often to presuppose one's identity as an American. In this way, claiming a regional identification can be a mark of one's racial privilege. Just as the category of "American" has often taken for granted a particular racial identification, so, too, have regional categories like "southerner" or "westerner." To define who belongs to a place or a community, after all, is also to define who does not. Regions thus represent the shifting dynamics of national identity, and in doing so, they constitute important spaces that allow us to scrutinize the extent to which it is possible, and to which it is not, to transcend, to reach beyond, one's own group.

Notes

INTRODUCTION

1. Quoted in Bentley, "Hunting for the Real," 64.

2. Quoted in Harvey, *Redefining the American Dream,* 7.

3. Fairweather, "Inclusive and Exclusive Pastoral," 278.

4. Wharton, *Backward Glance,* 7, 21. Subsequent references will be cited parenthetically in the text.

5. Wharton, *Age of Innocence,* 88.

6. Glasgow, *Woman Within,* 217. Subsequent references will be cited parenthetically in the text. All three writers date the transformation of upper-class status based on birth to that based on wealth in the turn-of-the-century period rather than in the post–Civil War era, even though that is when the very changes of which they speak began to take hold. As Richard Brodhead notes, the upper class of the postbellum years "was not an already integrated 'group' but a group in the process of self-grouping, a coming-together of elements with a common need to identify themselves as superior" (*Cultures of Letters,* 123). The tone of gentle mockery they take to the nineteenth-century elite's complaints of being infiltrated by outsiders makes plain just how powerful these writers thought the social changes of modernity to be.

7. Cather, "Nebraska: The End of the First Cycle," 2, 3, 7. Subsequent references will be cited parenthetically in the text.

8. Cather, *Willa Cather in Person,* 72.

9. Grammer, *Pastoral and Politics,* 11.

10. R. Williams, *Country and the City,* 77.

11. Cather, *Willa Cather on Writing,* 24.

12. Trachtenberg, *Incorporation of America,* 147.

13. Wharton, *Letters,* 99.

14. Ibid., 424.

15. Glasgow, *Life and Gabriella,* 480.

16. Cather, *Willa Cather in Person,* 157, 167. This association of the novel with modern American democracy explains why I have chosen to focus on that genre rather than the considerable amount of short fiction and poetry also produced by these three writers.

17. Bauer, *Edith Wharton's Brave New Politics,* 124.

18. Adams, *Epic of America,* 415.

19. Following Jacobson's *Whiteness of a Different Color,* I use the term "race" to refer to groups now seen as "white" and "racial difference" to distinguish Europeans from one another as well as from non-Europeans. As Jacobson writes, contemporary scholarship has "conflated race and color, and so has transported a late-twentieth-century understanding of 'difference' into a period whose inhabitants recognized biologically based 'races' rather than culturally based 'ethnicities'" (6). When terms such as "race or ethnicity" are used, they are meant to reflect the ambiguity that racial classification—especially whiteness—engendered.

20. Kallen, *Culture and Democracy,* 43.

21. Stoddard, *Racial Realities,* 112.

22. Stoddard, *Rising Tide,* 264.

23. Grant, introduction to Stoddard's *Rising Tide,* ix.

24. Gossett, *Race,* 136. See Wendell's *Literary History of America* and *Barrett Wendell and His Letters.*

25. Pimple, "Edith Wharton's 'Inscrutable Totem Terrors,'" 140–41.

26. Quoted in Painter, *Standing at Armageddon,* 152.

27. Turner, *Frontier in American History,* 266.

28. Such positions, of course, could uphold racial privilege by subscribing to the notion that ethnic or racial others, whose cultures might indeed infuse Anglos with the antidotes for advanced civilization, were lower on the evolutionary scale, a position most notable in the twenties craze for the "primitive."

29. Kallen, *Culture and Democracy,* 11.

30. Ibid., 43. Note that Kallen associated racial and ethnic diversity with individuality rather than with groupthink, as many other Americans of his time did.

31. Bourne, "Trans-National America," 249.

32. Ibid., 250.

33. Du Bois, *Souls of Black Folk,* 162.

34. Wendell, *Literary History,* 502.

35. Bourne, "Trans-National America," 253.

36. Kallen, *Culture and Democracy,* 97.

37. Frost, *Never One Nation*; see especially chapters 1, 4, and 5.

38. Cather, *Willa Cather on Writing,* 92–93.

39. Wharton, *Letters,* 54, 91.

40. Campbell, *Resisting Regionalism,* 149.

41. In her introduction to *Ethan Frome,* Wharton accuses writers who came before her of creating a New England that "bore little—except a vague botanical and dialectical—resemblance to the harsh and beautiful land as I had seen it" (i).

42. Cather, *Not Under Forty,* 85, 84. Subsequent references will be cited parenthetically in the text.

43. Cather's most obvious way of suggesting that Jewett's work is both great (for what it is) and limited arises in her comparison between Jewett and Henry James, "the commanding figure in American letters" at the time Jewett was writing; this comparison, in fact, seems reinforced by Cather's frequent quoting of James's opinions of Jewett and her work (*Not Under Forty,* 91).

44. Inness and Royer, eds., Introduction, *Breaking Boundaries,* 2, 7.

45. Foote, *Regional Fictions,* 19.

46. Zagarell, "Troubling Regionalism," 645, 649.

47. Glazener, *Reading for Realism,* 116.

48. Stokes, *Color of Sex,* 13.

49. Newman, *White Women's Rights,* 19–20. Sometimes this meant claiming their own rights through reform work (most notably in settlement houses) on behalf of other oppressed groups; often it meant directly pitting themselves as white women against class or racial others, a staple strategy of some of the most well-known suffrage activists of the day. At other times white women tried, with varying degrees of success, to divorce the causes they espoused from racial and class issues, insisting they had no official opinion on such matters. Another strategy involved making oblique references to racialism. Francis Willard's temperance phrase "a white life for two," for example, drew upon associations of whiteness with respectability and cleanliness.

50. In their most recent work on women's regional writing, *Writing Out of Place,* Judith Fetterley and Marjorie Pryse maintain that "the extent to which race emerges as a concern within a tradition defined primarily by gender and the degree to which gender as a category of analysis facilitates or obstructs a critique of hierarchies based on race has led us to complicate our understanding of the interweaving of gender and race in the discourse of region and nation" (26). Yet they nonetheless continue to assert that "regionalism engages in white and male critique as a critique of nation" (28–29), and that regionalist writers "set up conditions for empathy to cross lines of race, class, gender, and region" (281). See also Kaplan, "Nation, Region, Empire," and Brodhead, *Cultures of Letters.* Other treatments of regionalism that complicate feminist critical analyses such as those of Fetterley and Pryse include Campbell, *Resisting Regionalism*; Foote, *Regional Fictions*; Zagarell, "Troubling Regionalism"; Robison, "'Why Do We Not Write Our Side?'"; and Glazener, *Reading for Realism.*

51. This is true except when the writer portraying a particular city is part of a racial or ethnic minority. Hence for Fetterley and Pryse, Wharton is not a regionalist of New York, but Anzia Yezierska is.

52. Bentley, "Wharton, Travel, and Modernity," 149.

53. Donaldson, *Decolonizing Feminisms,* 6.

54. As David Martin ("'Regionalist Fiction'") has shown, regional writing manifests many of the same concerns as ethnography in that it elucidates the rituals, customs, and everyday life of societies associated with a specific geography. This same kind of ethnographic vision, as Bentley's *Ethnography of Manners* illustrates, is at the heart of Wharton's creation of elite New York. It is also at the heart of Glasgow's South (hence her claim of having written a "social history" of Virginia) and of Cather's West.

CHAPTER 1

1. "Rich and Poor Marched Together," 7.

2. The *New York Times'* claim that Glasgow attended the march cannot be substantiated by any statements Glasgow herself made, according to Pamela R. Matthews, Glasgow's biographer (personal communication). For Glasgow's statements on New York's influence on her work, see *A Certain Measure.*

3. Yezierska, "The Lost 'Beautifulness,'" in *How I Found America,* 32.

4. Glasgow, *Life and Gabriella,* 426–27, 490. Subsequent references will be cited parenthetically in the text.

5. Quoted in Benstock, *No Gifts from Chance,* 34.

6. Wharton, *Letters,* 84.

7. Wharton, *Age of Innocence,* 20; *House of Mirth,* 248. Subsequent references to both novels will be cited parenthetically in the text.

8. Kaplan, *Social Construction of American Realism,* 102.

9. Le Bon, *The Crowd,* v. Subsequent references will be cited parenthetically in the text.

10. Burrows and Wallace, *Gotham,* 737, 1114; Lankevich, *American Metropolis,* 122.

11. Burrows and Wallace, *Gotham,* 790.

12. Taylor, *In Pursuit of Gotham,* 35.

13. Burrows and Wallace, *Gotham,* 691.

14. Quoted in Taylor, *In Pursuit of Gotham,* 111.

15. Ewen, *Immigrant Women,* 24.

16. Taylor, *In Pursuit of Gotham,* xvi.

17. Ibid., 25.

18. Quoted in Burrows and Wallace, *Gotham,* 695; James Baldwin, *Another Country,* 570.

19. Quoted in Burrows and Wallace, *Gotham,* 1083.

20. Burrows and Wallace, *Gotham,* 1087. It is an unfortunate irony that Seligman was tutored by Horatio Alger Jr., the juvenile novelist and promoter of the American Dream.

21. Bentley, *Ethnography of Manners,* and "Hunting for the Real," 47–67.

22. Glasgow, *Virginia,* 303. Subsequent references will be cited parenthetically in the text.

23. Thiébaux, *Ellen Glasgow,* 7.
24. Cahan, *Rise of David Levinsky,* 355.
25. Campbell, *Resisting Regionalism,* 54.
26. Fetterley and Pryse, *Writing Out of Place,* 28.
27. Glasgow, *Descendant,* 17. Subsequent references will be cited parenthetically in the text.
28. Thiébaux, *Ellen Glasgow,* 36.
29. Saks, "Representing Miscegenation Law," 63.
30. Bentley, *Ethnography,* 12.
31. Campbell, *Resisting Regionalism,* 77.
32. Riis, *How the Other Half Lives,* 61, 13.
33. Jacobson, *Whiteness of a Different Color,* 174.
34. Morrison, *Playing in the Dark,* 67.
35. Peiss, "'Charity Girls,'" 159.
36. Riegel, "Rosedale and Anti-Semitism," 222.
37. See especially Grant's 1921 edition of *The Passing of the Great Race.*
38. Erenberg, *Steppin' Out,* 10.
39. Hoeller, "'The Impossible Rosedale,'" 15.
40. Erenberg, *Steppin' Out,* 34. For further discussion of Wharton's use of hotels, see chapter 6.
41. Gair, "Crumbling Structure of 'Appearances,'" 366.
42. I should note here that some critics, J. R. Raper among them, have speculated that Michael is Jewish; both his proper name and his nickname (Shem) hint this. I have chosen not to focus on Michael's possible Jewishness because he is primarily defined, I think, as a mix of classes. I have also not pursued this line of analysis because those who do so claim that Michael is Jewish by his father, assuming that his father belongs to a much lower class than the novel seems to suggest. See Raper's *Without Shelter.*
43. Bederman, *Manliness and Civilization,* 93. Pairings of an adult other and a white child are common at this time, as I discuss in chapter 3. The anthropological language of the day (primitives as evolutionary children) as well as the upbringing of upper-class whites (i.e., Wharton's relationship with her nurse, "Doyley," and Glasgow's with her black mammy) both contribute to this image's frequency.
44. Kassanoff, "Extinction," 62.
45. Ammons, "Edith Wharton and the Issue of Race," 80.
46. Kassanoff, "Extinction," 61.
47. Ammons, "Edith Wharton and the Issue of Race," 79.
48. Campbell, *Resisting Regionalism,* 9.
49. Wharton, *Custom of the Country,* 50. Subsequent references will be cited parenthetically in the text.
50. Wharton, *Backward Glance,* 7. On Wall Street as a region of strangers, see also chapter 6.
51. Cahan, *Rise of David Levinsky,* 443, 33.

52. Burrows and Wallace, *Gotham,* 783.

53. Glasgow, *Certain Measure,* 100.

54. Ibid., 102.

55. Bederman, *Manliness and Civilization,* 26. This argument was common enough to generate multiple responses by feminist activists of the day. Charlotte Perkins Gilman's *Women and Economics,* for example, takes the correspondence between civilization and gender differentiation directly to task. In Gilman's revision of social evolution theory, gender differentiation is a necessary step to a race's becoming "civilized," but one that must be transcended to further advance.

56. Thiébaux, *Ellen Glasgow,* 116. Glasgow herself thought that Gabriella's choice to marry O'Hara would be construed by her contemporaries as a radical one; as she humorously recounts in *A Certain Measure,* her more traditionally minded friend James Lane Allen asked her, "Would any Southern lady have so far forgotten herself as to run after a wild Irishman?" (101).

CHAPTER 2

1. Quoted in Bauer, *Edith Wharton's Brave New Politics,* 58. Wharton's final trip to the United States was in June 1923. See Benstock, *No Gifts from Chance,* 381.

2. De Jongh, *Vicious Modernism,* 9. Interestingly, Ellen Glasgow also weighed in on *Nigger Heaven,* summing up her reaction in a review of the novel for *The Bookman* thus: "A thrilling, a remarkable book. There is fire at the heart of it" ("Soul of Harlem," 509). Although her take on the book echoes the praise for the primitive that Van Vechten's novel sparked in others, Glasgow finds *Nigger Heaven* to be a "sincere interpretation of life," particularly because it eschews the Uncle Tom sentimentalism of southern whites' portrayals of African Americans (510). Despite Wharton's disdain for the novel, *Nigger Heaven* actually has much in common with her own works, especially its interest in portraying social mores and the shifting dynamics of class. To cite just one example, Mary Love's response to the other guests at Adora Boniface's party is very much like Lily Bart's response to the "social Coney Island" that the Gormers' parties create (*House of Mirth,* 181). See Charles Scruggs's "Crab Antics and Jacob's Ladder" for other points of comparison between Wharton's and Van Vechten's novels.

3. Hughes, *Big Sea,* 227.

4. See Kathleen Pfeiffer's introduction to the University of Illinois Press edition of *Nigger Heaven.* Subsequent references to the novel are to this edition and will be cited parenthetically in the text.

5. Hughes, *Big Sea,* 270. This explains, perhaps, why many maps of New York include Harlem before the 1920s, whereas maps made during and after the Jazz Age do not. See the examples in Eric Homberger's *Historical Atlas of New York City,* for instance.

6. Hughes, *Big Sea,* 271.

7. The phrase is Van Vechten's, from a letter he wrote to Gertrude Stein quoted

in Pfeiffer's introduction to the University of Illinois Press edition of *Nigger Heaven,* xxiii.

8. Ibid., 254–55. Responses to Van Vechten and *Nigger Heaven* have been intense and various, ranging from Hughes's argument that the novel was a satire with an unfortunate title (*Big Sea,* 270), to the charge that it plays up the stereotype of blacks as exotic primitives (Singh, "Black-White Symbiosis," 68, is a representative example), to the notion that it is overly didactic (see, for instance, Bruce Kellner's essay "'Refined Racism,'" 130).

9. Johnson, "Harlem," 301.

10. The implied criticism in Byron's remark may help to account for Wharton's extremely negative response to *Nigger Heaven.*

11. Wharton, *Letters,* 99.

12. Wharton, *Twilight Sleep,* 15. Subsequent references will be cited parenthetically in the text.

13. Burrows and Wallace, *Gotham,* 721.

14. Bederman, *Manliness and Civilization,* 202.

15. Goodwyn, *Edith Wharton,* 55. Goodwyn's characterization of Pauline applies to many other westerners in Wharton's works, as I argue in chapter 6.

16. Bauer, *Edith Wharton's Brave New Politics,* 166, 58.

17. Cooley, "In Pursuit of the Primitive," 85.

18. Kassanoff, "Extinction," 61.

19. Fass, *The Damned,* 20.

20. Erenberg, *Steppin' Out,* 170.

21. Larsen, *Passing,* 235. Subsequent references will be cited parenthetically in the text.

22. Erenberg, *Steppin' Out,* 115.

23. Ibid., xiii, 154.

24. The word derives from the French *gigole,* a prostitute or dance-hall call girl. See Erenberg, *Steppin' Out,* 114.

25. Erenberg, *Steppin' Out,* 80.

26. Quoted in Erenberg, *Steppin' Out,* 81.

27. "Ellin Mackey," 1.

28. Ibid., 2, 1.

29. Adickes, *To Be Young,* 28–29.

30. In *The Big Sea* Hughes describes "lindy-hoppers" who "had cards printed with their names on them and became dance professors teaching the tourists. Then Harlem nights became show nights for the Nordics" (226). The lindy-hop was named after Charles Lindbergh, whose ancestry was Scandinavian, which helps to explain why Harlem's "dance professors" chose that particular dance to appeal to "Nordic" "tourists."

31. Ogren, "Controversial Sounds," 160.

32. Rogers, "Jazz at Home," 217.

33. See Gubar, *Racechanges.*

34. McKay, *Home to Harlem,* 107. Subsequent pages will be cited parenthetically in the text.

35. Rogers, "Jazz at Home," 217, 224.

36. Burrows and Wallace, *Gotham,* 1087; Morrison, *Playing in the Dark,* viii.

37. Fass, *The Damned,* 116; Chinitz, "Langston Hughes," 62.

38. The repeated use of the word "nigger" in *Twilight Sleep* by a variety of characters indicates Wharton's interest in delving into Harlem's influence on New York, for uses of the word in other works is extremely rare.

39. Mumford, *Interzones,* 154.

40. The Housetop may also be a parody of cabarets like the Cotton Club (hence the New Orleans cotton market), although Wharton makes a point of noting that the Housetop's patrons are of several races, whereas the Cotton Club famously excluded blacks except as performers. *Twilight Sleep* leaves unclear whether Wharton understood that some nightclubs excluded customers on the basis of class as well as race and that different cabarets were associated with different groups, as McKay's novel, for instance, makes amply clear.

41. Quoted in Bauer, *Edith Wharton's Brave New Politics,* 98.

42. Wegener, "'Form,'" 117; Clubbe, "Interiors," 545.

43. Bentley, *Ethnography,* 81, 82.

44. Ibid., 47.

45. Lewis and Ardizzone, *Love on Trial,* 161–62.

46. Ibid., 156–57. Alice's act proved her point, but as Lewis and Ardizzone write, it "thrust [her] into a long history of race and color" marked by the rape, torture, and exploitation of black women (157). Lewis and Ardizzone argue that Kip's elite status ultimately helped to turn the tide of public opinion against him and toward Alice, for his wealth appeared to many to make him flawed and decadent.

47. Ibid., 238.

48. Saks, "Representing Miscegenation Law," 58, 53.

49. Lewis and Ardizzone, *Love on Trial,* 140–41. The details that follow are also discussed in Lewis and Ardizzone's work.

50. Quoted in Lewis and Ardizzone, *Love on Trial,* 228. Lewis and Ardizzone detail other ways the press treated the case, arguing that both the content and the point of view toward it ranged from region to region, even in African American media venues. Alice's initial reluctance to identify herself as black met with criticism in this era of burgeoning race pride. The *Richmond Planet,* for instance, protested that if Alice wanted to be white, she was welcome to that racial category (quoted in *Love on Trial,* 77). Still other African American writers satirized white male sexuality: "Alice had a little Kip," the *New York Amsterdam News* quipped, "His brain was LIGHT as snow,— / And everywhere that Alice went, / For years he tried to go" (quoted in *Love on Trial,* 133).

51. For a fuller discussion of Larsen's use of the Rhinelander case in *Passing,* see Madigan, "Miscegenation."

52. Benstock, *No Gifts from Chance,* 342–43. It is a historical oddity that Alice

and Kip associated the Rhinelander name, Wharton's mother's maiden name, with scandal, since Alice's name, Jones, was Wharton's own maiden name.

53. Quoted in Lewis and Ardizzone, *Love on Trial*, 232.

54. Ibid., 56–57.

55. Saks, "Representing Miscegenation Law," 53.

56. See Doyle's *Bordering on the Body.*

57. Cooley, *Savages and Naturals*, 9.

58. At the end of the novel, when Nona jokes about joining a convent, Pauline experiences a twinge of anti-Catholicism, "the old Puritan terror of gliding priests and incense and idolatry," which Nona thinks constitutes the "only solid fibre left" in Pauline and which, for the novel itself, represents the only purely American thing about her (315).

59. See Chinitz, "Langston Hughes."

60. Hughes, "Rejuvenation through Joy," 71, 72, 73. Subsequent references will be cited parenthetically in the text.

61. As Chinitz points out, Hughes "has actually left the question [of Lesche's race] uneasily open." See "Langston Hughes," 75.

62. Wegener points out that Wharton associated Egypt with the "growth of empire, commercially if not territorially." "Rabid Imperialist," 799.

63. Singh, "Black-White Symbiosis," 65.

64. Johnson, "Harlem," 310.

CHAPTER 3

1. Baldwin, "Stranger in the Village," from *Notes of a Native Son*, in *Collected Essays*, 129. Subsequent references will be cited parenthetically.

2. Both slaves and English women first arrived in Virginia in the same year, 1621, a historical coincidence that would prove critical to the kind of "blood relationship" Baldwin describes.

3. For a discussion of the antebellum concept of a "family black and white," see Elizabeth Fox-Genovese, *Within the Plantation Household.*

4. Glasgow, *Battle-Ground*, 86. Subsequent references will be cited parenthetically in the text.

5. Dennis, "Seeing Hampton Plantation," 84.

6. Quoted in Dabney, *Virginia*, 393.

7. Cohen, *At Freedom's Edge*, 217. The validity of Jim Crow laws had already been upheld in the 1896 *Plessey v. Ferguson* decision.

8. Hale, *Making Whiteness*, 3.

9. Bair, "Remapping the Black/White Body," 399.

10. McDonald, *Stuff of Our Forebears.* Although McDonald's assessment of Cather's southern heritage is valid in the main, it often veers into a characterization of Reconstruction ("the scourge of ruthless carpetbaggers," as she calls it [51]) that differs fundamentally from my own argument about the region.

11. Quoted in Marcus, "Pull of Race," 99.

12. Ibid.

13. See James Woodress's *Willa Cather: A Literary Life* (Lincoln: University of Nebraska Press, 1987), for example, for a discussion of the photograph, as well as MacDonald's *Stuff of Our Forebears* for a discussion of Cather's poem of the Civil War, "The Namesake" (23).

14. Baldwin, *The Devil Finds Work,* in *Collected Essays,* 533.

15. Hale, *Making Whiteness,* 101.

16. Urgo, "'Dock Burrs in Yo' Pants,'" 27.

17. Cather, *Sapphira and the Slave Girl,* 281. Subsequent references will be cited parenthetically in the text.

18. See, for instance, her "Nebraska" essay.

19. Quoted in MacDonald, *Stuff of Our Forebears,* 89.

20. Brundage, "White Women," 115; Hoelscher, "White-Pillared Past," 50.

21. Quoted in MacDonald, *Stuff of Our Forebears,* 97.

22. Morgenstern, "'Love Is Home-sickness,'" 196.

23. Urgo, *Novel Frames,* 158.

24. Glasgow, *The Deliverance,* 51. Subsequent references will be cited parenthetically in the text.

25. Glasgow, *Collected Stories,* 146.

26. Morrison, *Playing in the Dark,* 27–28.

27. Glasgow, *Voice of the People,* 91. Subsequent references will be cited parenthetically in the text.

28. The use of a slave or former slave as a mouthpiece for elite whites' class prejudice is not confined to *Sapphira* or to Glasgow's works, of course. This attribution of class bias to such characters not only seems to shift blame from whites but also, because it is usually associated with supposedly "aristocratic" servants like Till, tends to grant higher status to the enslaved over the emancipated African American.

29. Rabinowitz, *Race Relations,* 22.

30. Quoted in Cohen, *At Freedom's Edge,* 250.

31. Hale, *Making Whiteness,* 120.

32. Morgenstern, "'Love Is Home-sickness,'" 189.

33. Faulkner, *Sound and the Fury,* 267. Subsequent references will be cited parenthetically in the text.

34. Examples include Betty Ambler of *The Battle-Ground,* Maria Fletcher of *The Deliverance,* and (briefly) Eugenia Battle of *Voice,* in addition to *Barren Ground*'s Dorinda Oakley.

35. Dailey, *Before Jim Crow,* 95.

36. Glasgow, *Barren Ground,* 5. Subsequent references will be cited parenthetically in the text.

37. Sawaya, "'Problem of the South,'" 136.

38. Cohen, *At Freedom's Edge,* 240–41, table 12.

39. Ibid., xiv.

40. Ibid., 38.
41. Ibid., 128, 17.
42. Hale, *Making Whiteness,* 112.
43. Matthews, *Ellen Glasgow,* 161.

CHAPTER 4

1. Roosevelt, *It Seems to Me,* 43, 30–31.
2. In her novels of modern southern politics, *The Builders* (1919) and *One Man in His Time* (1922), Glasgow, too, critiques the Solid South, but unlike Roosevelt, she does so because she believes that racial issues unnecessarily divide whites and therefore hamper regional and national progress.
3. Roosevelt, *Tomorrow Is Now,* 50; excerpted in *Courage in a Dangerous World* under the title "The Social Revolution" (300). Subsequent references will be cited parenthetically in the text.
4. Black, *Casting Her Own Shadow,* 87.
5. Quoted in Roosevelt, *If You Ask Me,* 68.
6. *Alabama Sun,* April 28, 1944. Black discusses this edition of the paper in chapter 4 of *Casting Her Own Shadow.*
7. Black, *Casting Her Own Shadow,* 87.
8. Simon, "Race Reactions," 239.
9. Morgenstern, "'Love Is Home-sickness,'" 191.
10. Hale, *Making Whiteness,* 54.
11. Marcus, "'Pull of Race,'" 117.
12. Caldwell, "*South in the Revolution,*" 7, 14. Subsequent references will be cited parenthetically in the text.
13. Quoted in Silber, *Romance,* 142.
14. Painter, *Southern History,* 118.
15. Chesnutt, *Marrow of Tradition,* 469. Subsequent references will be cited parenthetically in the text.
16. Fetterley and Pryse, *Writing Out of Place,* 25.
17. By the mid-twentieth century, though, African American domestics had become the privilege of whiteness per se. For her *Telling Memories,* Susan Tucker interviewed African Americans who spoke of their refusal to work for poor whites, or their relief that they hadn't worked for them; those who did claimed that even though their employers were poor, these white women could get jobs in public spaces like restaurants and stores that they could not.
18. Graves, "What Ellen Glasgow Meant by 'Average,'" 70.
19. In the Old Dominion edition of the novel, published later, in 1933, Glasgow would revise her description here to read "the great, free, ignorant, and deluded people" (262).
20. Michaels, *Our America,* 43.
21. Chesnutt's language here forces us to question the existence of this "initmate

knowledge" that Ellis's acquiantances claim to possess, which makes Ellis himself look all the more open-minded in his own refusal to assume such authority.

22. Interestingly, white elite men of the decadent aristocracy compete with plain men for the affection of a genteel white woman in both novels, and both texts signal the superiority of the plain man by having them intervene in mob violence sparked by the supposed rape of a white woman by a black man.

23. This is contrary to historical evidence, as historians have shown that more lynchings were supposed punishment for murder than for other crimes. See, for instance, Brundage, *Lynching*.

24. Fewer African American men were lynched in Virginia than in other southern states, but the state was hardly free of these crimes. According to Brundage, 70 African Americans were lynched in Virginia between 1880 and 1930, compared to Georgia's 441 victims in the same years, and *at least* one lynching was committed in Virginia every year from 1880 to 1894 and from 1897 to 1905, except 1903. See *Lynching,* appendix 1.

25. Ibid., 177.

26. White, *Man Called White,* 59.

27. The phrase from which I take my chapter title is part of Judge Bassett's indictment of the Readjusters who assumed power in the late 1870s and early 1880s, before Nick is supposed to have left Kingsborough and achieved his success. According to their opponents, the Readjusters tried to institute "negro rule" by building interracial coalitions and by appointing African Americans to positions of authority, most notably on the Richmond school board. See Dailey's *Before Jim Crow.*

28. Rachleff, *Black Labor,* 30–31, 32.

29. Fetterley and Pryse, *Writing Out of Place,* 25.

30. Sundquist, *To Wake the Nations,* 394.

31. White, *Man Called White,* 83–84.

32. Brown, *Eradicating This Evil,* 173, 187; White, *Man Called White,* 59.

33. Brown, *Eradicating This Evil,* 289.

34. Gossett, *Race,* 426. For a discussion of the influence of such thinkers on Cather's West, see chapter 5.

35. Jacobson, *Whiteness of a Different Color,* 248.

36. Glasgow, *In This Our Life,* 138. Subsequent references will be cited parenthetically in the text.

37. Glasgow, *Woman Within,* 140.

38. Hale, *Making Whiteness,* 195–96.

39. Brundage, *Lynching,* 57.

CHAPTER 5

1. Cather, *O Pioneers!* 274. Subsequent references will be cited parenthetically in the text.

2. Kocks, *Dream a Little,* 29.

3. Robbins, *Colony and Empire,* 152.

4. Fowler is quoted in Riley, *Women and Indians,* 14. Both Rice (*Racial Hygiene*) and Stoddard (*Racial Realities in Europe*) make this argument.

5. Wister, *Virginian,* 400. Wister's novel is another example of the new regionalism I have associated with Cather, Glasgow, and Wharton, as its main characters are a southerner and an easterner who take their regions' values with them to the West. The convention of the eastern schoolmarm as a civilizing agent originated in Bret Harte's "The Idyl of Red Gulch" (1869).

6. Tompkins, *West of Everything,* 155; Wister, *Virginian,* 409.

7. Welke, *Recasting American Liberty,* 53; Adickes, *To Be Young,* 82.

8. Malone and Peterson, "Politics and Protest," 508.

9. Hine and Faragher, *American West,* 354.

10. Kocks, *Dream a Little,* 30.

11. Pascoe, *Relations of Rescue,* xvii.

12. Simonson, *Beyond the Frontier,* 11.

13. Allen, *Invention of the White Race,* 153, 152.

14. Robbins, *Colony and Empire,* 72.

15. Hine and Faragher, *American West,* 343, 334.

16. Horsman, *Race and Manifest Destiny,* 134–35.

17. Stoddard, *Racial Realities,* 6. Subsequent references will be cited parenthetically in the text.

18. The Johnson-Reed Act instituted a quota system that, being based on the 1890 census, favored old immigrant groups over new immigrant groups from southern and eastern Europe. See Jacobson, *Whiteness of a Different Color,* 82–85.

19. Ibid., 4, 42–43.

20. Strong, *Our Country,* 60–61.

21. See, for example, Stoddard's *Racial Realities,* 79–80. For a discussion of images of Czech immigrants in relation to *My Ántonia,* see Tim Prchal's "The Bohemian Paradox."

22. Rice, *Racial Hygiene,* 307. Subsequent references will be cited parenthetically in the text.

23. Hingham, *Strangers,* 42–43.

24. Quoted in Jacobson, *Whiteness of a Different Color,* 83.

25. Cather, *Willa Cather in Person,* 9.

26. Prchal, "Bohemian Paradox," 6; Sergeant, "Toilers of the Tenements," 232.

27. Irving, *Immigrant Mothers*; Moseley, "New World Symphony"; Reynolds, *Willa Cather in Context,* 10; Lindemann, *Willa Cather: Queering America,* 40.

28. Cather, *Willa Cather in Person,* 71–72.

29. Ross, *Changing America,* 3. Subsequent references will be cited parenthetically in the text.

30. Ross, *Old World,* 24. Subsequent references will be cited parenthetically in the text.

31. Turner, *Frontier in American History,* 3. Subsequent references will be cited parenthetically in the text.

32. Cather, *Willa Cather on Writing,* 16–17.

33. Riley, *Women and Indians,* 105.

34. Kocks, *Dream a Little,* 38.

35. According to Rice, new immigrants like Frank "are fired with an unusual, and to them unnatural, ambition to rise" in socioeconomic status (300). On Slav men's abuse of women, see Ross, *Old World,* 129.

36. Rölvaag, *Their Fathers' God,* 264. Subsequent references will be cited parenthetically in the text.

37. Although Peder is drawn to politics by a seemingly innate and sincere concern for his region's welfare, he is often less idealized than Cather's Alexandra is. In fact, while he resembles Alexandra in some respects, in his emotional outbursts he also resembles Alexandra's brothers, who manifest the less desirable qualities associated with Swedes.

38. Cather revises the usual gendering of those possessing the "best" white traits by contrasting Alexandra with her brothers, Lou and Oscar. In both cases Swedishness lends itself to Americanization, but Alexandra assimilates in a more positively portrayed way than her brothers do. While Alexandra becomes a strong, independent individual via her Americanization, Lou and Oscar become a part of the homogenizing, materialist middle class.

39. Elsbree, "Our Pursuit of Loneliness," 41.

40. Kocks, *Dream a Little,* 38.

41. Ryan, "Enclosure of America," 276.

42. Lindemann, *Willa Cather: Queering America,* 42.

43. Jacobson, *Whiteness of a Different Color,* 8.

44. Fischer, "Pastoralism," 31.

45. Cather, *My Ántonia,* 108. Subsequent references will be cited parenthetically in the text.

46. Skaggs, *After the World,* 15.

47. Hyde, *American Vision,* 123–30.

48. Sally Allen McNall's "Immigrant Backgrounds" makes a similar point (26).

49. Stoddard, *Racial Realities,* 15.

50. Ross likewise maintained that Slav women, "what with caring for their large families, . . . usually lose their attractiveness early," as indeed Ántonia does (*Old World,* 128).

51. Jim's assessment here is especially interesting in light of Cather's critique of American materialism. Where, one wonders, is the line between such economic success—between the hired girls' or Alexandra's material triumphs—and the money grubbing, material-accumulating obsessions we see lambasted in such novels as *One of Ours* and *The Professor's House*? This conceptual dividing line has as much to do with race as it does with class, in that it relates to debates about the roots of white racial greatness in the Old World (with its class rigidity) or in the new (with its supposed classlessness).

52. Tellefsen, "Blood in the Wheat," 234.

53. Mrs. Harling, one of Black Hawk's most respectable women despite being an

immigrant, is an example of how the same rhetoric that placed into doubt Slav and other new immigrant groups' racial predisposition for American citizenship could also unite northern Europeans and Anglo-Americans around their common Nordic "gift" for democracy.

54. Jacobson, *Whiteness of a Different Color,* 20.

55. This paradigm is also, of course, often a sexist one, wherein men are the mind and women the body of the same "race."

56. If the novel portrays the tramp as a bitter enigma, migratory workers riding the trains from job to job were a familiar feature of western life, especially after the 1893–94 economic depression. The tramp's suicide gestures toward the desperate and dangerous life that real itinerant workers led: between 1901 and 1905 an estimated twenty-five thousand of them died riding the railroads in search of work. See Hine and Faragher, *American West,* 295.

57. Stout, *Willa Cather,* 156. The riding circle described in book 1 simultaneously highlights Native Americans' presence in the prairie of the past and their absence in the West of the present.

58. In *Redefining the American Dream* Sally Harvey maintains that Blind d'Arnault, "through his desire and talent, asserts his individuality" (57.) Yet his talent springs not from his individuality but his race; individuality itself, not to mention the American Dream Harvey claims he achieves, stands in opposition to his blackness (57).

59. Tellefsen, "Blood in the Wheat," 235.

60. Quoted in Hine and Faragher, *American West,* 421.

61. Unlike Lena, whom we never see speak any language but English (the closest she comes is listening to Ole Benson speak Norwegian [274–75]), Ántonia, as she tells Jim in the last section of the novel, rarely speaks the language of her adopted country (324).

62. Rosowski, *Birthing a Nation,* 77; *Dictionary,* quoted in Jacobson, *Whiteness of a Different Color,* 80.

63. Conzen, "Sage of Families," 319.

64. Irving, *Immigrant Mothers,* 98.

65. Graulich, "'O Beautiful for Spacious Guys,'" 187.

CHAPTER 6

1. Limerick, *Legacy of Conquest.*

2. Will, "Nervous Origins," 299. This is where Turner's thinking, which is generally opposed to that of the eugenicists, starts to echo the same kinds of assumptions they had, for in both cases there is a lack of confidence that the "best" races (for Turner, frontier whites) were the same as the fittest or most able to survive. According to the eugenicists, the more evolved a race was, the more in danger it was of being subsumed by lesser races that were conditioned to withstand depravations and harsh conditions.

3. Quoted in Robbins, *Colony and Empire,* 63.

4. Dorst, *Looking West,* 112. Wilson is quoted in Robbins, *Colony and Empire,* 8.

5. Welke, *Recasting American Liberty,* 258.

6. Bogne, "Agrarian Empire," 287; Malone and Peterson, "Politics and Protest," 503. According to Malone and Peterson, it was widely rumored that the Burlington and the Union Pacific, Nebraska's largest railroad lines, divided the state's two senate seats between them.

7. Quoted in Hine and Faragher, *American West,* 274–75; Rohnbough, "Continuing Search," 135.

8. Trachtenberg, *Incorporation of America,* 9.

9. Nicholson, *Valley of Democracy,* 56. Subsequent references will be cited parenthetically in the text.

10. Bourne, "Mirror of the Middle West," 266. Subsequent references will be cited parenthetically in the text.

11. Gonzáles, Chapter Three Commentary, 103.

12. Robbins, *Colony and Empire,* xii.

13. Bauer, *Edith Wharton's Brave New Politics,* 146.

14. Stout, *Willa Cather,* 93.

15. Trout, *Memorial Fictions,* 42.

16. Cather, *Lost Lady,* 3. Subsequent references will be cited parenthetically in the text.

17. In Niel's remark that the western elite came to "'develop our great West,' as they used to tell us," Cather may be inserting a sarcasm, hinting at the paternalistic assumptions of those who held the most power in directing the forms that settlement of the region would take (3). But if that is the case, the sarcasm is directed toward the innocence of men like Captain Forrester, not toward the power they yield over others, as my discussion of the novel will illustrate.

18. As we saw in Glasgow's characterizations of them in *The Descendant,* Germans (particularly in comparison to the Irish, and especially before the war) were said to be essentially conservative and respectful of the existing social order.

19. Robbins, *Colony and Empire,* 110, 120.

20. Ibid., 118.

21. Zettsu, "Slavery, Song, and the South," 98.

22. Urgo, "How Context Determines Fact," 185. As Stout points out, we have to wonder how Ivy's way of getting land from Native Americans in Wyoming differs from the way the Captain got his land from Natives in Nebraska. See *Willa Cather,* 222.

23. Cather, "Nebraska," 7; Cather, *Lost Lady,* 56.

24. Hoffman, *The Twenties,* 332.

25. Wolff, *Feast of Words,* 233, 243; Ammons, *Edith Wharton's Argument,* 107; Wershoven, *Female Intruder,* 136.

26. These examples are from *Twilight Sleep, Custom of the Country,* and *Hudson River Bracketed,* respectively. Cecelia Tichi also discusses Wharton's use of satirical

names for "outlanders" in her essay "Emerson, Darwin, and *The Custom of the Country,*" 95.

27. Conzen, "Sage of Families," 325.

28. Tichi, "Emerson, Darwin," 110.

29. Waid, *Edith Wharton's Letters,* 153–54, 123.

30. Wershoven, *Female Intruder,* 591; Marconi Transatlantic Wireless Telegraph, "American Girls Are Popular in Berlin," n.p.

31. Stout, *Willa Cather,* 93.

32. Showalter, "Custom of the Country," 92–93. In chapter 1 I argued that Regina Beaufort in *Age of Innocence* forfeits her own status in marrying a Jew, but that *Custom*'s Ralph, as a man, does not. At the beginning of *Custom* it seems that Clare Van Degen has thoroughly assimilated her vulgar husband Peter's values, but as their marriage becomes more strained and as she draws closer to Ralph, her gentility once again surfaces in a way that it never does in Regina's case.

33. See chapter 1 for a discussion of Glasgow's character.

34. Kassanoff, *Edith Wharton and the Politics of Race,* 22.

35. Gair, "'Crumbling Structure of 'Appearances,'" 355.

36. Tichi, "Emerson, Darwin," 97.

37. Wharton and Codman, *Decoration,* 25.

38. Nicholson, *Valley of Democracy,* 13; Boydston, "'Grave Endearing Traditions,'" 35.

39. Wharton, *Letters,* 99, 91.

40. Quoted in Lewis, *Edith Wharton,* 424.

41. Quoted in D. Williams, *Not in Sisterhood,* 29.

42. Wharton, *Hudson River Bracketed,* 190. Subsequent references will be cited parenthetically in the text.

43. Bauer, *Edith Wharton's Brave New Politics,* 116; Nicholson, *Valley of Democracy,* 77.

44. Vance's comparison of "Instead" to a "movement" that bears ships to sea reinforces the association of Alida Lorburn with Jewett, whose *Painted Firs* features retired sea captains and their past experiences at sea.

45. Wharton, *Gods Arrive,* 372.

CONCLUSION

1. This tendency toward comparison makes the regional works of writers such as Cather, Glasgow, and Wharton relevant to the transnational approaches currently being taken to the study of American literature.

2. Anderson, *Imagined Communities.*

3. Fetterley and Pryse, *Writing Out of Place,* 3–4.

4. Ibid., 27.

5. In *Cosmopolitan Vistas* Tom Lutz argues that identification with one region consistently furnishes an opposition with which American writers valorize cosmo-

politanism; my own analysis of Wharton, Glasgow, and Cather suggests that for these three women, cosmopolitanism is actually a function of a character's association with a particular region.

6. Russ, "'There's No Place Like Home,'" 358. See also Rosenblatt, *Black Fiction,* 90. Fetterley and Pryse, as I mentioned earlier, see Chesnutt as a rare example of a male regionalist. I might argue that Chesnutt's rarity comes from his portrayal of Uncle Julius as so thoroughly native, at least from the perspective of the white narrator of "Goophered Grapevine." Of course, Julius himself complicates his own insider status with his stories of slavery, when the master's manipulation of slaves continually displaces them, a displacement central to the black experience as *Marrow* portrays it.

7. Baldwin, "The Harlem Ghetto," in *Collected Essays,* 52.

Bibliography

Adams, James Truslow. *The Epic of America.* Boston: Little, Brown, 1934.
Adickes, Sandra. *To Be Young Was Very Heaven: Women in New York before the First World War.* New York: St. Martin's, 1997.
Alabama Sun. April 28, 1944.
Allen, Theodore W. *The Invention of the White Race.* London: Verso, 1994.
Ammons, Elizabeth. "Edith Wharton and the Issue of Race." In Bell, *Cambridge Companion to Edith Wharton,* 68–86.
———. *Edith Wharton's Argument with America.* Athens: University of Georgia Press, 1980.
Anderson, Benedict. *Imagined Communities: Reflections on the Origin and Spread of Nationalism.* Rev. ed. London: Verso, 1991.
Bair, Barbara. "Remapping the Black/White Body: Sexuality, Nationalism, and Biracial Antimiscegenation Activism in 1920s Virginia." In *Sex, Love, Race: Crossing Boundaries in North American History,* edited by Martha Hodes, 399–413. New York: New York University Press, 1999.
Baldwin, James. *Another Country.* 1962. In *Baldwin: Early Novels and Stories.* New York: Library of America, 1998.
———. *Baldwin: Collected Essays.* New York: Library of America, 1998.
Bauer, Dale. *Edith Wharton's Brave New Politics.* Madison: University of Wisconsin Press, 1995.
Bederman, Gail. *Manliness and Civilization: A Cultural History of Gender and Race in the United States, 1880–1917.* Chicago: University of Chicago Press, 1995.
Bell, Millicent, ed. *The Cambridge Companion to Edith Wharton.* New York: Cambridge University Press, 1995.
Benstock, Shari. *No Gifts from Chance: A Biography of Edith Wharton.* New York: Scribner's, 1994.
Bentley, Nancy. *The Ethnography of Manners.* New York: Cambridge University Press, 1995.

———. "'Hunting for the Real': Wharton and the Science of Manners." In Bell, *Cambridge Companion to Edith Wharton*, 47–67.

———. "Wharton, Travel, and Modernity." In Singley, *Historical Guide to Edith Wharton*, 147–79.

Black, Allida M. *Casting Her Own Shadow: Eleanor Roosevelt and the Shaping of Postwar Liberalism.* New York: Columbia University Press, 1996.

Bogne, Allan. "An Agrarian Empire." In Milner, O'Connor, and Sandweiss, *Oxford History of the American West*, 275–313.

Bourne, Randolph. "A Mirror of the Middle West." In *The Radical Will: Selected Writings, 1911–1918*, 265–70. New York: Urizen Books, 1977.

———. "Trans-National America." In *The Radical Will: Selected Writings, 1911–1918*, 248–264. New York: Urizen Books, 1977.

Boydston, Jeanne. "'Grave Endearing Traditions': Edith Wharton and the Domestic Novel." In *Faith of a (Woman) Writer*, edited by Alice Kessler-Harris and William McBrien, 31–40. New York: Greenwood, 1988.

Brodhead, Richard H. *Cultures of Letters: Scenes of Reading and Writing in Nineteenth-Century America.* Chicago: University of Chicago Press, 1993.

Brown, Mary Jane. *Eradicating This Evil: Women in the American Anti-Lynching Movement, 1892–1940.* New York: Garland, 2000.

Brundage, W. Fitzhugh. *Lynching in the New South: Georgia and Virginia, 1880–1930.* Urbana: University of Illinois Press, 1993.

———. "White Women and the Politics of Historical Memory in the New South, 1880–1920." In Dailey, Gilmore, and Simon, *Jumpin' Jim Crow*, 115–39.

Burrows, Edwin G., and Mike Wallace. *Gotham: A History of New York City to 1898.* New York: Oxford University Press, 1999.

Cahan, Abraham. *The Rise of David Levinsky.* 1917. New York: Harper & Row, 1966.

Caldwell, Joshua W. *"The South in the Revolution" and "The Patriotism of the South": Addresses by Joshua W. Caldwell.* Privately printed.

Campbell, Donna M. *Resisting Regionalism: Gender and Naturalism in American Fiction, 1885–1915.* Athens: University of Ohio Press, 1997.

Cather, Willa. *A Lost Lady.* 1923. New York: Vintage, 1990.

———. *My Ántonia.* 1918. Lincoln: Bison/University of Nebraska Press, 1997.

———. "Nebraska: The End of the First Cycle." *Nation* 117 (1923): 236–38. Reprinted in *Roundup: A Nebraska Reader*, edited by Virginia Faulkner, 1–8. Lincoln: University of Nebraska Press, 1957.

———. *Not Under Forty.* 1936. Lincoln: University of Nebraska Press, 1988.

———. *O Pioneers!* 1913. Lincoln: Bison/University of Nebraska Press, 1997.

———. *Sapphira and the Slave Girl.* 1940. New York: Vintage, 1975.

———. *Willa Cather in Person: Interviews, Speeches, and Letters.* Edited by L. Brent Bohlke. Lincoln: University of Nebraska Press, 1986.

———. *Willa Cather on Writing.* Lincoln: University of Nebraska Press, 1988.

Chesnutt, Charles W. *The Marrow of Tradition.* 1901. In *Three Classic African American Novels,* edited by Henry Louis Gates Jr. New York: Vintage, 1990.

Chinitz, David. "Rejuvenation through Joy: Langston Hughes, Primitivism, and Jazz." *American Literary History* 9 (1997): 60–78.

Clubbe, John. "Interiors and the Interior Life in Edith Wharton's *The House of Mirth.*" *Studies in the Novel* 28 (1996): 543–64.

Cohen, William. *At Freedom's Edge: Black Mobility and the Southern White Quest for Racial Control, 1861–1915.* Baton Rouge: Louisiana State University Press, 1991.

Conzen, Kathleen Neils. "A Sage of Families." In Milner, O'Connor, and Sandweiss, *Oxford History of the American West,* 317–57.

Cooley, John R. "In Pursuit of the Primitive: Black Portraits by Eugene O'Neill and Other Village Bohemians." In Kramer and Russ, *Harlem Renaissance Re-Examined,* 83–95.

———. *Savages and Naturals: Black Portraits by White Writers in Modern American Literature.* Newark: University of Delaware Press, 1982.

Dabney, Virginius. *Virginia: The New Dominion: A History from 1607 to the Present.* 1971. Charlottesville: University Press of Virginia, 1983.

Dailey, Jane. *Before Jim Crow: The Politics of Race in Postemancipation Virginia.* Chapel Hill: University of North Carolina Press, 2000.

Dailey, Jane, Glenda Elizabeth Gilmore, and Bryant Simon, eds. *Jumpin' Jim Crow: Southern Politics from the Civil War to Civil Rights.* Princeton, NJ: Princeton University Press, 2000.

De Jongh, James. *Vicious Modernism: Black Harlem and the Literary Imagination.* New York: Cambridge University Press, 1990.

Dennis, Samuel F., Jr. "Seeing Hampton Plantation: Race and Gender in a South Carolina Heritage Landscape." In Schein, *Landscape and Race in the United States,* 73–94.

Donaldson, Laura. *Decolonizing Feminisms: Race, Gender, and Empire-Building.* Chapel Hill: University of North Carolina Press, 1992.

Dorst, John. *Looking West.* Philadelphia: University of Pennsylvania Press, 1993.

Doyle, Laura. *Bordering on the Body: The Racial Matrix of Modern Fiction and Culture.* New York: Oxford University Press, 1994.

Du Bois, W. E. B. *The Souls of Black Folk.* 1903. New York: Norton, 1999.

"Ellin Mackey Calls Cabarets a Refuge." *New York Times,* November 26, 1925.

Elsbree, Langdon. "Our Pursuit of Loneliness: An Alternative to the Paradigm." In Mogen, Busby, and Bryant, *Frontier Experience and the American Dream,* 31–49.

Erenberg, Lewis. *Steppin' Out: New York Nightlife and the Transformation of American Culture, 1890–1930.* Westport, CT: Greenwood, 1981.

Ewen, Elizabeth. *Immigrant Women in the Land of Dollars: Life and Culture on the Lower East Side, 1890–1925.* New York: Monthly Review Press, 1985.

Fairweather, Colin. "Inclusive and Exclusive Pastoral." *Studies in Philology* 97, no. 3 (2000): 276–307.

Fass, Paula. *The Damned and the Beautiful: American Youth in the 1920s.* New York: Oxford University Press, 1977.

Faulkner, William. *The Sound and the Fury.* 1929. New York: Vintage/Random House, 1990.

Fetterley, Judith, and Marjorie Pryse. *Writing Out of Place: Regionalism, Women, and American Literary Culture.* Urbana: University of Illinois Press, 2003.

Fischer, Mike. "Pastoralism and its Discontents: Willa Cather and the Burden of Imperialism." *Mosaic* 23 (1990): 31–44.

Foote, Stephanie. *Regional Fictions: Culture and Identity in Nineteenth-Century American Literature.* Madison: University of Wisconsin Press, 2001.

Fox-Genovese, Elizabeth. *Within the Plantation Household: Black and White Women of the Old South.* Chapel Hill: University of North Carolina Press, 1988.

Frost, Linda. *Never One Nation: Freaks, Savages, and Whiteness in U.S. Popular Culture, 1850–1877.* Minneapolis: University of Minnesota Press, 2005.

Gair, Christopher. "The Crumbling Structure of 'Appearances': Representation and Authenticity in *The House of Mirth* and *The Custom of the Country.*" *Modern Fiction Studies* 43 (1997): 349–73.

Gilman, Charlotte Perkins. *Women and Economics.* Boston: Small, Maynard, 1898.

Glasgow, Ellen. *Barren Ground.* 1925. San Diego: Harvest/Harcourt Brace, 1985.

———. *The Battle-Ground.* 1902. Tuscaloosa: University of Alabama Press, 2000.

———. *A Certain Measure: An Interpretation of Prose Fiction.* New York: Harcourt, Brace, 1938.

———. *The Collected Stories of Ellen Glasgow.* Edited by Richard K. Meeker. Baton Rouge: Louisiana State University Press, 1966.

———. *The Deliverance.* New York: Doubleday, Page, 1904.

———. *The Descendant.* 1897. New York: Harper, 1905.

———. *In This Our Life.* 1941. Mattituck, NY: Amereon, n.d.

———. *Life and Gabriella: The Story of a Woman's Courage.* Garden City, NJ: Doubleday, Page, 1916.

———. *Phases of an Inferior Planet.* New York: Harper, 1898.

———. "The Soul of Harlem." Rev. of *Nigger Heaven,* by Carl Van Vechten. *The Bookman* 64 (December 1926): 509–10.

———. *Virginia.* 1913. New York: Penguin, 1989.

———. *The Voice of the People.* New York: Doubleday, Page, 1900.

———. *The Voice of the People: The Old Dominion Edition of the Works of Ellen Glasgow.* Garden City, NY: Doubleday, 1933.

———. *The Woman Within.* 1954. Charlottesville: University Press of Virginia, 1994.

Glazener, Nancy. *Reading for Realism: The History of a U.S. Literary Institution, 1850–1910.* Durham, NC: Duke University Press, 1997.

Gonzáles, Rosalinda Mendez. Chapter Three Commentary. In *Western Women: Their Land, Their Lives,* edited by Lillian Schlissel, Vicki Ruiz, and Janice Monk, 99–105. Albuquerque: University of New Mexico Press, 1988.

Goodwyn, Janet. *Edith Wharton: Traveler in the Land of Letters.* New York: St. Martin's, 1990.

Gossett, Thomas F. *Race: The History of an Idea in America.* 1963. New York: Oxford University Press, 1997.

Grammer, John M. *Pastoral and Politics in the Old South.* Baton Rouge: Louisiana State University Press, 1996.

Grant, Madison. 1961. *The Passing of the Great Race; or, the Racial Basis of European History.* New York: Scribner's, 1921.

Graves, Mark A. "What Ellen Glasgow Meant by 'Average': Southern Masculinity and the Rise of the Common Hero." In *Regarding Ellen Glasgow: Essays for Contemporary Readers,* edited by Welford Dunaway Taylor and George Longest, 63–70. Richmond: Library of Virginia, 2001.

Graulich, Melody. "'O Beautiful for Spacious Guys': An Essay on the 'Legitimate Inclinations of the Sexes.'" In Mogen, Busby, and Bryant, *Frontier Experience and the American Dream,* 186–201.

Gubar, Susan. *Racechanges: White Skin, Black Face in American Culture.* New York: Oxford University Press, 1997.

Hale, Grace Elizabeth. *Making Whiteness: The Culture of Segregation in the South, 1890–1940.* New York: Pantheon, 1998.

Harvey, Sally Peltier. *Redefining the American Dream: The Novels of Willa Cather.* Rutherford, NJ: Associated University Presses, 1995.

Hine, Robert V., and John Mack Faragher. *The American West: A New Interpretive History.* New Haven, CT: Yale University Press, 2000.

Higham, John. *Strangers in the Land: Patterns of American Nativism, 1860–1925.* 1955. New Brunswick, NJ: Rutgers University Press, 1988.

Hoeller, Hildegard. "'The Impossible Rosedale': 'Race' and the Reading of Edith Wharton's *The House of Mirth.*" *Studies in American Jewish Literature* 13 (1994): 14–20.

Hoelscher, Steven. "The White-Pillared Past: Landscapes of Memory and Race in the American South." In Schein, *Landscape and Race in the United States,* 39–72.

Hoffman, Frederick. *The Twenties: American Writing in the Postwar Decade.* New York: Viking Press, 1955.

Homberger, Eric. *The Historical Atlas of New York City: A Visual Celebration of Nearly 400 Years of New York City's History.* Alice Hudson, Cartographic Consultant. New York: Owl/Henry Holt, 1994.

Horsman, Reginald. *Race and Manifest Destiny: The Origins of American Racial Anglo-Saxonism.* Cambridge, MA: Harvard University Press, 1981.

Howells, William Dean. *A Hazard of New Fortunes.* 1890. New York: Modern Library, 2002.

Hughes, Langston. *The Big Sea.* 1940. New York: Hill and Wang, 1993.

———. "Rejuvenation through Joy." In *The Ways of White Folks,* 69–98. 1933. New York: Vintage/Random House, 1990.

Hyde, Anne Farrar. *An American Vision: Far Western Landscape and National Culture, 1820–1920.* New York: New York University Press, 1990.

Inness, Sherrie A., and Diana Royer, eds. *Breaking Boundaries: New Perspectives on Women's Regional Writing.* Iowa City: University of Iowa Press, 1997.

Irving, Katrina. *Immigrant Mothers: Narratives of Race and Maternity: 1890–1925.* Urbana: University of Illinois Press, 2000.

Jacobson, Matthew Frye. *Whiteness of a Different Color: European Immigrants and the Alchemy of Race.* Cambridge, MA: Harvard University Press, 1998.

Johnson, James Weldon. "Harlem: The Cultural Capital." In Locke, *New Negro,* 301–11.

Kallen, Horace. *Culture and Democracy in the United States: Studies in Group Psychology of the American Peoples.* 1924. New York: Arno Press, 1970.

Kaplan, Amy. "Nation, Region, Empire." In *Columbia History of the American Novel,* edited by Emery Elliot, 240–66. New York: Columbia University Press, 1991.

———. *The Social Construction of American Realism.* Chicago: University of Chicago Press, 1988.

Kassanoff, Jennie. *Edith Wharton and the Politics of Race.* Cambridge: Cambridge University Press, 2004.

———. "Extinction, Taxidermy, Tableaux Vivants: Staging Race and Class in *The House of Mirth.*" *PMLA* 115 (2000): 60–74.

Kellner, Bruce. "'Refined Racism': White Patronage in the Harlem Renaissance." In Kramer and Russ, *Harlem Renaissance Re-Examined,* 121–32.

Kocks, Dorothee. *Dream a Little: Land and Social Justice in Modern America.* Berkeley: University of California Press, 2000.

Kramer, Víctor A., and Robert A. Russ, eds. *Harlem Renaissance Re-Examined.* Troy, NY: Whitston, 1997.

Lankevich, George. *American Metropolis: A History of New York City.* New York: New York University Press, 1998.

Larsen, Nella. *Passing.* 1929. In *Quicksand and Passing,* edited by Deborah McDowell. New Brunswick, NJ: Rutgers University Press, 1996.

Le Bon, Gustave. *The Crowd: A Study of the Popular Mind.* 1896. 2nd ed. Dunwoody, GA: Norn S. Berg, 1968.

Lewis, Earl, and Heidi Ardizzone. *Love on Trial: An American Scandal in Black and White.* New York: Norton, 2001.

Lewis, R. W. B. *Edith Wharton: A Biography.* New York: Harper Colophon, 1975.

Limerick, Patricia Nelson. *The Legacy of Conquest: The Unbroken Past of the American West.* New York: Norton, 1987.

Lindemann, Marilee. *Willa Cather: Queering America.* New York: Columbia University Press, 1999.

Locke, Alain. *The New Negro.* 1925. New York: Touchstone, 1997.

Lutz, Tom. *Cosmopolitan Vistas: American Regionalism and Literary Value.* Ithaca, NY: Cornell University Press, 2004.

Madigan, Mark J. "Miscegenation and 'the Dicta of Race and Class': The Rhinelander Case and Nella Larsen's *Passing*." *Modern Fiction Studies* 36 (1990): 523–28.

Malone, Michael, and Ross Peterson. "Politics and Protest." In Milner, O'Connor, and Sandweiss, *Oxford History of the American West*, 501–33.

Marconi Transatlantic Wireless Telegraph. "American Girls Are Popular in Berlin: 'Dollar Princesses' the Centres of Attention in Aristocratic Society There." *New York Times*, January 28, 1912.

Marcus, Lisa. "'The Pull of Race and Blood and Kindred': Willa Cather's Southern Inheritance." In Romines, *Willa Cather's Southern Connections*, 98–119.

Martin, David. "'Regionalist' Fiction and the Problem of Cultural Knowledge." In *A Sense of Place: Re-Evaluating Regionalism in Canadian and American Writing*, edited by Christian Riegel, Herb Wyile, Karen Overbye, and Don Perkins, 35–50. Edmonton: University of Alberta Press, 1998.

Matthews, Pamela R. *Ellen Glasgow and a Woman's Traditions*. Charlottesville: University Press of Virginia, 1994.

McDonald, Joyce. *The Stuff of Our Forebears: Willa Cather's Southern Heritage*. Tuscaloosa: University of Alabama Press, 1998.

McKay, Claude. *Home to Harlem*. 1928. Foreword by Wayne F. Cooper. Boston: Northeastern University Press, 1987.

McNall, Sally Allen. "Immigrant Backgrounds to *My Ántonia*: 'A Curious Social Situation in Black Hawk.'" In *Approaches to Teaching* My Ántonia, edited by Susan Rosowski, 22–30. New York: Modern Language Association, 1989.

Michaels, Walter Benn. *Our America: Nativism, Modernism, and Pluralism*. Durham, NC: Duke University Press, 1995.

Milner, Clyde, II, Carol O'Connor, and Martha Sandweiss, eds. *The Oxford History of the American West*. New York: Oxford University Press, 1994.

Mogen, David, Mark Busby, and Paul Bryant, eds. *The Frontier Experience and the American Dream: Essays on American Literature*. College Station: Texas A&M University Press, 1989.

Morgenstern, Naomi. "'Love Is Home-sickness': Nostalgia and Lesbian Desire in *Sapphira and the Slave Girl*." *Novel* 29 (1996): 184–205.

Morrison, Toni. *Playing in the Dark: Whiteness and the Literary Imagination*. New York: Vintage/Random House, 1993.

Moseley, Ann. "A New World Symphony: Cultural Pluralism in *The Song of the Lark* and *My Ántonia*." *Willa Cather Pioneer Memorial Newsletter* 39, no. 1 (1995): 1, 7–12.

Mumford, Kevin. *Interzones: Black/White Sex Districts in Chicago and New York in the Early Twentieth Century*. New York: Columbia University Press, 1996.

Newman, Louise Michele. *White Women's Rights: The Racial Origins of Feminism in the United States*. New York: Oxford University Press, 1999.

Nicholson, Meredith. *The Valley of Democracy*. New York: Scribner, 1919.

Ogren, Kathy. "Controversial Sounds: Jazz Performance as Theme and Language in the Harlem Renaissance." In *The Harlem Renaissance: Revaluations,* edited by Amritjit Singh, William S. Shiver, and Stanley Brodwin, 159–85. New York: Garland, 1989.

Painter, Nell Irvin. *Southern History across the Color Line.* Chapel Hill: University of North Carolina Press, 2002.

———. *Standing at Armageddon: The United States, 1877–1919.* New York: Norton, 1987.

Pascoe, Peggy. *Relations of Rescue: The Search for Female Moral Authority in the American West, 1874–1939.* New York: Oxford University Press, 1990.

Peiss, Kathy. "'Charity Girls' and City Pleasures: Historical Notes on Working-Class Sexuality, 1880–1920." In *Unequal Sisters: A Multicultural Reader in United States Women's History,* edited by Ellen Carol Dubois and Vicki Ruiz, 157–66. New York: Routledge, 1990.

Pimple, Kenneth. "Edith Wharton's 'Inscrutable Totem Terrors': Ethnography and *The Age of Innocence.*" *Southern Folklore* 51 (1994): 137–52.

Prchal, Tim. "The Bohemian Paradox: *My Ántonia* and Popular Images of Czech Immigrants." *MELUS* 29, no. 2 (2004): 3–25.

Rabinowitz, Howard. *Race Relations in the Urban South, 1865–1890.* New York: Oxford University Press, 1978.

Rachleff, Peter J. *Black Labor in Richmond, 1865–1890.* Urbana: University of Chicago Press, 1989.

Raper, J. R. *Without Shelter: The Early Career of Ellen Glasgow.* Baton Rouge: Louisiana University Press, 1971.

Reynolds, Guy. *Willa Cather in Context: Progress, Race, Empire.* New York: St. Martin's Press, 1996.

Rice, Thurman. *Racial Hygiene: A Practical Discussion of Eugenics and Race Culture.* New York: Macmillan, 1929.

"Rich and Poor Marched Together in Suffrage Parade." *New York Times,* May 12, 1912.

Riegel, Christian. "Rosedale and Anti-Semitism in *The House of Mirth.*" *Studies in American Fiction* 20 (1992): 219–24.

Riis, Jacob. *How the Other Half Lives.* 1890/1901. New York: Dover, 1971.

Riley, Glenda. *Women and Indians on the Frontier, 1825–1915.* Albuquerque: University of New Mexico Press, 1984.

Robbins, William G. *Colony and Empire: The Capitalist Transformation of the American West.* Lawrence: University of Kansas Press, 1994.

Robison, Lori. "'Why, Why Do We Not Write Our Side?': Gender and Southern Self-Representation in Grace King's *Balcony Stories.*" In Inness and Royer, *Breaking Boundaries,* 54–71.

Rogers, J. A. "Jazz at Home." In Locke, *New Negro,* 216–24.

Rohnbough, Malcolm. "The Continuing Search for the American West: Historians Past, Present, and Future." In *Old West/New West: Quo Vadis?* edited by Gene M. Gressley, 123–46. Worland, WY: High Plains Publishing, 1994.

Rölvaag, O. E. *Their Fathers' God.* 1913. Translated by Trygve M. Ager. Lincoln: Bison/University of Nebraska Press, 1983.

Romines, Ann, ed. *Willa Cather's Southern Connections: New Essays on Cather and the South.* Charlottesville: University Press of Virginia, 2000.

Roosevelt, Eleanor. *Courage in a Dangerous World: The Political Writings of Eleanor Roosevelt.* Edited by Allida M. Black. New York: Columbia University Press, 1999.

———. *If You Ask Me.* New York: D. Appleton-Century, 1946.

———. *It Seems to Me: Selected Letters of Eleanor Roosevelt.* Edited by Leonard C. Schlup and Donald W. Whisenhunt. Lexington: University Press of Kentucky, 2001.

———. *Tomorrow Is Now.* New York: Harper and Row, 1963.

Rosenblatt, Roger. *Black Fiction.* Cambridge: Harvard University Press, 1974.

Rosowski, Susan. *Birthing a Nation: Gender, Creativity, and the West in American Literature.* Lincoln: University of Nebraska Press, 1999.

Ross, Edward. *Changing America: Studies in Contemporary Society.* New York: Century, 1912.

———. *The Old World in the New: The Significance of Past and Present Immigration to the American People.* New York: Century, 1914.

Russ, Robert A. "'There's No Place Like Home': The Carnival of Black Life in Claude McKay's *Home to Harlem.*" In Kramer and Russ, *Harlem Renaissance Re-Examined,* 355–73.

Ryan, Melissa. "The Enclosure of America: Civilization and Confinement in Willa Cather's *O Pioneers!*" *American Literature* 75 (2003): 275–303.

Saks, Eva. "Representing Miscegenation Law." *Raritan* 8, no. 2 (1998): 39–69.

Sawaya, Francesca. "'The Problem of the South': Economic Determination, Gender Determination, and Genre in Glasgow's *Virginia.*" In *Ellen Glasgow: New Perspectives,* edited by Dorothy M. Scura, 132–45. Knoxville: University of Tennessee Press, 1995.

Schein, Richard, H., ed. *Landscape and Race in the United States.* New York: Routledge, 2006.

Scruggs, Charles. "'Crab Antics and Jacob's Ladder': Aaron Douglas's Two Views of *Nigger Heaven.*" In Kramer and Russ, *Harlem Renaissance Re-Examined,* 149–81.

Sergeant, Elizabeth Shepley. "Toilers of the Tenements: Where the Beautiful Things of the Great Shops Are Made." *McClure's,* July 1910.

Showalter, Elaine. "The Custom of the Country: Spragg and the Art of the Deal." In Bell, *Cambridge Companion to Edith Wharton,* 87–97.

Silber, Nina. *The Romance of Reunion: Northerners and the South, 1865–1900.* Chapel Hill: University of North Carolina Press, 1993.

Simon, Bryant. "Race Reactions: African American Organizing, Liberalism, and White Working-Class Politics in Postwar South Carolina." In Dailey, Gilmore, and Simon, *Jumpin' Jim Crow,* 239–59.

Simonson, Harold P. *Beyond the Frontier: Writers, Western Regionalism, and a Sense of Place.* Fort Worth: Texas Christian University Press, 1989.

Singh, Amritjit. "Black-White Symbiosis: Another Look at the Literary History of the 1920s." In Kramer and Russ, *Harlem Renaissance Re-Examined,* 65–74.

Singley, Carol, ed. *The Historical Guide to Edith Wharton.* New York: Oxford University Press, 2003.

Skaggs, Merrill Maguire. *After the World Broke in Two: The Later Novels of Willa Cather.* Charlottesville: University Press of Virginia, 1990.

Stoddard, Lothrop. *Racial Realities in Europe.* New York: Scribner's, 1924.

———. *The Rising Tide of Color against White World-Supremacy.* New York: Scribner's, 1920.

Stokes, Mason. *The Color of Sex: Whiteness, Heterosexuality, and the Fictions of White Supremacy.* Durham, NC: Duke University Press, 2001.

Stout, Janis P. *Willa Cather: The Writer and Her World.* Charlottesville: University Press of Virginia, 2000.

Strong, Josiah. *Our Country: Its Possible Future and Its Present Crisis.* Rev. ed. New York: Baker & Taylor/American Home Missionary Society, 1891.

Sundquist, Eric J. *To Wake the Nations: Race in the Making of American Literature.* Cambridge, MA: Belknap/Harvard University Press, 1994.

Taylor, William. *In Pursuit of Gotham: Culture and Commerce in New York.* New York: Oxford University Press, 1992.

Tellefsen, Blythe. "Blood in the Wheat: Willa Cather's *My Ántonia.*" *Studies in American Fiction* 27 (1999): 229–44.

Thiébaux, Marcelle. *Ellen Glasgow.* New York: Frederick Ungar, 1982.

Tichi, Cecelia. "Emerson, Darwin, and *The Custom of the Country.*" In Singley, *Historical Guide to Edith Wharton,* 89–114.

Tompkins, Jane. *West of Everything: The Inner Life of Westerns.* New York: Oxford University Press, 1992.

Trachtenberg, Alan. *The Incorporation of America: Culture and Society in the Gilded Age.* New York: Hill and Wang, 1982.

Trout, Steven. *Memorial Fictions: Willa Cather and the First World War.* Lincoln: University of Nebraska Press, 2000.

Tucker, Susan. *Telling Memories among Southern Women: Domestic Workers and Their Employers in the Segregated South.* Baton Rouge: Louisiana State University Press, 1988.

Turner, Frederick Jackson. *The Frontier in American History.* New York: Henry Holt, 1920.

Urgo, Joseph. "'Dock Burrs in Yo' Pants': Reading Cather through *Sapphira and the Slave Girl.*" In Romines, *Willa Cather's Southern Connections,* 24–37.

———. "How Context Determines Fact: Historicism in Willa Cather's *A Lost Lady.*" *Studies in American Fiction* 17 (1989): 183–92.

———. *Novel Frames: Literature as Guide to Race, Sex, and History in American Culture.* Jackson: University Press of Mississippi, 1991.

Van Vechten, Carl. *Nigger Heaven.* 1926. Introduction by Kathleen Pfeiffer. Urbana: University of Illinois Press, 2000.

Waid, Candace. *Edith Wharton's Letters from the Underworld: Fictions of Women and Writing.* Chapel Hill: University of North Carolina Press, 1990.

Wegener, Frederick. "'Form,' 'Selection,' and Ideology in Edith Wharton's Antimodernist Aesthetic." In *A Forward Glance: New Essays on Edith Wharton,* edited by Claire Colquitt, Susan Goodman, and Candace Waid, 116–38. Newark: Delaware University Press, 1999.

———. "'Rabid Imperialist': Edith Wharton and the Obligations of Empire in Modern American Fiction." *American Literature* 72 (2000): 783–812.

Welke, Barbara Young. *Recasting American Liberty: Gender, Race, Law, and the Railroad Revolution, 1865–1920.* Cambridge, UK: Cambridge University Press, 2001.

Wendell, Barrett. *Barrett Wendell and His Letters.* Edited by M. A. DeWolfe Howe. Boston: Atlantic Monthly Press, 1924.

———. *A Literary History of America.* New York: Scribner's, 1900.

Wershoven, Carol. *The Female Intruder in the Novels of Edith Wharton.* Rutherford, NJ: Fairleigh Dickinson University Press, 1982.

Wharton, Edith. *The Age of Innocence.* New York: D. Appleton, 1920.

———. *A Backward Glance.* 1933. New York: Touchstone/Simon & Schuster, 1998.

———. *The Custom of the Country.* 1913. London: Oxford University Press, 1995.

———. *The Gods Arrive.* New York: D. Appleton, 1933.

———. *The House of Mirth.* 1905. New York: Norton, 1990.

———. *Hudson River Bracketed.* 1929. New York: Charles Scribner's Sons, 1985.

———. Introduction. *Ethan Frome.* 1911. New York: Scribner's, 1922.

———. *The Letters of Edith Wharton.* Edited by R. W. B Lewis and Nancy Lewis. New York: Scribner's, 1988.

Wharton, Edith, and Ogden Codman Jr. *The Decoration of Houses.* 1897. New York: Norton, 1998.

White, Walter. *A Man Called White: The Autobiography of Walter White.* 1948. Foreword by Andrew Young. Athens: University of Georgia Press, 1995.

Will, Barbara. "The Nervous Origins of the American Western." *American Literature* 70 (1998): 293–316.

Williams, Deborah Lindsay. *Not in Sisterhood: Edith Wharton, Willa Cather, Zona Gale, and the Politics of Female Authorship.* New York: Palgrave/St. Martin's, 2001.

Williams, Raymond. *The Country and the City.* New York: Oxford University Press, 1973.

Wister, Owen. *The Virginian.* 1902. New York: McMillan, 2002.

Wolff, Cynthia Griffin. *A Feast of Words: The Triumph of Edith Wharton.* New York: Oxford University Press, 1977.

Yezierska, Anzia. *How I Found America: The Collected Short Stories of Anzia Yezierska.* New York: Persea, 1991.

Zagarell, Sandra. "Troubling Regionalism: Rural Life and the Cosmopolitan Eye in Jewett's *Deephaven.*" *American Literary History* 10, no. 4 (1998): 639–63.

Zettsu, Tomoyuki. "Slavery, Song, and the South: Cather's Refiguration of Stowe and Forster in *A Lost Lady.*" *Arizona Quarterly* 52, no. 1 (1996): 104.

Index

Adams, James Truslow, 6
African Americans: in democracy, 17, 75, 86–87, 99–101, 104–5; eugenicists on, 7; and jazz, 59–61; and labor issues, 17, 93–94; political activity of, 75, 92–93, 117; and white southerners, 12, 17, 73–76, 192n28, 103–4, 109n17; in white southern women's writing, 92–93
American Dream: and new immigrants, 138; and New York, 25, 30; and race, 186n20, 197n58; and the West, 133
American "race," 7–8, 9, 136–38, 157–58, 159
Ames, Jessie Daniel, 121
Anderson-McCormack election law (Virginia), 75
Anglo-Saxons: and cultural pluralism, 9, 18; decadence of, 8, 9–10, 66; democratic "fitness" of, 7, 13, 33; eugenics on, 33, 134, 168; in the South, 104; as superior race, 9, 17, 23, 24; in the West, 158. *See also* Nordics; whites; white women
Association of Southern Women for the Prevention of Lynching (ASWPL), 121

Baldwin, James: on New York, 26; on race relations in America, 17, 73–74, 100; on race relations in the South, 77, 78, 91; on white racial privilege, 181–82; on white southern identity, 73–74, 78, 91, 98
Belmont, Alva, 21
Berenson, Bernard, 25
Berlin, Irving, 65, 66
Black Hawk (Sauk Chief), 153–54
Boas, Franz, 121
Bohemians. *See* Slavs
Bourne, Randolph, 9, 159, 168–69
Boutmy, Emile, 158

cabarets, 17, 51, 56, 58–59, 62n40
Cahan, Abraham, 28–29, 46, 181
Caldwell, Joshua, 104, 111
Canby, Henry, 5
Castle, Irene, 56–57, 58, 61
Cather, Willa: on African Americans, 76, 78–79, 98; on class, 18, 46, 84, 136, 140, 147n51; on cultural pluralism and eugenics, 18, 136–37, 138–39, 140; on democracy, 5–6, 12–14; development as a writer, 78–79; on immigrants, 3–4, 136–37, 138–39, 179–80; on the Irish, 180; on modern American culture, 1–6, 183n6; on New Women, 139, 180; on nineteenth-century American culture, 1–4; on Nordics, 139; on the Old South, 79–80; on the pioneers, 3–4; on regionalism, 10–16, 18, 177–78, 180; review of George Bernard Shaw, 1; on Slavs, 139; on the social position of white women, 14, 15–18, 79,

98, 177–78, 180; on the West, 3–4, 14, 131–32, 133, 136, 160–61; and white southern identity, 76, 78–79, 82–83, 98
Cather, Willa, works of
  Alexander's Bridge, 10
  A Lost Lady: 18, 80, 160, 170; the American Dream in, 162; class in, 161–64; the Irish in, 161–65; white racial divisions in, 161–62, 163; white womanhood in, 161–62, 164–65
  "Miss Jewett," 11–12
  My Ántonia: 16, 78, 134, 139, 165; African Americans in, 149–50; Anglo-Americans in, 144–45, 147, 148, 150, 151; class in, 145–46, 148–49; cultural pluralism and eugenics in, 18, 154; immigrant diversity in, 80, 147–48, 160; the Irish in, 151; Native American removal in, 149, 153–54; nativism in, 136, 147, 148–49, 154, 161; New Women in, 151–52, 154; Scandinavians in, 147n53, 151–52; Slavs and new immigrants in, 135, 144–145, 150–51, 153–54; whiteness in, 144, 148, 152–54; white womanhood in, 148–50
  "My First Novels," 10
  "Nebraska: The End of the First Cycle," 3–4, 140
  One of Ours, 161
  O Pioneers!: 16, 80, 134, 136, 156; and Cather's development as a writer, 10–11, 78; cultural pluralism and eugenics in, 18, 140; diversity in, 141, 142–44; Native American removal in, 139; pioneers in, 131; Scandinavians in, 141, 142; Slavs in, 139–40; whiteness in, 142–43
  Sapphira and the Slave Girl: 16, 17, 78, 180; African Americans in, 86–87, 101–4, 106, 179; class in, 83–85; the "family black and white" in, 80–81, 83, 86–91, 102–3, 127; interracial sex in, 88–89, 90; the Old South in, 91, 105; slavery in, 80–81, 83–85, 91; white womanhood in, 83, 88–89, 103
  Shadows on the Rock, 138
  The Song of the Lark, 80
Chesnutt, Charles: "The Goophered Grapevine," 105–6, 119, 128; *The Marrow of Tradition,* 105, 106–8, 111–20, 127; and regionalism, 180–81
Chopin, Kate, 92, 93
class: and democracy, 6, 9, 23; and consumer culture, 12, 25; and gender, 58, 146, 150; and immigration, 135, 147–48; in New York, 25–26, 32, 34; in regionalism, 13, 14; in the South, 75–76, 105, 111; in the West, 133, 157–58, 160
CORE (Congress of Racial Equality), 99
cultural pluralism, 8–9, 18, 136
Czechs. *See* Slavs

Dabney, Virginius, 74
dancing. *See* cabarets
democracy: and class, 6–9, 24, 157; cultural effects of, 6, 25; and diversity, 6, 8–9, 13, 16–17, 137; and evolution, 8; and immigrant assimilation, 7–8; and modern American culture, 6–7, 11, 13, 23–24, 75, 121; in New York, 25–26, 30; Nordics and, 136, 141, 142, 153; in the North, 104; qualities associated with, 6–7; and race, 7–9, 18, 23, 147–48, 153; and region, 9–10, 100; and regionalism, 13; and segregation, 17, 75, 76, 104–5; Slavs and, 135, 137, 138, 196n50; in the South, 74, 91, 99; in the West, 137–38, 159–60; and whiteness, 7, 10, 13, 18, 100
Dewitt, William, 26
divorce, 18, 159–60
Du Bois, W. E. B., 9, 65–66

Emancipation Proclamation, 133
eugenics: on democracy and racial difference, 7, 8, 9, 18, 135–36, 147–48, 153; on divisions within the white race, 134–38, 153, 157n2, 168; on Nordics, 7, 8, 9, 135, 136, 141, 142, 145, 152; on the role of women in new territories, 132; on Slavs, 9, 134, 135, 137–40, 145, 196n50

Faulkner, William, 25, 91–92
flappers, 51, 58, 60
Fowler, William, 132
Freeman, Mary Wilkins, 11

Gale, Zona, 172
Gast, John, *American Progress,* 156–57, 159
Germans, 10, 33, 162
gigolos, 58, 59
Glasgow, Ellen: on African Americans, 76–78, 98, 120–21; on class, 3, 12, 14, 24, 105; on democracy, 5–6, 12–14, 49; development as a writer, 77–78; on the "family black and white," 91, 92; on modern American culture, 1–6; on the New South, 105; on New Women, 16, 29; on New York, 21–24, 28–29; on *Nigger Heaven* (Van Vechten), 188n2; on the Old South, 1–3, 79–80; on regionalism, 10–17, 18, 177–78, 180; on segregation, 121; on the social position of white women, 14, 15–17, 18, 79–80, 98, 177–78, 179, 180; on the Southern Lady, 27–28, 85–86, 123; on white southern identity, 76–77, 79–80, 98
Glasgow, Ellen, works of
  Barren Ground: 16, 120; African Americans in, 93–96; Anglo-Saxon supremacy in, 96; class in, 97; the "family black and white" in, 94–96, 97, 122; feminism of, 96; imperialism in, 96–97; interracial sex in, 97; New Women in, 92–93; white womanhood in, 92–93, 96, 179–80
  The Battle-Ground: the "family black and white" in, 74, 81, 82–83, 85; the Old South in, 82, 91; white womanhood in, 82–83
  Beyond Defeat: 128, 179
  The Builders, 110
  A Certain Measure, 21; 49n56
  The Deliverance, 82, 85–86, 122
  The Descendant: 28, 29; Anglos in, 17; class in, 30–33, 35, 36–37, 39–40; ethnicity in, 33; hybridity in, 31; the Irish in, 32–33, 164; naturalism of, 30–31, 36–37, 39–40, 109–110; New Women in, 35; New York in, 30–31; Virginia in, 30; white manhood in, 35, 37, 39
  In This Our Life: African American narrator in, 126–27; African American response to racism in, 127–28, 179; class in, 122; examination of white privilege in, 124–28; the "family black and white" in, 121–22, 124–28; interracial identity in, 124–26; the Southern Lady in, 123–24; white womanhood in, 123–24, 179; white racial decline in, 122–23
  Life and Gabriella: 5, 28, 40; Anglos in, 22, 47–49; class in, 40, 42, 46–49; the Irish in, 22, 42, 46–49, 164; New York in, 42–43
  One Man in His Time, 110
  Phases of an Inferior Planet, 28
  Virginia: 27–28; Anglos in, 27; interracial sex in, 89–90, 97; the "family black and white" in, 89–90; the Southern Lady in, 28; white womanhood in, 28, 179
  The Voice of the People: 99; African American citizenship in, 114–17; African American servants in, 106; Anglo-Saxon supremacy in, 96, 110–111, 114–15, 124; class in, 108–110, 112; democracy in, 110, 114; the "family black and white" in, 85, 87–88, 105, 109, 119, 122; mob violence in, 114–15; southern regionalism in, 105, 115
  "Whispering Leaves," 82
  The Woman Within, 1, 5, 11, 76
Grant, Madison, 7, 9, 35, 121

Homestead Act, 133–34
Hoover, J. Edgar, 101
Howells, William Dean, 13, 41
Hughes, Langston, 51, 52, 68–69
Hurston, Zora Neale, 65

Irish, 33, 47, 48, 134, 164
Italians, 7, 24, 33, 104, 134, 137

James, Henry, 11, 12n43
jazz, 25, 51, 58, 59–61
Jewett, Sarah Orne, 11–12, 14
Jews, 12, 24, 26, 99
Johnson, James Weldon, 52, 70
Johnston, Mary, 21
Jolson, Al, 65, 66

Jones, Alice. *See* Rhinelander, Leonard Kip, annulment suit against
Jones, Lizzie, 77–78, 128

Kallen, Horace, 7–10, 13, 136
Knopf, Alfred A., 52

Lapsley, Galliard, 50
Larsen, Nella, 51, 57–58, 66, 180
Le Bon, Gustave, 23–24, 31, 32, 35
Lippmann, Walter 25
local color. *See* regionalism
Locke, Alain, 60, 70
lynching and mob violence, 114–15

Manifest Destiny, 156–57, 168
McKay, Claude, 51, 60–61, 180
Mitchell, Margaret, 92, 93, 95

naturalism, 17, 29
new immigrants, 7, 134–38. *See also* Italians; Slavs; whites: divisions among
New Women: in New York: 29, 58; in the South, 92–93; in the West, 152, 159–60
Nicholson, Meredith, 159, 163, 167, 171, 173
Nineteenth Amendment, 133
Nordics: 7, 8, 9, 135, 136, 141, 142, 145, 152. *See also* Anglo-Saxons; whites

O'Neill, Eugene, 96

pastoral, 2–4, 11, 27, 39, 45, 53, 76, 111, 156–57, 176
Populism, 133
Progressive Era, 6, 51, 57, 133, 134

Readjusters, 115
"race suicide," 54, 66
Reconstruction, 75, 133
Redeemers, 75
regionalism: 10; and immigrant writers, 181; and lynching, 115; politics of, 14–17, 18, 177–78; and writers of color, 180–81
Rhinelander, Leonard Kip, annulment suit against Alice Jones, 64–66
Rhinelander, Newbold, 66
Rice, Thurman, 135, 140
Riis, Jacob, 32
Rogers, Joel, 60, 61
Rölvaag, O. E., 140–41, 142, 181
Roosevelt, Eleanor: 99–101, 120, 121, 128; "Eleanor Clubs," 101, 103
Roosevelt, Theodore, 8, 54
Ross, Edward: on democracy and race: 137–38, 157, 159; on divisions within the white race, 140; on Nordics, 142, 151; on Slavs: 139, 140, 146

Scandinavians, 10, 135–36
Sergeant, Elizabeth Shepley, 136, 138
Shuffle Along, 59
Slavs: democratic "fitness" of, 135, 137, 138, 146n50; eugenics on, 9, 134, 140, 145; as materialist, 137
Stoddard, Lothrop: on democracy and race, 7, 9, 136–38, 141, 142, 153; on divisions within the white race, 134, 135; on the failure of democracy, 7; on Nordics, 136, 142; and scientific racism, 121; on Slavs, 135, 140, 145
Strong, Josiah, 135
Suffrage: African American, 117; restrictions to African American suffrage, 75; Woman Suffrage, 133

Turner, Frederick Jackson: on the American "race," 9, 137–38, 157, 159, 161, 172; on democracy, 8, 158–59; on masculinity in the West, 132; on western materialism, 158, 159, 171

United States Committee on Selective Immigration, 136

Van Vechten, Carl: 62; *Nigger Heaven*, 50–52, 57, 59–61

Washburn, Emelyn, 22
Wendell, Barrett, 7, 9
Wharton, Edith: on the American Dream, 54; on democracy, 5–6, 12–14, 49; on divorce, 53; on Harlem, 50–51; on modern

American culture, 1–6; on New Women, 29; on New York, 22–23, 28–29; on *Nigger Heaven* (Van Vechten), 50–51; on Old New York society, 2–3, 26–27, 162; on regionalism, 10–17, 11n41, 16n54, 18, 177–78, 180; on the social position of white women, 14, 15–16, 18, 177–78, 180; on the West, 160–61, 165–68, 171–72
Wharton, Edith, works of
The Age of Innocence: 52; class in, 2, 22; elite white womanhood in, 23, 26, 27, 178–79; erosion of social boundaries in, 40; marriage in, 43–46; New York in, 41, 43; Old New York society in, 29–30, 53, 105; orphan figure in, 64; white racial decline in, 169
A Backward Glance, 2, 4, 11
The Buccaneers, 166
Bunner Sisters, 29
The Children, 53
The Custom of the Country: 52; class in, 18, 41, 45, 166–68, 168–71; divorce in, 53, 167–68, 171; erosion of social boundaries in, 41, 53; hotels in, 170–71; the Irish in, 164, 168, 169; Old New York society in, 41, 45, 169; westerners in, 166–71; white racial decline in, 169–170
The Decoration of Houses (with Ogden Codman), 170
Ethan Frome, 16
French Ways and Their Meaning, 171
The Gods Arrive, 172, 175
The House of Mirth: 52; Anglos in, 34–36, 38–39; elite white womanhood in, 17, 36, 38–39, 178–79; erosion of social boundaries in, 5, 22, 26, 29, 53, 63; hotels in, 36, 170; Jews in, 33–35, 37–39, 169; naturalism of, 17, 36, 39–40; New Women in, 58; New York street life in, 61; Old New York society in, 30; racial mixing in, 35, 63; and Wharton's career, 11; white manhood in, 35; white racial decadence in, 15, 38, 169; westerners in, 166
Hudson River Bracketed, 166, 171–76, 178–79
"Mrs. Mainstay's View," 29
Old New York, 22
Sanctuary, 166
Summer, 16
Twilight Sleep: 17, 50, 53; African Americans in, 52, 55–56, 62, 67–70; cabarets in, 52, 61–62, 62n40, 66–67; democracy in, 55; divorce in, 53, 64; the flapper in, 56–58, 62; the Harlem Renaissance in, 51, 55–56, 67–70; Italians in, 67; jazz in, 59–62, 68; Jews in, 67; modernism in, 62–63; New Women in, 51, 57–58; racial ambiguity in, 64; *Rhinelander v. Jones* case in, 65, 66–67, westerners in, 54–55, 166, 167, 172, 175; white racial decline in, 52, 55, 123, 169; white womanhood in, 58, 61, 62, 64, 66–67, 69–70
whites: decadence of, 9, 54, 159; democratic "fitness" of, 6, 10, 13, 100; divisions among, 6, 7, 10, 6n19, 48, 134–36, 134n18; and the Harlem Renaissance, 50–51, 58, 59–61; in New York, 55; in the North, 104; racial privilege of, 9, 37, 56, 73, 121; in the South, 17, 73–76, 77, 81–82, 99, 103–5; in the West, 18, 133. *See also* American "race"; Anglo-Saxons; Nordics; white women
White, Walter, 99, 115, 121
white women: in New York, 58–59, 65; in the South, 79–80, 92–93; social position of, 13–17, 66, 177–78; and suffrage, 133; in the West, 18, 131–33, 156–57, 159. *See also* New Women
Wilson, Woodrow, 158
Wister, Owen, 132, 133
Writers' League Against Lynching, 121

Yezierska, Anzia, 22